Yale French Studies

NUMBER 83

Post/Colonial Conditions: Exiles, Migrations, and Nomadisms
Volume 2

Yale French Studies

Françoise Lionnet and Ronnie Scharfman, *Special editors for this issue*
Liliane Greene, *Managing editor*
Editorial board: Hillari Allred, Denis Hollier (Chair), Peter Brooks, Shoshana Felman, Christopher Miller, Kevin Newmark, Charles Porter, Amy Reid, Suzanne Toczyski
Staff: Cynthia Mesh, Kathryn Oliver
Editorial office: 82-90 Wall Street, Room 308.
Mailing address: 2504A-Yale Station, New Haven, Connecticut 06520.
Sales and subscription office:
  Yale University Press, 92A Yale Station
  New Haven, Connecticut 06520
  Published twice annually by Yale University Press

Designed by James J. Johnson and set in Trump Medieval Roman by The Composing Room of Michigan, Inc.
Printed in the United States of America by the Vail Ballou Press, Binghamton, N.Y.

ISSN 044-0078
ISBN for this issue 0-300-05397-5

FRANÇOISE LIONNET AND
RONNIE SCHARFMAN

Editors' Preface

This is the second volume of a double issue concerning issues of identity, language, and modernity in a postcolonial Francophone context. It
is organized according to a specifically geographic focus, but it also
expands and refines the theoretical perspectives developed in volume one.

Part One, "Maghrebian Pluralities: Geographies of the Postcolonial
Subject," includes writing by a major figure in North African liter-
ature, Abdelkebir Khatibi, who meditates as he wanders through the
colonial city (the French quarter, the *mellah*, and the *medina*) with its
French, Jewish, and Arab inhabitants. The second essay, by Lucy Stone
McNeece, is a deconstructive analysis of Khatibi's autobiographical
novel *La Mémoire tatouée.* Thomas Spear's interview with Tahar Ben
Jelloun was done in Paris after the Gulf War, and covers a variety of
topics including Jean Genet, the Palestinian question, and the place of
Maghrebian literature in the definition of a Maghrebian identity. Réda
Bensmaïa's Deleuzian approach to Nabile Farès' discourse reads it as a
paradigm for the revolutionary transformation of minority populations in Algeria. H. Adlai Murdoch's essay on the foremost Algerian
woman novelist and filmmaker, Assia Djebar, examines her discursive
strategies as bicultural, postcolonial subject, and Hédi Abdel-Jaouad
shows how the Russian-born nomad Isabelle Eberhardt made herself
into a Maghrebian writer, using thematic and formal means which will
later be echoed by the indigenous writers of the Maghreb.

In Part Two, "Poetics of the Archipelago: Transatlantic Passages,"
Guadeloupean novelist and essayist Maryse Condé questions the ways

YFS 83, *Post/Colonial Conditions*, ed. Lionnet & Scharfman, © 1993 by Yale
University.

1

in which Caribbean literature, especially writing by women, has been evaluated by her compatriots. In an interview with prize-winning Haitian poet and novelist René Depestre, critic Joan Dayan explores the literary consequences of exile, and in her essay on *Hadriana*, she reveals what the reception of this novel in France means about the ideological underpinnings of Depestre's modes of representation. Mireille Rosello studies the intertextual references to Baudelaire's "L'Albatros" in Aimé Césaire's *Cahier d'un retour au pays natal*, and shows how the Antillean poet appropriates the French poetic tradition. We conclude this volume with two essays that summarize many of the intellectual problematics raised by the other contributors of this double issue. The poetics and esthetics of exile and errancy are examined by Elisabeth Mudimbe-Boyi as she juxtaposes two women novelists— an African and a Caribbean—using formal categories of analysis. The French Jewish writer André Schwarz-Bart is the subject of the last essay by Bella Brodzki who sheds light on his pained attempt to link the history of slavery with the suffering of the Holocaust. With this essay on André Schwarz-Bart, we come full circle with our investigation of exiles, migrations, and nomadisms since this writer exemplifies the problem of origins and belonging, of cultural appropriation and linguistic nationalism.

I. Maghrebian Pluralities: Geographies of the Postcolonial Subject

ABDELKEBIR KHATIBI

A Colonial Labyrinth

Now if the colonial city was to be divided into three parts, one would see, in one section, the residence of the French called "pieds noirs" [black feet] (certainly due to racism in metropolitan France); in another, the mellah;* and the medina inhabited by the largest population. Three communities, that is, three gazes graduated according to the principle of light and shade, in a country called, one should remember, "Sunset."† I fall asleep in the dreams of this beautiful name.

Lyautey‡ militarily surrounded the medina to break up its anarchic proliferation and its apparent illogicality. I grew up in this anarchy and this illogicality while practicing the covert glance. A covert glance common to the Jew and the Muslim who, because of the arrogance of the conqueror, were obliged to internalize the brightness of the sun, to tan, in a way, by the strength of the heart.

I could recognize this covert glance while walking in the narrow streets of the mellah where the second wife of my maternal grandfather would embroider in the company of some Jewish neighbors whom she had invited over. Embroidery went together with the rites of passage and borders that each sorority adorned with its beautiful gaze—in the margin of the Book. These illiterate women, a little blurred in my memory, were learning the fundamentals of weaving silence, of awakening in men unbridled desires. One of my relatives loved a Jewish woman. They were married without scandal. She

*The Jewish Quarter.—Translator's note.
†Maghreb, in Arabic means "sunset," "West"—Translator's note.
‡Maréchal Lyautey organized the French protectorate in Morocco in 1912.—Translator's note.

YFS 83, *Post/Colonial Conditions,* ed. Lionnet & Scharfman, © 1993 by Yale University.

changed her religion and her name, she took them back when they separated. These were like a vestment, a symbolic ornament whose color and perfume changed with the seasons of the body.

If I tie and untie this rug of ancient images, like a deck of postcards that a dazed, slightly drunk postman (maybe a crimson angel!) distributes randomly to permutable addresses, it is because I am trying to put some order, in counterpoint, to my perception of the colonial space and its obsolete folklore. Lyautey thought he could frame the medina (and he did it with art) by fixing it inside its walls and gates. But the whole space became "mural," riddled with holes of intense life, silence, humiliation, anger, boots, and grenades. In 1953, I almost was hit by one in the middle of my body. I immediately jumped into the labyrinth of the medina. This bullet, lost in time, trained me to have the thought of instantaneous death in the back of my mind, and to keep a space open to war. And now, behind my friendly appearance, I cannot conceal this part of myself.

At first, I see the blind murality in the brush strokes of the amateurish painters and folklorists of that time. I am not thinking of these orientalist odalisks that one can see in museums, in brothels, or in luxurious drawing rooms; nor of Delacroix's admirable sketches done during his travels in Morocco. I am thinking rather of the frivolous art of the brush stroke or the drawings representing the streets and the scenes of the medina that are reproduced like postcards and not the other way around as any good artist would have done. Since photography was born after the beginning of French colonization, the image that the conqueror had of the Algerian and the African, of the Muslim and the Jew, was bound to multiply itself with the mechanical, then automatic, view-finder of prejudice and jeers.

The vocabulary of "colors" is used when one talks about racism but is it not a disaster of language! A minority community, victim of racism, is a *stain*, an ink stain so unreadable, so blinding for the racist that it drives him crazy. The racist, in fact, confuses colors whereas he thinks that he is distinguishing and mastering them in the delight of this dual hate: hate for others and hate of the self. It is the archaic passion of an invertebrate death that recurs beneath the glacial fury of his gaze, without a glimmer of light that could temper the barbarian word. Word without scream, scream without word: disaster of racism and destruction—real and imaginary—the objects of his unrelenting hatred.

The "yellow" race has cultivated the art of the body as ornament, a composition in a range of colors, a veiling, a tattooing of signs. And thus, yellow is the secret paradigm of a civilization, and not at all a shameful or abject stigma. It occupies a beautiful ritual space in a ceremony enacted by the graduated colors that the Japanese memory has scattered in costumes, paintings, floral art and in processions of familial and public festivals.[1]

Let's return to the colonial city. A labyrinth binds the *"pieds noirs"* districts to the medina and the mellah. Roger Caillois warns us: It behooves us to be aware of the fact, although only a few have noticed it, that the word "labyrinth" embraces two opposite ways of perceiving a maze. In one instance, the itinerary is endless and tortuous, but compulsory. Hesitation is impossible. Only one corridor is available at any given instant, although it is always curved and thus gives the impression to anyone taking it that he is simply retracing his steps. In fact, it forces him to traverse successively all the points of the exploited area. The other kind, by contrast, is formed only by crossroads. Every fragment of gallery starts from a crossroad, identical to the previous one. The wanderer is thus thrown from one perplexity to another, all of them equally insoluble. He has no way of deciding whether the crossroad where he ends up is not one of those through which he has already passed. He has no way of knowing whether or not he has progressed. In the first type of labyrinth, it is impossible for some progress not to be achieved; whoever ventures in inevitably makes his way toward the exit, or if he turns back, toward the departure point."[2]

Here is one possible entrance into the colonial labyrinth: on Islamic land, the Christians and the Jews had a status of *dhimmis.** They paid a tithe to the king and to the governors. Then came colonization: France imposed what it called the "Protectorate" on Tunisia and Morocco. *Dhimmi*, protection: two words not to be forgotten in the lexicon of this memory.

Morocco inherited from its distant past a remarkable Jewish community. I do not know since what obscure time these Jewish peasants and shepherds, who could be found right up to the Sahara, have existed. Their presence there gives the strange feeling that primitive Judaism,

1. Abdelkebir Khatibi, *Ombres japonaises* (Montpellier: Fata Morgana, 1988).
2. Roger Caillois.
*A non-Muslim subject of a Muslim country.—Translator's note.

by staying close to the land, desired to break with its obsession with money and to fuse itself, right there, with the roots of its native land, its landscapes, and immemorial myths. I am thinking of the legend that can be found in a popular tale about a pious Jewish *marabout* who, in order to have his death believed to be miraculous, transformed himself into a migratory bird around an eternally lit candle facing the sunset, the very name of Morocco: *al-maghrib.*

The mellah was as poor as the medina. The poorest among the Jews would enter the proletariat by going into exile in the land of Israel. The second generation of these people exiled by force and fear, gave birth to a marginal political movement that was quickly suppressed: the Black Panthers, who had nothing to do with the revolt of black Americans (the Falashas from Ethiopia know something about that now). I had met some of the members of this small movement in Paris, in 1975, after the publication of my book *Vomito blanco.*[3] I learned that this book, distributed in Israel, had been rapidly sold; after its disappearance from the market, it had been photocopied by the members of this movement, Moroccan in origin, and distributed by a parallel circuit. I must say that this act of small piracy delighted me.

Let's keep walking in the mellah's small streets, repeating what I once wrote to Jacques Hassoun:* "What I mean is that this so-called labyrinth is also a cultural way of treating space, of learning, how shall I put it, a psychology and strategy of walking, of meeting, of avoiding, of fighting, of fleeing, of all the displacements of the body when it is caught in a social network such as this one. One learns in these variously shaped neighborhoods a movement of nimbleness of the mind, if not a certain malice. The obstacle is not always visible: it may jump out at a street corner. And night becomes a pretext for some witchcraft of our senses, our fears. In these small streets, then, a whole mobility of pretending, of avoiding is set into action. And many rituals of courtesy are necessary, have been necessary to exorcise the very short distance between people, crowds. That is the reason that I always have liked this movement of deambulation that allows one to find the rhythm of space and to look well at what is happening at one and the same time. A slow

---

3. Abdelkebir Khatibi, *Vomito blanco: Le Sionisme et la conscience malheureuse* (Paris: 10/18, 1974). This is Khatibi's discussion of the Palestinian Question.

*Egyptian-born psychoanalyst and writer, living in Paris.—Translator's note.

rhythm is necessary, a step that one can suspend in order to exchange a few words, some ritual sentences, but in fact also to neutralize the narrowness of the space, its promiscuity, the too closely intertwined situations that are suffocating at times. I have internalized, as have all the Jews of the mellah and each inhabitant of the medina, this psychology of detour. Indeed, for a long time we have been walking in the same space, in the same topographical fiction, even if the mellah has been separated from the medina since the fifteenth century. But it has, in fact, produced the same structure, a microstructure for the minority that had to preserve and protect its difference. This space, imposed here, has reproduced the medina from the inside, like a reflection in a mirror. A vanishing reflection—this is the history of the diaspora in Arab land. It is the reflection of a common history, a memory that turns into a psychoanalyst's dream. I speak to you very directly. I come back once more to the notion of the labyrinth. There is a counterapprenticeship where one learns tactics, and the strategy of *contours*, of the *drapé* [fluidity] of the walk. I am convinced that the nostalgia for this space is not a mere cry out of the past but really *the trace of a trauma*, of a lost land. In order for the Jew to rediscover the Letter, he must lose his land (that is the tragic sense of the diaspora), but if he find both the Land and the Letter, the third term must always be available as a signature: *Yahweh*. Perhaps (and I say this very quickly) what binds Jews and Arabs together is this: they both love *the name (the signature) more than their own image*. They sign after God. Theirs is a different kind of narcissism: Arabs and Jews look at the chiasma of their names, the erasure, the third term split in its division of intolerance. An exhausting, interminable experience."[4]

Therefore, tolerance, intolerance, and their borders combine themselves into an art of living. We tolerate the other only if he does not threaten to disturb our territory, our singularity, and our memory. This is often an untenable position for the reason that the conflict between real or imaginary territories is a relation of power either "implosive," "explosive," or "alternating."

The "implosive" movement of a memory refers to a past that is no longer sustained by today's reality. It refers to a lost model, lost forever: a theological unity between the city of God and the city of men, or a "strict equality" between the forces of life and death.

It is thus a dream perpetuated from century to century. This mem-

4. Abdelkebir Khatibi and Jacques Hassoun, *Le Même livre* (Paris: Editions de l'Eclat, 1985), 130–32.

ory is deadly. It is identified with a model of civilization that is no longer viable while the world in a state of becoming obeys a new language, experimental and exploratory.

Instead of transforming itself, of developing according to the reality of the world, this memory finds its strength in the nostalgia for the past. But that is a past without a past. In other words, the memory survives in melancholy. Let me explain myself. The social structures, models of power, culture, and imagination perpetuated by a civilization are an adaptation to its will to live and survive on earth, and not in religious heaven. There is no accommodation possible between heaven and earth.

The implosive memory dreams up therefore an imaginary exchange. It implodes in two ways: on the one hand, it closes itself in the nostalgia of a dead time and its entropy; on the other hand, it *endures* the present as if it were a dream, or rather a nightmare. But both past and present can exist only if they are transformed, enriched by the exploration of new and practical thoughts. The past comes back in our memory through metamorphosed forms.

This is the reason why the movement of nostalgia and melancholy implodes. Confronted with a changing potential, it is defenseless in the face of thought and of the world. To go backward? But where? Repeating what is definitely over results, finally, in the self-destruction of the being, and of the personality.

In principle, each nation is a plurality, a mosaic of cultures, if not a plurality of languages and genealogies. This plurality is never set in a real relationship of equality (between groups, cultures, sexes, powers) but in one of hierarchy and *asymmetry*. Intrinsically, the State (centralized or decentralized) must administer over the paradoxical process of this asymmetry.

There is thus always an implosive conflict between the components of a nation. As soon as one group loses its bearings in time and space, it explodes because of its will to live and survive.

But memory is changing all the time. It accumulates the advances that global civilization provides. By exploring new thoughts and new practices, it learns to better administer space, time, and its will to live. The best attitude, the most humble and efficacious one is the *apprenticeship* of tolerance. When I learn what you are saying, what you are doing, I increase my memory. Whoever accepts these facts and changes can negotiate his place wherever he is, in his own country or elsewhere, and with real partners. If he hasn't accepted himself as he is, how can he negotiate? How can he confront the powers of life and death?

I have said already that space, like memory, is in the process of becoming. It is a matter of strategy, of geopolitics, of international environment. Arab space, for example, consists in a collection of territories and civilizations. But we know that a land is not a land anymore, it is not a mere area added to another area. A new strategic language (military, political, economical, scientific, of the media) explores the models of power affecting men.

How can you act, or think while acting, if you do not have the key to read these transformations? To understand before acting, to learn before understanding, to consolidate the force of one's memory and of one's space: this is the paradigm of lucidity and of the face to face.

Lucidity comes after the melancholy and apocalyptic obsession of torture, asphyxiating gasses, destruction, the war of stones. To think after Auschwitz and Hiroshima entails moving aside from the thought that has become the cult of the dead. And each thought contains in itself the seeds of its own decomposition. In order to be able to conceive of the barbarism of the other and to make it accessible to thought, we have to accept the thought that is *latent* in us: our temptation for disaster.

Perhaps then, we would be attentive to the message that the Israeli writer Amos Oz addresses to his people: "Every one of the engaged factions does not fight against its enemy but against the neurotic shadows of its own past. The Arabs do not see us, they see the French, the English, the Turks. We do not see the Arabs at all, but the Russians, the pogroms, Hitler."

September 1988

—Translated by Catherine Dana

LUCY STONE McNEECE

Decolonizing the Sign: Language and Identity in Abdelkebir Khatibi's *La Mémoire tatouée*

For Maghreb writers of the postcolonial period, the dilemma that underlies the more obvious political, economic, and cultural issues is their problematic relation to the French language. It is commonplace to assert that values and ideology are encoded into language, and that to learn a foreign language is not merely a linguistic leap but a cultural one as well. We may therefore expect the drama of cultural difference, as of cultural identity, to be played out at the level of language itself. Is it possible to express the experience of exile and alienation in the language of the oppressor? Can a writer become the subject of his own discourse in a language that has been and is being used to define his culture from outside? It is not accidental that the growing interest in Francophone literature has coincided with the dismantling of the Cartesian subject in French theoretical discourse.

Abdelkebir Khatibi's *La Mémoire tatouée* addresses many of these critical issues.[1] Born in Morocco in 1938, Khatibi attended both Koranic and French schools, and, like many of his generation, went to France for graduate study. *La Mémoire tatouée*, first published in 1971, is part autobiographical narrative, part parable, part poem, part dialogue, and part commentary. Written in French, it is permeated by

1. Abdelkebir Khatibi, *La Mémoire tatouée* (Paris: UGE, 1971); (Collection 10/18, 1979). Henceforth referred to in the text. Other texts by Khatibi that directly or indirectly address questions of cultural identity and bilingualism include, *La Blessure du nom propre* (Paris; Denoël, 1974); *Le Roman maghrébin*, (réédition), (Rabat; SMER, 1979); *Le Livre du sang* (Paris: Gallimard, 1979); *Amour bilingue* (Paris: Fata Morgana, 1983); *Maghreb pluriel*, (Paris: Denoël, 1983); *Le Même livre* (avec Jacques Hassoun) (Paris: édition de l'Eclat, 1985). Translations from the French are mine.

YFS 83, *Post/Colonial Conditions*, ed. Lionnet & Scharfman, © 1993 by Yale University.

cadences and expressions from both the Koran and Khatibi's native dialect. It is both polymorphic and polyphonic, shifting frequently among voices and grammatical subjects. The text is full of surprising visual imagery, musical phrasing and repetition, incantations, word-play, and subtle shifts from the literal to figurative levels of meaning. Its tone moves effortlessly between irony and pathos, between violence and lyricism. At once heterogeneous and heretical, Khatibi's text subverts the common assumptions about the experience of exile, cutting across typical oppositions of value associated with East and West, colonizer and colonized, primitive and civilized, nature and culture. The style is consummately self-conscious, yet gains its urgency from the sense it conveys that everything is risked in the process of writing itself. At moments the narration approaches the kind of disintegration associated with schizophrenic discourse, before it regains penetrating lucidity. As the author himself asks, "Mais quoi, l'écriture, n'est-elle pas travaillée par la folie, le mal, le suicide?" (209) [But after all, isn't writing shaped by madness, evil, suicide?]. Khatibi's novel invites the reader to become fully aware of what it means to write in a postcolonial context, and how close indeed writing is to one's sense of self and one's desire. He demonstrates that writing in the language of another culture involves no less than the sacrifice and the recreation of the self.

The work's title indicates the way in which Khatibi concretizes the most elusive concepts, affirming the relation of the body and desire to language and writing. The title also establishes the primacy of the sign, or rather of the material signifier, in the formation of personal identity. By the conjunction of "mémoire" and "tatouée," Khatibi articulates the degree to which memory is not cognitive but corporeal, sensuous, and indelible. The emblem of the persistence of sensory impressions is the tattoo, whose markings are a focus of the narrator's early perceptions. A symbol of writing and of magic, the tattoo is a sign of the sacred, mysterious and sensual. The boy associates tattoos with henna-colored hands and with women's gestures—at once eloquent and indecipherable—which govern his desire. Among the many references associated with the word "tattoo" there are two which seem particularly relevant to Khatibi's text: the inscribing of pictures on the skin in black, a notion that suggests defamation and the disruption of the opposition of the sacred to the profane, and, etymologically (from an early English form, "tapto" or "tatu"), a shutting off or silencing, originally a signal given to soldiers or sailors to return to camp after encoun-

ters with local women.[2] This latter connotation foreshadows, indirectly, the submersion of the narrator's early history as he enters
Western culture. More generally, it refers to the "silencing" of the
colonized under colonial rule, when the indigenous culture quite literally "loses a voice" in its cultural destiny.

Khatibi identifies the Berber language as the Maghreb peoples'
"mother tongue," both because it is the earliest code of exchange, and
because it is learned directly from the mother in a physical, sensuous
manner. The Lacanian paradigm can be useful here: the oral dialect and
all that surrounds it is tied to the Imaginary, while the French culture
and language belong to the Symbolic. Arabic partakes of both realms
because of its oral (dialectal) and its written forms, but under colonial
occupation, it would be increasingly on the side of the Imaginary. The
critical discontinuity described by Lacan as one enters the Symbolic is
therefore augmented for the Maghreb people, because the leap into
language does not bring access to the discourse, which remains twice
alien to them. According to Lacan, when the child enters social discourse in his own culture he necessarily surrenders or represses his
authentic desire. This is so because he must constitute himself as a
grammatical subject ("je"). Represented by a material signifier, he is
caught up in a relay of shifters that leads him towards the signifieds of
the Other encoded in the language. The Maghreb subject, therefore,
surrenders his desire but is denied any compensation in the form of
participation in the official culture.[3]

La Mémoire tatouée illustrates what Khatibi asserts in *Maghreb
pluriel*, namely, that the language of early life is never fully erased,
though other "languages" may appear to have effaced it: "Son déracine-
ment même le fait travailler dans la dis-ruption . . . le parler maternel,
parce que justement non écrit et non élevé au concept de texte, main-
tient la mémoire d'un récit et sa primauté généalogique . . . (193–94),
[Its very deracination causes it to work towards disruption . . . the
mother's dialect, precisely because not written and not raised to the

2. *Webster's Unabridged Dictionary,* Second Edition (New York: Simon &
Schuster, 1983).

3. Jean Amrouche identifies the crisis of the Maghreb subject and its relation to
language in *Colonisation et langage* (intervention at the Congrès méditerranéen de la
Culture, Florence, October 1960, reproduced in *Etudes méditerranéennes,* 11, 1963,
116–17), cited by Jacqueline Arnaud in *La Littérature maghrébine de langue française,
1,* Publisud; 1986, 85: "For the language must be for him not only a collection of
forms . . . which he will use . . . knowing of its rules. . . . The entire range of meanings, the whole semantic depth of this language must be felt by him in the depths of his
being."

concept of text, maintains the memory of a story, and its genealogical primacy].

As the narrator becomes immersed in French culture and ideology, his native language and culture seem to recede. He moves further away from his past as the demands of acculturation increase. Yet while his exile involves an eradication of cognitive data, it begins to liberate affective material and sensory associations. Memory and forgetting begin to assume a relation of interdependence instead of one of exclusion: forgetting may well be a condition for retaining what is indispensable.

Khatibi's text, like a palimpsest, is layered with echoes and traces of other texts. It has no clear boundaries, no beginning and no end. Every text, as Khatibi states in *Maghreb pluriel,* has already begun long before it is opened:

> Début du livre: commencement sans commencement, temps de l'écriture et dont le livre—ouvert ou pas—n'est qu'une traversée, une sorte de halte, marquée, démarquée et emportée par l'écriture qui travaille pour son compte . . . le commencement a eu lieu dans un ailleurs sans cesse reculant vers l'inouï, là où l'effacement du sujet se joue de toutes les manières. [*Maghreb pluriel,* 180].

> The opening of the book: a beginning without a beginning, a time of writing of which the book—open or not—is but a passage, a kind of way-station, marked, demarcated and carried away by the writing which works for itself . . . the beginning occurred in an elsewhere ceaselessly receding towards the extraordinary, where the subject's effacement is at stake in every case.

This question of beginnings is central to Khatibi's project; it draws attention to two important features of his unorthodox use of language: that knowledge of ourselves and of others is a function of our relation to signs that operate differentially and diversely in every culture; that the languages we presume to use to create meaning in fact inscribe meanings upon us. It also prefigures the intertextual nature of all writing, and implies the presence of traces of previous encounters with other languages and other cultures. Potentially subversive of authoritarian institutions, such a concept is already a subtle critique of any pretense to ideological purity or integrity. It lays the groundwork for the dismantling of cultural imperialism, wherever it is to be found.

Khatibi's work is an inquiry into the way language structures one's perception of the world. It is an adventure in the most serious sense, a journey whose outcome is highly ambiguous. In fact, *La Mémoire tatouée* has neither resolution nor closure. The narrator's quest remains unfinished; his inquiry confronts an enigma whose answer is always another question. He declares at the outset that writing in another's language is a defiance of death, not unlike the stories told by Sheherazade in *Les Mille et une nuits:* "ce principe infiniment exclusif . . . doit, à mon sens, conduire tout narrateur vers le lieu de sa transfiguration: image d'un tombeau irradié d'où s'élèvera—peut-être—le chant du poème et de la pensée" (9) [this infinitely exclusive principle . . . should, as I see it, lead every narrator towards the place of his transformation: the image of a transparent tomb from which will arise—perhaps—the hymn of the poem and of the thought]. Everything is balanced on the "peut-être," and the space of that suspension is the space of the material sign, constantly threatening to fall towards the referents of the Other, "la signature d'un mort" (11) [the signature of a dead person]. Khatibi's enterprise is an attempt to reclaim the signs and values of his culture that have been appropriated by the French and hence cut off from their complex structure of reference.

The author's venture carries the menace of a symbolic death. Writing in the French language entails the risk of the loss of self, the effacement of subjectivity, because the ideological perspective of the colonizer is always present in the forms of its language. The odyssey of Khatibi's narrator is a quest for self-possession and self-knowledge that paradoxically involves a form of self-abandonment, a doubling that demands the surrender of his real self for the sake of a simulacrum which is a grotesque parody of the authentic reality he seeks. The *persona* the narrator assumes,—a cause of what Khatibi elsewhere terms "cet exil intérieur" [this inner exile]—is born of a desire to bridge the abyss between his native language (already a transcription of Berber dialect into Arabic) and the imposed language and culture of the West.

Franz Fanon explains one aspect of this phenomenon when he states that the colonized subject feels compelled to assume the disdainful perspective of the colonizer toward himself to avoid the pain of humiliation.[4] He longs, literally, to become white, because the white race, besides disposing of power over his culture, appears to possess an authenticity he believes he lacks. But to see himself through the eyes of the Other, he must enter the Other's imaginative space, assume its values, and provisionally at least, disown his own. The irony of this

4. Frantz Fanon, *Peau noire, masques blancs* (Paris: Seuil, 1952), 51, 89.

mutilating self-deformation is that it is subversive of both systems. It is also a process of revelation: it exposes those elements in each culture that, for political and economic reasons, have remained hidden and unidentified. Writing in another's language, besides unveiling aspects of the Other's culture that are devalued or denied, highlights those features of one's own culture that are either invisible because too familiar, or so perturbing to the structures of power that they must be repressed.

La Mémoire tatouée is unlike any conventional autobiography. Although written in the first person, it is not confessional, and the author does not provide his readers with either realistic scenes of the past, or a coherent psychological portrait of his narrator. He does not present a logical sequence of events that might serve to explain or to legitimize present attitudes. The absence of such a structure of cause and effect deters us from reading the story as a naturalistic tale. Khatibi's protagonist is a construct, not only because he is the personal invention of the author, but because he is a cultural invention in an extreme sense, an artifact of the colonial imagination. His novel, in part, is an autobiography of the non-I, or "alterbiography." We tend to think of autobiography as a vehicle of individual authenticity, and read it for the vicarious pleasure of gaining access to the intimate world of another's self. Khatibi's novel denies us that seductive illusion, dramatizing instead the impossibility of knowing another person as a subject, and exposing the inauthenticity that often characterizes our relations with ourselves as well as others.

The postcolonial subject, moreover, is condemned to live almost entirely in this mode, deprived of the sanction that is normally provided by cultural identification. Khatibi's narrator, lacking an authenticating frame of reference, is like the illegitimate son of an interracial union, obliged to contemplate himself from the outside, as an object rather than as the subject of his own life.[5]

The details Khatibi chooses to include are immensely significant, but not as causative, psychological factors. Rather, they function as poetic indicators of the changing relation of the narrator to signs and meanings in a process whereby he is abstracted from his familiar world and becomes the almost purely formal representation of the desire of the Other, in this case, the French culture.

5. In *Le Roman maghrébin*, op. cit., 39, Khatibi cites Jean Amrouche: " . . . The colonised has received the benefit of the language of a civilisation of which he is not the legitimate heir. And consequently he is a sort of bastard," 39.

La Mémoire tatouée amply testifies to the difficulty of speaking or writing from the point of view of an integrated or grounded subject. The novel is an inquiry into the problem, at once epistemological and ontological, of knowing oneself with respect to the Other. It is a meta-discourse about writing and its subjects, in the sense of being both about authorship and about the objects of its narration within the context of a postcolonial society. The process of writing inevitably raises the issue of position and placement. The changing relation of subject to object, of mind to world, of sign to referent, are aspects of a long-standing problem of Western metaphysics that here finds a new and critical reformulation. Khatibi has understood the particular importance of this issue for the postcolonial sensibility. Acutely aware of the fact that political independence in no way guarantees cultural freedom, Khatibi knows that the writer is the one who must assume the task of exploring the implications of the problem, and must be prepared to sacrifice himself, if need be, for those who cannot or dare not pose the questions that must be asked.

The opening of the story introduces one of the central themes of the work: the relation of the sign to a process of division, doubling, and death. The author tells us that his name refers to the holy day of Aid-el-Kebir which commemorates Abraham's sacrifice of his son, Isaac: "Rien à faire, même si ne m'obsède pas le chant de l'égorgement, il y a, à la racine, la déchirure nominale" (17) [Nothing to be done even if I weren't obsessed by the hymn of the slaughter, there is, at the source, a tear in the name].

In *Maghreb pluriel,* as in *La Blessure du nom propre,* Khatibi speaks of the symbolic function of names and of the deformations they inevitably undergo when translated from one language to another. Khatibi's analysis recalls Proust's treatment of names as phonetically suggestive of sensory associations and therefore connected to imaginary visions formed in early life, but simultaneously as the emblem of familial and social identity, and thus expressive of a collective ideology rather than of personal values. Names represent that fulcrum between self and Other upon which our identity is perilously balanced.

Khatibi's text is divided into three parts. The first describes the narrator's childhood as a Maghreb boy growing up under colonial occupation. The second includes the narrator's experience as an exile in Paris, and the third, after a brief interlude in which the action is suspended, encompasses a long, cross-continental journey that leads the narrator back to his native Morocco. The narrative structure is dialectical and foregrounds the dominant themes of cultural and psychic division and exile. The dialectic is established immediately at every level. In the first part, there are primarily two imaginative spaces, one belonging to the highly eroticized environment of home, women, the streets, and the tribal traditions, the other belonging to the rigidly structured space of French schools attended by the narrator. The opposition between these two environments is expressed by different uses of language, narrative voice, and tone.

In the streets, unseen female voices using the sexually suggestive "tu" form address the boy directly:

> Enfant, vois le jour faste, va une fois par an à la foire rurale de la tribu. Traîne ton regard sur la poussière, flotte furtivement avec la foule, au bord de la plage rocheuse, voisine de la foire . . . Passe devant le maïs grillé ou le nougat enroulé, passe devant le kaléidoscope, mais arrête-toi devant le conteur. [74]

> Child, see the fortunate day, go once a year to the tribal country fair. Let your gaze linger on the dust, float furtively with the crowd, on the edge of the rocky beach, next to the fair. . . . Pass by the roasted corn or the rolled nougat, pass by the kaleidoscope, but stop in front of the storyteller.

At once protective and challenging, the voices encourage the boy to surrender to his senses and intuition, to open himself to sounds and odors around him. Using the "tu" and the imperative form, the tribal voices suggest an intimate, rather than alien, authority opposed to that of the colonials, whose use of the familiar "tu" is a means of patronizing the colonized.[6] The tribal voices articulate the paradox of the boy's apparently ambiguous status within his own culture: that of man and boy, individual and tribal member, possessing "masculine" and "feminine" traits. The voices suggest a crossing of the many boundaries— rooted in a binary and exclusionary logic—that sustain the West's hegemony.

In calling the boy to his responsibility as a member of the community, they encourage a behavior that is easily perceived as "dissolute" by the colonials. Events described by storytellers are participatory rituals like dances in which the teller mimics sounds and gestures integral

---

6. Marc Gontard, *La Violence du texte* (Rabat: L'Harmattan, 1981). In that work, Gontard analyzes the form of Khatibi's discourse, comparing its rhetorical strategies to those of the Koran.

to the tale. Gesture and sound take precedence over narrative details, creating a kinesthetic effect on the group that underscores the corporeal nature of the boy's involvement in his tradition.

The language used to express the tribal culture is rife with poetic effects such as alliteration, repetition, pronounced rhythms, and unusual phonetic patterns. The lexical choices include words transliterated from dialect and are rich in sensory and physical references. The language is opalescent, fluid, sensual, and erotic, and its intonation and rhythms have a kinesthetic impact upon the reader. Khatibi manages to turn the West's dreams about the Arab world artfully against itself; he infuses the French language with a mysticism and sensuality that may also be read as signs of infection menacing an inviolate ideal. In so doing, he exposes the fear that informs the West's most seductive fantasies, revealing its underlying disdain.

At times we hear voices of the French colonials and see the narrator's culture through their paternalistic gaze:

> Et quoi! Les Arabes aiment regarder des roses en papier, ou en plastique, la nature leur a échappé d'entre les doigts, ils croupissent, grisés par le thé et l'absinthe. Et pour cacher leur misère, ils forniquent toute la journée. Il faut créer des jardins rationnels, des villes géométriques, une économie en flèche, il faut créer des Paradis sur terre, Dieu est mort, vive le colon! [53]

> Well! The Arabs like to look at roses made of paper, or of plastic, nature has slipped through their fingers, they stagnate, intoxicated by tea and absinthe. And to hide their destitution, they fornicate all day long. Rational gardens must be created, geometrical cities, a booming economy, earthly Paradises must be created. God is dead; long live the colonizer!

Khatibi's satire of the colonial will to power and its smug self-consecration clarifies the delusion behind essentializing myths about the Other. The language associated with the colonials translates the rationalistic mentality of the dominant culture: it is dry, transparent, explicit, and cognitive. Its syntax is logical, direct, and often monotonously symmetrical. There are harsh consonants, polysyllabic words, and little sensuality. That Khatibi makes these different attitudes speak in direct, rather than indirect, discourse, allows us to experience some of their seductive force upon the child, and to comprehend his inability to integrate these disparate perspectives.

This linguistic and rhetorical opposition reflects a dialectical—as opposed to simply binary—narrative structure that recounts the boy's growing exile within a colonized society. The French occupation sets up artificial barriers and constraints, making it increasingly difficult for the boy to reconcile the environments of home and school. He slips in and out of each world, beginning to dissemble and deceive. Shuttled between his family and his aunt, between two mothers, two towns, three languages (his oral dialect, written Arabic, and French), the boy quickly learns to adopt outward forms at the expense of inner belief. Attending a variety of French schools, the boy plunges into a world of intellectual order but emotional and spiritual chaos.

Khatibi's use of differing narrative voices and varying syntactical and rhetorical structures redefines and gradually disrupts the conventional opposition of "civilized" and "primitive." The Moslem culture reveals itself to be predicated upon very different, but equally elaborate, principles as those of the West. We begin to understand that signs function differently in the narrator's culture: they constitute a coherent fabric of belief that informs the rituals of daily life. Their authority is collective and bound to the past. In the West, the individual, while constrained by certain laws, is free to manipulate signs according to his needs, to exchange and to reinterpret them within a more open system.

Signs for the narrator are linked to the sacred, a concept completely alien to the rationalized version of the holy found in Western Christianity. The sacred is at once mystical and erotic, and its signs dense and polyvalent, irreducible to any single meaning. They radiate by association, representing valued relationships and connections rather than explicit definitions, and serve to bind the individual to a collective history. By contrast, religion in the West is cut off from social and personal life; its signs have become reduced to simple equivalents or symbols of specific aspects of a religious myth so secularized that it has lost much of its spiritual force. The sacred in the Maghreb culture retains the element of violence that industrial societies have managed to eliminate from their rituals. Violence has a constructive function for tribal societies; it is both cathartic and curative for the community as a whole, and it informs sacred ceremonies with energy and seriousness.[7] The violence we observe in the novel is of two kinds: the

---

7. René Girard, *Violence and the Sacred* (Baltimore: Johns Hopkins University Press, 1977), 143–68. Girard discusses sacrificial rituals and the ritualization of violence in general as a means both of preserving the community, guaranteeing its solidarity, and of keeping random violence outside the group.

ritualized violence of the tribal celebrations, and the "discrete," often invisible, violence committed against the imagination of the Maghreb people as an instrument of colonial domination.

The narrator's entry into French schools marks his entrance into a desacralized culture where intellectual formulations about the world are wholly divorced from his direct experience. The sense of guilt he feels is tied to this sense of loss, in which he feels somehow implicated. It marks a shift from a world dominated by the authority of one book, the Koran, whose verses and graphics are inscribed on objects all around him, to a world of many books, and the gross proliferation of abstract signs:

> Chant d'abord, le Coran s'apprend par coeur . . . à côté du Coran, il y avait le talisman et la magie des femmes, par le henné aussi et le ta-touage. C'est pourquoi, signe des signes, le sexe est la fin de la mémoire désordonnée. [67]

> First a hymn, the Koran is learned by heart . . . besides the Koran, there was the talisman and women's magic, by means of henna and tattooing. That is why, sign of signs, sex is the end of the disordered memory.

Sex is a meta-sign because it embodies the difference upon which all signification is founded. Sexuality is mystical, linked to the sacred, because it involves the surrender of the individual to something beyond himself. Sex is "la fin" because it involves a momentary death of consciousness akin to mystical ecstasy, and also an *end* in the sense of goal, a symbol of spiritual synthesis, and an indirect means of re-establishing broken connections in the narrator's tattered memory. Later in the story, when the narrator desperately seeks out the company of women, often prostitutes, we recognize that he is really in search of a fabric of life that is lost to him. He has been deprived of the coherent society of his youth, where women marked with henna protected him and initiated him into the mysteries of the sacred. Indeed, sexuality—understood as a sensual orientation to the world—may be seen as a basic organizing figure both of the psyche of Khatibi's narrator, and of the text's elements as a whole. The coherence of the text's representations does not lie in the logic of episodes or psychological "development": instead, it arises out of a network of poetic values and motifs that form a multivalent signifying structure.

The paradoxical early life of Khatibi's protagonist is expressed poetically in an allusion to a myth which synthesizes his contradictory vision of his culture. He remembers his mother telling him that Morocco's independence was a loss for the French analogous to that of being weaned from a mother's breast. The boy envisions his mother imagining herself as the nymph Calypso who held Ulysses prisoner in her cave:

> La fraîcheur mythique de cette rencontre avec l'Occident me ramène à la même image ondoyante de l'Autre, contradiction d'agression et d'amour. Adolescent, je voulais me définir dans l'écoute nostalgique du mythe initial. [23]

> The mythic freshness of this encounter with the Occident takes me back to the same fluctuating image of the Other, a contradiction of aggression and love. As an adolescent, I wanted to define myself in a nostalgic harkening to a myth of origins.

The myth, which returns at the end of the text in an altered form, is a remarkable condensation of many of the motifs circulating throughout the novel. The most obvious feature of the myth is that it has its origins in the Western tradition, although the boy identifies it as a myth that describes his own beginnings ("le mythe initial"). Secondly, the boy recalls his mother telling him that the French were the weak, or "dependent," people in the colonial situation, an image that inverts the conventional hierarchy. The myth states that Ulysses and Calypso made love the night before he left for home, a detail that implies the European's susceptibility to values such as sensuality and passion, disdained by his rationalist principles. According to the myth, Calypso offers Ulysses (if he stays) immortality, a notion which constitutes a fantasy about progress and power entertained by both cultures about the West.

The mythical encounter crystallizes, in a poetic idiom, the shifting oppositions that the narrator must confront as a colonial subject. The "feminization" of the colonized, a frequent and complex distortion, implies at once desirability and weakness. The problem of sexual identity is tied inevitably to that of cultural identity and to the structures of power. Yet the boy's reading of the myth strains against such stereotypes, opening the way for a range of values usually absent from both sides of the equation. In fact, Khatibi's hero will at times embody aspects of both masculine and feminine, aggressor and victim, lover and beloved. The mixture of desire and hostility referred to by the boy expresses a conflict that necessarily ensues when the goal of one's desire (some form of recognition, validation, or power from the Other) is at odds with the means pursued to attain that goal (making oneself a desirable object, assuming the form of the Other's desire).

The narrator's education in French schools teaches him to acquire the forms of Western culture by imitation and imposture. Unable to comprehend their structure of reference, he develops a mimetic relation to forms of expression *per se*. His ignorance leads him unwittingly to detach words and gestures from their established connotations, a process that often becomes a source of high comedy. His ludic manipulation of Western conventions takes the form of a self-parody that is also a satire of France's "sacred" tradition:

> Maniaque dans les imitations, je racontais la suite de l'historie en alexandrins laborieux, torchés. Je voulais plaire au professeur de français, puisque par Corneille je serais entré dans l'éternité de l'Autre. L'Occident nous offrait ses paradis. [97]

> Meticulous in imitations, I told the rest of the story in laborious, scanned alexandrines. I wanted to please the French professor, since by means of Corneille I would enter into the Other's eternity. The West offered us its paradises.

While in class he is taught to memorize, to analyze, and to master an "écriture explicite" [explicit writing], the streets teach him a different lesson based on innuendo and suggestion:

> A l'extérieur, des chuchotements vagues, une extrême fragilité des mains, l'émergence, quelque part, de palpitations feutrées, éparses et secrètes. [87]

> Outside, vague whispers, extremely fragile hands, the emergence, somewhere, of muffled palpitations, scattered and secret.

The narrator's affair with French culture and language involves a sublimation that inverts the relation of writing to the body that obtains in his own culture. He is captivated by the evocative power of words rather than by their semantic values: "Devant l'explosion des sens, j'évitais de comprendre, j'y aurais laissé mon âme" (91) [Confronted by the explosion of meanings, I avoided understanding, I would have left my soul there]. French words have an exotic fascination for him that is sensory and formal rather than cognitive, but they draw him nonetheless away from his own frame of reference: "L'autre soir j'ai rêvé que mon corps était des mots" (89) [The other evening I dreamt that my body was words]. The dream succinctly articulates both the relation of writing to the body, and to what extent his journey has led him, paradoxically, away from, rather than toward, his desire. Here, instead of the sign being inscribed in the body as in the case of a tattoo, the body is inscribed in the sign, disembodied.

The dream confirms what we have observed, that the narrator has been "seduced"—however willingly—by Western culture into a state of abstraction. Yet we must also acknowledge that he has, in a sense, "prostituted" himself by imitation and imposture, entering into the commerce of signs. He has profanated himself in removing himself from his origins. Ironically, however, his entire culture is perceived as "profane" because marginalized by the West, excluded from the political space of administrative and cultural authority. The "rape" of the colonized people is more complex than often imagined, for it involves tacit collaboration between oppressor and oppressed. Khatibi demonstrates that there is seduction and betrayal on both sides. He also reveals a reciprocal effect of fertilization. Although the dream image alludes to the fragmentation of the body and the sublimation of desire, it also suggests a contrary metamorphosis: the reestablishment of the broken connection between the body and language, asserting the possibility—so diminished in the languages of empire—of concrete, polyvalent expression.

Khatibi's story is replete with paradox, both in its dialectical structure and in the use of rhetorical figures such as the oxymoron. The rhetorical figure that most aptly expresses his concept of bilingualism as paradox, (Gontard, La Violence du texte, 84). But the most telling evidence of its volatile bipartite-tripartite structure is expressed by the figure of the parabola, a graphic image present at every level of the text. A geometrical arc whose beginning and end form parallel, ever-opening lines, the parabola mirrors itself in infinite dispersion. This graphic form appears in Arabic script, and it "mimics" the recurring image of the flight of the swallow. This image occurs in conjunction with the sacred space in Maghreb culture, allied to a form of knowing opposed to the rationalistic cognition of the West. Representing the notion of mystical transcendence or spiritual quest, the parabola describes a departure and return analogous to the geographical and spiritual journey of the narrator. The figure also reproduces the rhetorical patterns of the novel's language, which, as I have remarked, at first oscillates between the disparate voices of the native and the colonial worlds. As the story progresses and the narrator becomes increasingly involved in French culture, the tribal voices diminish, only to reappear in an altered form at the end of the novel.

Articulating the paradox of identity and difference, the parabola is a structural principle of the text, in that the narrator's quest constitutes a parable (a word that derives from the same Greek root), or allegory. In "The Rhetoric of Temporality," Paul de Man defines allegory as "the unveiling of an authentic temporal destiny," a kind of "negative self-knowledge" that is the subject's awareness of his condition as determined by temporal realities beyond his control. This spiritual loss, this "death" of the transcendental subject (whose refuge, frequently, is myth) is expressed in allegory, a form that relies on no absolutes.[8] Unlike the symbol, which is predicated on the possibility of equivalence, identity, or coincidence, within a coherent system, allegory declares itself at a distance from an origin that is irretrievable. Allegory, or parable, is thus a meta-sign of difference, a difference that is concrete and insurmountable because embedded in a temporal frame. The narrator's story is a parable about the impossibility of abandoning one's native culture and assuming another, but it is also about the illusion of origins, of imagining the existence of some original, pure cultural identity that might then either be violated (by the colonizer) or contaminated (by the colonized).[9]

The narrator's desire to grasp the West's intellectual tradition as a way of legitimizing his precarious identity has a paradoxical effect upon both cultures. Instinctively, he perceives what might be termed the "unconscious" dimension of Western discourse, the anxiety latent in its rhetoric of certitude. He exposes the unspoken, or unspeakable, (l'indicible) in the Western system. He is attuned to material features of its language that contradict the rigidity of its ideological position: "Mon accord allait au bruissement des mots, à la métaphore outrée, à la sinusoïde" (117) [My consent went to the murmuring of the words, to the outrageous metaphor, to sinusoid contorsions.]

Khatibi's narrative is also an ironic allegory that plays upon familiar tenets of Koranic doctrine. Koranic law dictates that one should make a pilgrimage to the holy city of Mecca, where one must cast off native clothing and don the simple dress of that city. Khatibi's narrator will

<hr />

8. Paul de Man, *Blindness and Insight* (Minneapolis: University of Minnesota Press, 1981), 207–09.

9. In the chapter entitled "Pensée autre," Khatibi states that the notion of cultural unity in the Maghreb, a notion linked to that of theocracy, is a thing of the past. Citing the numerous tribal, national, and class differences within the Maghreb culture, he identifies as illusory the nostalgia for an original, ideal and totalizing entity. *Maghreb pluriel*, op. cit., 13.

perform a profane inversion of this holy pilgrimage: he travels to Paris, the Mecca of Western civilization, where he sheds his native clothes and dresses like a Dandy, that perfect caricature of the Western civilized intellectual. But the more he appears to approach the center of French culture, the more he confirms his spiritual distance. We are, in fact, obliged to rethink the relation of similarity to difference: the desire for identity, or "sameness," leads to a pseudoidentity that denies difference; real difference is a constituent of identity. Like a photographic negative, Khatibi's narrator remains separated from Western culture and from himself by the ontological abyss between facsimile and fact, appearance and reality.

In Paris, a city of myriad images, inscriptions and signs, values circulate as commodities for consumption, changing and being exchanged according to social inclination and individual need, divorced from any basis in experience or structure of belief. Paris is profane, not because it is a locus of debauchery, but rather because it is a city radically cut off from its vital sources. It is profane because of a deflation of meaning, not a lowering of moral standards. As Khatibi's narrator observes, all its inhabitants are exiles:

> Tout y est rendu au signe de la transparence, à la méditation enfumée, au papillonnement saisonnier des idées, rendez-vous de l'homme, en tant qu'addition de simulacres. [153]

> There everything is exhausted by the sign of transparence, by the seasonal fluttering of ideas, the meeting of men as an accumulation of simulacra.

Although unable to decipher the multitude of codes and signs that surround him, living a half-life in which he feels dispossessed of agency and validation, Khatibi's narrator unwittingly begins to reclaim signs from their presumed transparency in the West, destabilizing the edifice upon which its colonialism relies: the complicity between signs and referents deemed to be absolute.

Towards the end of the novel, after a journey across several continents, the narrator returns to his native Morocco where his voice suddenly resounds with authentic passion. Addressing the West, he rewrites the mythical encounter between Ulysses and Calypso in violent terms:

> Que vienne le Jour de la Très Grande Violence! Je tiens ta hanche dans le sable, je recroqueville ton corps à l'évasion la plus irruptive et j'attends:

tout se passe par-delà les épices, le cri de l'enfance. Je tatoue sur ton sexe, Occident, le graphe de notre infidélité, un feu au bout de chaque doigt. Point nodal, crac! [189]

Let the day of great violence come! I hold your hip in the sand; I curl up your body for the most explosive escape and I wait: everything occurs beyond the spices, the childhood cry. I tattoo on your sex, Occident, the graph of our infidelity, a fire at the tip of each finger. The nodal point, bang!]

The final image in this passage testifies to the paradoxical character of Khatibi's text. The "infidélité" refers to betrayal of the Other and betrayal of oneself. It refers to each culture's pretense to cultural purity and its denial of its own difference. The image of burning the tattoo on the nude body of the West suggests a subtle parody of the Judeo-Christian concept of "The Word became Flesh." The tattoo is a graphic sign that encodes sacred history as it is known through the senses. Like memory, it conserves and orders experience around affective values that are connected to graphic images rather than to rational meanings.

Khatibi's book is a tattooed memoir in that it tells a tale of alienation and exile that carries within it both its roots and its history, traced in its rhetorical figures and linguistic patterns. The narrator's repressed culture and his desire are, in fact, present throughout the novel, not only in tribal voices, but in the sensual imagery, rhymes, and musics of the language itself. It is evident in the "parabolic" involutions of his phrasing and syntax, in its echoes and repetitions. The sensory character of the text reaffirms the relation of writing to the body, and in so doing, represents the hope of repossessing the sign. If colonization involves the appropriation and fixing of the signs of another culture within one's own, then decolonization demands the liberation of the sign.

At the end of the narrative, Khatibi leaves his reader to contemplate an enigma: "Une rosace en mosaïque: je suis fasciné chaque fois que j'y jette un regard. Quelle pensée de pierre me hante?" [212] [A rose window in mosaic form: I am fascinated each time I glance at it. What thought of stone haunts me?]. The "pensée de pierre" suggests ancient inscriptions, perhaps those of the rosetta stone. The verb "hanter" echoes the words of a man who gave the narrator a talisman as a boy: "Il dit: tu es divisé de part et d'autre du corps . . . Il dit: tu es hanté" (52) [He says: you are divided on either side of your body. He says: you are haunted]. "Hanter" condenses the theme of doubling, conveying both a shadow outside the self and a level of subconscious experience within.

It suggests both the specter of the Other and the mask of repression. It recalls the voluptuous tribal voices who, throughout the narration, have reminded the narrator of his origins. Articulating both the way desire is governed by the Other and the way identity is founded upon difference, the verb "hanter" effectively sums up the dynamics of the text.

The design of the "rosace" is the very image of the signifier. Made of overlapping parabolic arcs in a circle, it is like a knot, an enigma without end. In its density and concentration, it is a heterogeneous sign, embedded in various forms in both the Arabic and Christian traditions as a symbol at once mystical and erotic. Echoing the Latin "sub rosa," it suggests the skin, the body, and desire. It recalls the image of the tattoo.

In Khatibi's text, the "rosace" thus signals the liberation of the sign from colonial servitude. The author/narrator has defied madness and death to demonstrate that colonization is ultimately an epistemological assault on a culture's sign-system. Yet writing operates to transfigure the effects of this confrontation with mortality. Liberating the repressed elements of the narrator's forgotten history, writing redeems his lost origins through an insistent pattern of sounds and rhythms across the text. Predicated upon difference, the writer's identity is always that of a ventriloquist speaking in many voices. Khatibi's tale of estrangement can now be understood as an allegory of the inevitable and necessary exile of the writer from a narrow, univocal concept of psychological or cultural identity. By reaffirming the primacy and autonomy of the signifier, Khatibi and his double have begun to reclaim their language and culture from the shadow of empire. In so doing, they have restored writing to its sacred function.

THOMAS SPEAR

Politics and Literature: An Interview with Tahar Ben Jelloun

On May 25, 1991, Tahar Ben Jelloun addressed the public at the open-ing session of a three-day conference, the "Journées Internationales Jean Genet," at the Odéon Theater in Paris. Ben Jelloun told how Jean Genet had phoned him after reading his first novel, Harrouda, *in 1973. Because of several issues of mutual concern—racism in France, the status of immigrant workers, and the Palestinian people—, Genet decided that the two writers should collaborate (see* Le Monde diplo-matique, *July 1974), which they did on several occasions until Genet's death in 1986.*

Several days later, Ben Jelloun granted me an interview to con-tinue the discussion about Genet and to answer questions regarding his experiences as a prominent critic and writer. Among the projects preoccupying Ben Jelloun in late May was the translation of La Re-montée des cendres, *a poem inspired, or rather "provoked," by the Gulf War, and scheduled to appear in a bilingual (French-Arabic) edition. The artist Edmond Baudouin was also completing illustra-tions to accompany a new edition of* Harrouda, *which would soon appear in the "Futuropolis" series (Gallimard, 1991). What follows is an abridged and translated version of our interview.*

MAGHREBINE IDENTITY AND THE TERRITORY OF LITERATURE

Thomas Spear As a Moroccan, do you identify yourself as African? Do you view Morocco as African?

YFS 83, *Post/Colonial Conditions,* ed. Lionnet & Scharfman, © 1993 by Yale University.

Tahar Ben Jelloun No. In Morocco one tends to feel more Arab than African. We're really in the northernmost part of Africa and we have a very different history. Personally, I don't feel at all African. That's not a pejorative or mean statement, but I don't feel African because I have no ties to Africa.

TS In the middle of your most recent novel, *Les Yeux baissés*, when the narrator returns to Morocco, why does she say that "the country is a fiction"?

TBJ Because she has been away from it for a long time. She has continued to imagine a country that, in fact, has progressed in certain areas and regressed in others. Her village has fallen into ruin, into a sort of degradation.

TS When you write, is Morocco sometimes for you a country of fiction?

TBJ It's a country that *gives* me fictions. That feeds me fictions. It's fabulous. I regret only that I don't have more time to write, because I have so many stories to tell, so many things to say.

TS In an interview published in *Notre librarie* (N⁰ 103), you said of Moroccan writers that "our only identity is as writers, our only territory is literature." Certainly, if one is really a good writer, one is beyond territories. But do you still identify yourself as Maghrebine?

TBJ Yes, of course. But I say that so as to stop this sort of perpetual questioning that asks, "Hey, why are you writing in French? you're an Arab!" I don't have a problem with identity. When you get down to it, what matters to me is what I produce, what I write. So if what I write can be associated with a place, which is necessarily Morocco, that's good. But my ambition is that this "place" should be everyone's place.

TS One must always have a particular perspective when one writes.

TBJ Exactly. If I talk about something very particular, about a tiny territory, from this point "there," it's crucial that readers in, say, Minnesota, be able to imagine, when they read what I've written, that that exists, without necessarily recognizing themselves in the character of the novel. It's sort of like me when I read Latin-American or Japanese novels. Japanese sensibility is completely different from mine, but for me, when a book is *good*, whatever its origin may be, it relates to my own situation. For instance, one of the books that I appreciate the most is Joyce's *Ulysses*. And God knows that there are continents between *Ulysses*, Ireland, Joyce, his writing, and me! But I would say that Joyce is someone who has helped me to write.

TS I find it unfortunate that Francophone literature from the Maghreb is so little-known in French Literature departments in French and American universities. The same "classics" are often read and taught. There seems to be so little interest in discovering, for example, the fresh imagination that you have to contribute.

TBJ No, in my opinion the French have come a long way on that score. In the past twenty years there has been enormous progress. I'm not talking about the press or about the universities; it's the general public who is interested. The press is following suit. Obviously, I myself was helped by the *Prix Goncourt*, which opened a lot of doors for me. But I'm not the only one. In 1987, when I was questioned about the impact of the *Prix Goncourt*, I said that what mattered most to me was that literature from the Maghreb was no longer going to remain "strange" or foreign, that it was going to become something. Now, just as I predicted, the others are being discovered after me: there is an Algerian writer named Rachid Mimouni who is extremely successful, and there is Tahar Djaout, for example. There is an interest in the others.

BEURS: FRANCO-MOROCCAN IDENTITY

TS Here in France, there is a community of people known as "Beurs." Do you have any particular ties to the Maghrebine community here?

TBJ I don't have any particular ties to it, no. I'm somewhat interested in its destiny. I watch a bit to see how things happen, how they develop, but I don't have any direct ties.

TS You know that they read you, probably . . .

TBJ Absolutely. But I don't have the impression that I express their universe, or their concerns. Others could prove me wrong, but that's just my own personal impression. For them, I express to a much greater extent their parents' homeland than the country they themselves have adopted. My most recent book, *Les Yeux baissés*, does raise this problem of identity and relations with the country of adoption, it's a book that touches on the problem of the transferal of identity.

TS The woman who narrates the novel, Fathma, settles permanently in France. You have said elsewhere that *Les Yeux baissés* is a book of "uprooting." Do you yourself feel as French as you do Moroccan? Do you not feel uprooted, or displaced, here in France?

TBJ I don't feel uprooted in the least here! I feel at ease here *and* in Morocco. My country is Morocco. I feel completely Moroccan. But in France I feel just as concerned by France and by what happens to it.

TS There are certain writers who live far from their country of origin for a very long time. Some of them, the writer René Depestre for example, are difficult to identify with a particular country. My Haitian students react rather strongly to him: they say that he hasn't seen Haiti for thirty years. Isn't that your case with Morocco?

TBJ No! I'm in direct contact with Morocco almost daily. I go there almost every two months and I spend about five months a year there.

TS Will your daughter be a "Beure," or will she be Moroccan?

TBJ She was born in France. I don't know. No, "Beur" is something very specific. Beurs are children of the subproletariat of immigrant workers and manual workers who have been raised here. I'm basically giving you a composite picture of the "Beur" or "the Beur generation." For example, children of Maghrebine lawyers or doctors living in France don't call themselves Beurs, because they've been raised in a more auspicious milieu. "Beur" automatically designates suburbia, delinquency, problems of assimilation, etc. There is a whole "Beur universe." You have, you know, the proletarian father, the mother who stays home, cramped quarters, lots of children . . . this isn't a caricature, it's the case of a lot of people. But if, for example, you look at the Paris phone book, you'll find that there are hundreds upon hundreds—perhaps even thousands—of Maghrebine professionals: doctors, lawyers, business executives. . . . With their families and their children, they live here like bourgeois French people. Can you call their children "Beurs"? . . . As far as my daughter is concerned, I don't know, I can't, already, put a label on her. I think that she will grow up in a Franco-Moroccan milieu. Partly in Morocco, partly in France.

FRENCH OR ARABIC?

TS Could you write in Arabic?

TBJ No.

TS French is your language of choice?

TBJ Yes. I can write articles, things like that, but I'm really not at ease in Arabic.

TS Last spring there was a colloquium held by the Conseil International d'Etudes Francophones, in Arizona, where I met the Moroccan writer Abdelhak Serhane, who also writes in French. I asked him if French is in fact a language much sought-after by Arab women, since one can speak more freely about the feminine condition in French than in Arabic. He told me that French is not only chosen for and by women, but by men *and* women, because Arabic is a sacred language; there are things that cannot be said in the language of the Koran.

TBJ Yes. I often say that the fact of writing in French is a way for us to be somewhat bold and also to be relevant, because, when one writes in Arabic, one is slightly intimidated by the language of the Koran. To my knowledge, there is no writer in Arabic, at least no modern writer, who has tried to do violence to the Arabic language. It's hard to do. There is no tradition in Arabic of *work* on language, as there is, for example, with Joyce or even Faulkner, or in France with . . .

TS Céline?

TBJ For instance. No, *we* don't have that tradition.

TS You don't allow yourselves to "twist" or disfigure [*tordre*] the language?

TBJ No. Arabic is a very beautiful language, very strong and solid. It is not at all an easy language to twist, either. One has to be very strong to do that.

TRANSLATION AND PUBLISHING
IN THE ARABIC WORLD

TS I have read *Le Pain nu*, the novel by Mohammed Choukri that you translated. Could you talk about the difference, for you, between the work of the writer and the work of the translator?

TBJ I am not a translator. I've done an anthology of Moroccan poetry and I've translated quite a few Moroccan and Arab poets. Choukri's book was translated more in order to make Choukri known than to exercise the trade of the translator. Choukri was someone who was the victim of a sort of rejection. So I did that translation rather in the spirit of doing him a favor. Translation is something with which I'm not at ease. It's a very hard process for a writer because it's a work of creation. I say to myself, I may as well use this time to write something myself, rather than translate.

TS In the Foreword to *Le Pain nu*, you said that "publishing in the Arab world is above all conformist and commercial." Do you still hold that opinion?

TBJ I said that ten years ago. I don't know how things stand with publishing in the Arab world now. But I know that it obeys neither the same criteria nor the same rules as international publishing.

TS Doesn't "international" necessarily imply commercialization?

TBJ Yes, but I mean that certain extraliterary elements are taken into account in Arab publishing. A political and a moral censorship are present in the text which are not necessarily separate. But I know that certain books of mine in Arabic don't make it into certain countries for those reasons. On top of that, there is a lot of disorder in publishing in the Arab world. Literary piracy is very widespread. And Arab books are handicapped in their commercialization; one's book should be able to circulate freely through twenty countries; but that's not the case. There is censorship, surveillance; there's no real exchange between Arab countries.

TS It's sad. In written form, at least, you nevertheless have *one* common language among so many countries.

TBJ Yes. But there are always exceptions. Morocco, for example, is a great consumer of Arab books published in Lebanon or in Egypt. Morocco is a good market for those countries. But they are not necessarily a good market for Moroccan publishing. You see, no piracy takes place in Morocco, but books published in Morocco are pirated in Egypt or in Lebanon. There is a disorder and a lack of respect for texts in the Arab world as a whole.

TS Respect? Of rights, or respect of the text?

TBJ Both. Of rights, and of the text itself. The two times that I've had to deal with publishers directly—one was in Syria and the other was in Lebanon (and they were very aware of the fact that they could glean a profit from my books)—, they told me that they would publish me, but on the condition that this, that, and the other thing be taken out. . . . It was unbelievable. Every time the word "sex" came up it had to be taken out; every time there was a reference to Islam that could potentially offend Muslims, Fundamentlists . . . Finally I said no, thank you, I'd rather not be published.

TS But your work is nonetheless translated into Arabic . . .

TBJ Yes, my work is translated. That is, my books make it into those countries, but I don't have any information about them. For example, some of my books have been printed in Egypt. I've never seen a copy, I don't know how it was carried out, I've never received any royalties. Nothing. I gave up on Arab publishing a long time ago.

* * * *

THE KING OF MOROCCO

TS Gilles Perrault's book, *Notre Ami le roi,* caused a scandal last year here in France. What is the nature of your relationship with the King of Morocco? He can't appreciate you very much . . .

TBJ I don't know whether or not he appreciates me. I maintain a stance of freedom and independence vis-à-vis politicians, both in France and in Morocco. I don't enter into debates with them. And I don't have any particular relationship with the King of Morocco. He received me twice, it lasted a few minutes, and that's all there was to it. I think he knows what my position is on human rights; I've been very vocal about it in the press: I refuse to accept the fact that people are imprisoned for their ideas and that torture occurs within prisons. He knows that.

HUMAN RIGHTS, RACISM, PALESTINIAN PEOPLE

TS Speaking more specifically in political terms, do you think that France has changed since Mitterrand has been in power? Do you find that there have been any changes, positive or negative?

TBJ The first positive step taken by Mitterrand's government was in my opinion the abolition of the death penalty. That's not bad, not bad at all. This said, I'm extremely disappointed by French politicians' lack of progress as far as the Palestinian question is concerned.

TS Is there any cause in particular that you endorse at the moment?

TBJ One cause that is still unfortunately very much in the foreground is the cause of the Palestinians. And then, in Europe, there's the problem of racism. Racism in France, human rights in the Maghreb (and in the Arab world), and the enduring Palestinian question: those are three issues that affect me personally.

TS On Radio France Internationale in January, you stated that the situation in the Persian Gulf was like "a western where [there were] only bad guys."

TBJ It's true. I felt like defending neither Saddam Hussein, nor those old-fashioned Kuwaiti princes, nor the American and Western forces. It's true, it was as if we were all caught up in a sort of absurd scenario. And it's still going on.

TS Do you have any particular opinion of Americans? Your work is translated in the United States, but I wonder if you have the impression that you manage to have an effect on people there.

TBJ No, I don't have any illusions about the United States! I can get across to students or universities who are interested . . . but reaching the general public is out of the question. Not because I'm an Arab, but rather, I think, because literature from the Maghreb does not conform well to their universe. It's something that simply doesn't enter into their way of thinking. On the other hand, it seems to me that Americans are not very curious about what goes on outside of the United States. People don't realize what a closed country America is. Its borders are more or less open, . . . but one finds a rather violent intellectual closure there. At the same time, there are some very interesting things about the United States.

As far as the Palestinian question is concerned, the Americans are still chummy with the Israeli government. When one considers for a moment Israel's arrogance and its way of saying "no" to everything, whatever the situation, it's intolerable. I think that in the West—whether in Europe or in America—there is, in absolutely everything, a repressed entity: Palestine. This sentiment is very strong, in France in any case. It's less strong in countries like Italy or Spain. In France there is a very violent and very strong sort of Israeli lobby that doesn't let anything past it. They are constantly on the look-out, they are there, they are waiting. . . . The minute you say "It's raining in Israel," it's antisemitism. You'd better think twice before you say that the sky is cloudy over Israel. So there is this sort of caricature of absolute support that is quite troubling. It's much easier to have exchanges with Israeli intellectuals on their own turf than with Franco-Jewish intellectuals. When Israeli writers like Amos Kenan or Amos Oz (among others) come to Paris, I talk with them.

TS *They* are aware of what's really going on—

TBJ Of course.

GENET AND THE PALESTINIAN QUESTION

TS You say that French politicians are not making any progress concerning Palestinians.

TBJ There remains, in France, a rather fierce anti-Arab bias. It's not direct. Well, the *Front National* expresses it rather strongly. But so far *intellectual* circles have not acknowledged the Palestinian question. You may have noticed, for example, in the discussion on Genet the other day, that there was a problem with his position vis-à-vis Jews. There was a constant effort to make an antisemite of him. Whereas that *wasn't* the real problem with Genet. In a perverse and roundabout way, they were trying to say that *Le Captif amoureux* is an antisemitic text. When the book first came out, there were disgraceful articles written about it. Has it been published in the United States, or not?

TS No. Grove Press, which had the initial rights to Genet in English, was bought out a few years ago by people who refused to publish it. The translation has been published in England, but it still isn't available in the U.S.*

In a collection of poetry you have published, *A l'Insu du souvenir*, there is a text where you say, "Jean Genet is a scandalous man."

TBJ I wrote that text when all of Europe was up in arms against him because he had published the preface to the *Bande de Baader*. The text, "Violence et Brutalité," published in *Le Monde* (2 September 1977) triggered a wave of hatred and incomprehension against him. It was rather amazing. Twenty years later, Genet was encountering the same animosity he had known in the fifties and sixties. For the first time, I

---

*It now has been published by the University Press of New England, 1992.

saw Genet moved. Deeply moved. I saw him often and, in general, nothing bothered him. But he was battered and hurt by this sort of hatred directed against him. I wrote the little text called "Pour Jean Genet" to boost his morale, that's all.

*　*　*　*

THE PUBLIC, POLITICALLY ENGAGED WRITER

TS You have written, in the same text on Genet, that "For him, the writer is he who succeeds in no longer having a face."

TBJ That's a construction that I thought was pretty and that I had used a very long time ago, when I began to write. I believe it profoundly: I have said that I write so as no longer to have a face. I write not to display myself or to exploit literature for my own benefit, but rather to disappear and to leave the work in the foreground. It's a bit pretentious. At the same time, it's more modest than the opposite attitude, when people hold the stage and the book has to follow.

TS You are a media personality; you often put the face of Ben Jelloun before the public's eyes.

TBJ But always with reserve. I don't ask for it. I don't hunt down the powers that be or the media. I'm more or less in the background. They're the ones who come to me.

TS But you give interviews; you often appear on TV, for example. You talk about politics, about immigrant workers, about Palestinians. . . . What is your opinion of the "engaged" writer? Do your books imply a Sartrian engagement?

TBJ I deliberately make a distinction—an unequivocal one—between writing and everyday political engagement. When I write, I don't produce a text that is "engaged" in the militant sense of the word. I create a work that is much more in-depth. Although, as you will see, in the poem that I'm currently publishing (*La Remontée des cendres*), which was provoked, inspired, in me by the final images of the Gulf War, I don't talk about the Gulf, or about Saddam Hussein, or about Bush. I don't talk about that. But those who have read the text so far have been more overwhelmed by the emotion that I've attempted to restore than by any political analysis. I don't do political analysis in a poem. So it's not an "engaged" poem in the sense that it's not a thing-with-a-slogan:

"Down with x, y, or z." It's a text for the individual, for those who were massacred and about whom no one speaks. Therefore it can't be considered a political text. And yet, ultimately it is also political.

I appear in the media always with some reluctance, and it is because I am solicited to do so. But I try to avoid it; I never provoke it. I never say, "Hey, I think I'll be on TV or on the radio." It's something that I never ask for. But sometimes I become aware of the fact that it's necessary to speak. It's necessary to speak because, if I don't speak, the silence could be interpreted as an endorsement of such-and-such a situation. So because of my high visibility, I feel obliged to intervene in the realm of information and say what I think, so as not to let others say what I don't think. It's something that doesn't necessarily thrill me, but I feel obliged to do it. Although, during the Gulf War, contrary to the impression I may have given, I didn't really take the stage much compared with others.

TS Just before the war broke out, you spoke on the radio, on Radio France Internationale. And your short story, "Le Suspect," was printed in *Le Nouvel Observateur* in February. I used the story in my intermediate courses. Concurrently in the United States, there was very little written against the military intervention. After the war, I was happy to see your short story come out in English, in *The Nation*.

TBJ Yes, in the case of that story, for example, I couldn't confine myself to political discourse. I had to produce a work of fiction, in the same way that I wrote the later poem (*La Remontée des cendres*). I'd be unhappy if I had to limit myself to a single discourse, whether fictional or political. In fact, I sort of try to be in both domains at once. The minute people reproach me for speaking in excessively political terms on TV, they open the paper the next day and find a literary text.

THE RAW MATERIAL THAT EVERYONE HAS

TS You have said that you are not very interested in writing about your own life. And yet, to a certain extent, you do precisely that.

TBJ One draws inspiration from oneself, but that's not enough. *All* lives are interesting and *all* individuals are interesting. What is important is *how* to express those lives, *how* to express what they carry within them. That's what makes the difference between a writer and an amateur: the work performed on raw material that everyone has.

You have only to take any character in the street—just look around you—, delve into his or her life, and you will find enough to make a novel.

TS Maryse Condé also claims to be interested by those whom you call "beings marked by failure" (*Les Yeux baissés*, 237). She says that she favors those of her characters who are unsuccessful.

TBJ Characters who succeed are not interesting. Succeed at what, to do what? What is their life, anyway? It goes by so fast, what are they going to succeed at? What are we going to succeed at? But failure is interesting. There are flaws, there is passion. Injury is interesting as a condition because there is something in it that betrays a sort of calmness, or serenity.

THOSE WHO SUFFER

TS You have said that talking about others is not very interesting. In almost all of your books, there is a female narrator and the principal character is a woman. In your work there is a marked interest in the feminine condition. And that is precisely to go toward the other, to see the world through the other's eyes.

TBJ Exactly. I don't withdraw into myself. On the contrary, I go towards others. I go towards woman because, in our society, she is the victim of a not-so-nice situation. So I serve as her witness. But that also holds for children in our countries who are often mistreated. I don't embrace failure, but rather those who suffer, because they have been condemned to a sort of destitution or suffering. That's basically what captivates me.

TS And yet the condition of woman, more than of children, is really what interests you.

TBJ Yes, but through the condition of woman an entire world is reflected. It's not only woman; man isn't so great either. But it's true: I use myself as a starting point. I'm compelled to go back to my roots, my origins.

THE RUSHDIE AFFAIR AND CENSORSHIP

TBJ Take the writer Salman Rushdie. At the moment he's controversial, but before the controversy he was nevertheless someone I read. In

Midnight's Children or *Shame*, Rushdie makes reference to his own memory. *Satanic Verses* was also a way of settling scores with his society, even though he was living calmly in London at the time (now his life is no longer calm). I find him very interesting as a writer. Fortunately, I had known and discovered him well before the scandal broke out. Unfortunately, I have the impression that, now, Rushdie is a writer condemned to no longer being read—or to always being read in the wrong way. It's a shame for him.

TS Yes. It's curious to note that his book has been more disparaged than those by a lot of other writers (the reference to Mohammed aside, of course . . .). Once, on *Apostrophes*, you said that you visited a school in Morocco where there were young girls who knew passages of your books by heart. There must be a lot of people in Moroccan religious circles who are strongly opposed to what you do.

TBJ Yes, naturally. I'm not well liked at all. There are sermons against me in the mosque. I'm occasionally the bête noire of integrationists. Whether they are political or religious fundamentalists. It's self-evident. It doesn't surprise me. I've never asked a fanatic to like what I've written. That would be unthinkable. That would be like asking him to disown his mother. All I want is simply to have nothing to do with them; I'm not trying to provoke them. I don't force them to read my books. But, without even reading my books, they attack me in the mosques.

TS Are you familiar with the very interesting texts by Malek Chebel?

TBJ Yes.

TS As he puts it, one can find an open homosexuality in the Arab world and, at the same time, a prohibition against talking about it. You address homosexuality, the condition of women. . . . You claim that you don't aim to provoke. But you want to tell the truth.

TBJ When I write, I don't adopt an attitude of provocation. I follow my truth, I follow my emotions, and I tell. I don't have any ulterior motives. When I write, I don't know what I'm going to do. I don't have an agenda. I try to transpose the reality I come from, such as I live it and see it. The writer's role is to be a witness to that reality, an engaged witness, personal and sentimental and all that, but a witness nevertheless. If this testimony is badly received, I can't do anything about it. But Moslem Fundamentalists, for example, don't read. All one has to do is say to them, "Hey, there's a writer who insulted Islam." "Insulted Islam" isn't true, but it doesn't really matter, obviously. When one is dealing with fundamentalists, caricature always gains the upper hand. I don't have to justify myself. I only have to refer them to the text. If they returned to the text, they would be taking a step forward. They would be betraying their intransigence.

TS Knowing full well what it is.

TBJ Of course. They need guys like that to deliver their sermons.

LITERARY JOURNEYS, "REALISM"

TS *La Nuit sacrée* starts thus: "The truth is all that matters." In this novel you go beyond truth. That's what I find so admirable: the flights toward the imaginary and the fictive. Do you really want to bear witness to the truth?

TBJ That's a claim! Yes, I claim that extreme subjectivity, or extreme fiction, is more apt to bear witness to truth than any police or news investigation. I know a lot more about Brazil through reading Amado or other writers than by going there with people who know the country and who show me around. In a sense, one can no longer travel: there are novelists for that. When one travels, it's only to confirm or invalidate what one has read. What gives me information isn't the Blue Guide, but rather the way in which the imaginary is transposed in books.

I sometimes say that I don't do realism because realism is impossible. Those who say that it's possible to photograph or write reality are fooling themselves. Because reality is crazy, it's nuts. To go and capture it, neither photography nor cinema nor drawing—and especially not TV— . . . no one can do that. . . . Reality is something within us, it shifts, it is elusive. What upsets me the most, what irritates me, is when would-be writers try to practice realism, to relate man's little troubles. That's not realism. Absolutely not. What is crucial is to be equal to this madness, to this sort of delirium of reality. Reality is DE-LI-RI-OUS. In unhappiness or happiness, delirium is what matters. That's why in my books there is always a sort of breakaway, a flight toward the imaginary, there is a universe, how should I say, that escapes everything.

—Translated by Caren Litherland

RÉDA BENSMAÏA

The Exiles of Nabile Farès: Or, How to Become a Minority[1]

> Nombreux
> sont les Exils
> à l'intérieur de nos
> âmes
> de nos villages
> de nos champs.
>
> —Nabile Farès, *L'Exil et le Désarroi*[2]

Why have I singled out Nabile Farès's *Un Passager de l'Occident*[3] for particular attention in this issue on nomadism and exile in emerging modern literatures? First of all, among the works of Maghrebian writers, this text exemplifies an approach that directly tackles problems posited by what we may call a "literature of migration." These problems are not only psychological but linguistic, and in the final analysis, political as well. Farès writes like a walker and thinks like a migratory bird:

1. A shorter version of this article appeared in *Peuples méditerranéens*, 30 Jan. 1985, Paris. The first version of this article was translated by Mrs. Karen Mallone. My reading of Farès would have been impossible without the invaluable work of Gilles Deleuze and Félix Guattari on the status of minorities and so-called "minor" literature in *Mille plateaux: capitalisme et schizophrénie* (Paris: Editions de Minuit, 1980) [*A Thousand Plateaus: Capitalism and Schizophrenia*, trans. Brian Massumi (Minneapolis: University of Minnesota Press, 1987)] and in *Kafka: pour une littérature mineure* (Paris: Editions de Minuit, 1975) [*Kafka: Toward a Minor Literature*, trans. Dana Polan (Minneapolis: University of Minnesota Press, 1986)]. Parenthetical citations of *Mille plateaux* and *A Thousand Plateaus* will refer respectively to *"MP"* and *"TP."*

2. Nabile Farès, *L'Exil et le désarroi* (Paris: Maspéro, 1976), 84. Hereafter parenthetical citations will refer to this text as *L'Exil*. Translation of this and all other quotations from the work of Farès are by Jennifer Gage. For quotations from other authors cited in the present article, a published English translation is used when available, with page references provided both for the original French and the English translation.—Translator's note

3. Nabile Farès, *Un Passager de l'Occident ou, Ali-Saïd (le Chanceux)* (Paris: Seuil, 1971). Page numbers for quotations from *Un Passager de l'Occident* will be indicated parenthetically with the initials *"UPO."*

YFS 83, *Post/Colonial Conditions*, ed. Lionnet & Scharfman, © 1993 by Yale University.

C'est pourquoi:
Exils et Découvrements
Pouvoirs et Renoncements
Patrie et Turpitudes
Tout est jeté sur Nous
en Vrac, comme des vêtements
sans lendemain,
et Nous voilà Errants
—devenus Errants—à des milles du chemin accompli. . . .
[*L'Exil et le désarroi*, 15]

This is why:
Exiles and Discoveries
Powers and Renunciations
Fatherlands and Depravities
Everything is heaped upon us
Like worn-out clothes
and here we are, wanderers
—having become wanderers—many miles down the road.

I chose *Un Passager de l'Occident* not only because it so eloquently explores the shores of the "inner sea" and surveys the great transformations sweeping these boundaries—migration, peripheralization, acculturation, and so on, all veritable sea changes that swell the margins of this *Mediterranean*, the *inland* sea and the sea *within*—but also because it represents an immense labor of scriptural *mise en forme* of the "raw material" that every Maghrebian writer confronts in this "inner sea."

Beyond this, there are many reasons to examine closely this deceptively transparent text. Indeed, just when we think we have closed the circle, drawn the circumference of the Mediterranean, it turns out that Farès is not where we expect to find him, but always on the edge, in a margin or marginality where borderline phenomena "open up" the Mediterranean rather than delineate its closure. This open frontier or liminality—which at the end of the book assumes the enigmatic guise of a cosmic dialogue—compels us to return to this text whose philosophical and political effects have not been adequately assessed.

It would not be exaggerating to declare that of all Maghrebian writers, Nabile Farès has provoked the most political and ideological controversy and the least critical commentary.[4] There has been a polariza-

---

4. Notable exceptions are the studies by pioneers such as Antoine Raybaud "Le

tion in the reception of his work. On the one hand, there is what appears immediately "clear and communicable" in his work, what is assumed to be transparent in his political and ideological positions,— resulting in an image of Farès as the standard-bearer of the Berber cause. On the other hand, those elements of his work that seem to be "hermetic" or "obscure" or even "abstract" are often underrated or neglected, because of an apparent unwillingness to read them closely. It seems to me that most readers have confused the leopard with his spots. By "complicating" his writings, Farès casts a smokescreen over what he cannot or will not openly "express." It is precisely this process of exclusion—this "reduction reflex," to borrow a term from Philippe Sollers—that I wish to analyze here by isolating some of the principal axes of the "tactics" Farès has deployed in this text dealing with the "metastable" status of the Maghrebian writer, the West, and the Mediterranean. It is not my intention to provide "keys" for reading this complex work, but to sketch a map that will allow us to travel through the various regions that the text has secretly staked out for us.

> "In your battle against the world, sustain the world."
> —Franz Kafka, *Diaries*

What is particularly striking about *Un Passager de l'Occident* is its posture of true defiance toward any attempt to assign a fixed and homogeneous framework to the geographical and rhetorical wanderings of the writer.

First, geographical *loci:* this pseudobiographical novel begins in Paris and ends in the stratosphere. By journey's end, we have crossed the United States from north to south and swept the shores of the

---

travail du poème dans le roman maghrébin (II): l'exemple du *Champ des Oliviers* de Nabile Farès" and Anne Roche "Le Desserage des structures romanesques dans *Le Champ des oliviers* de Nabile Farès", both in *Itinéraires et Contacts de Cultures*, Centre d'Etudes Francophones de l'Université de Paris XIII, Littératures du Maghreb, Volumes 4–5 (Paris: Editions L'Harmattan, 1984), 105–47 and 147–73 respectively. See also Hédi Bouraoui's "La Littérature maghrébine de langue française et la critique actuelle," Charles Bonn's "Pour une théorie des lieux d'énonciation dans la communication littéraire maghrébine de langue française" and my "Les États du Livre: Nabile Farès, *L'Etat perdu, discours pratique de l'émigré*," in the proceedings of the *Congrès Mondial des Littératures de Langue Française*, ed. Jacqueline Leiner, Giuliana Toso Rodinis and Majid El Houssi (Università degli studi di Padova, Padua, 23–27 May 1983).

Mediterranean from Orense to the Cangas Peninsula in Spain, hovering along the way over various regions of Algeria. We must not believe, however, that this is the only voyage. Such continental wanderings are always accompanied by local wanderings, which can transform a street or bar in Paris (*La Romance,* for example) into a veritable transit station, one of many places where one travels (musically) at high speed—*without moving:* to Peru, Venezuela, Spain, Greece, Brazil . . .

Next, rhetorical *loci:* unlike the majority of well-known books on the Mediterranean, *Un Passager de l'Occident* is composed of a series of texts that do not all participate in a common scriptural economy. For example, if we set aside the purely narrative component (the meeting with Conchita and the journey to Spain), we realize that this heterogeneous text includes numerous passages written in the style of the philosophico-political essay, along with poems, fragments of diary, or confessional prose, and finally dramatic "dialogues" whose main "characters" are nonhuman entities (such as the "Dialogues de Terre et Crépuscule," [Dialogues of Earth and Twilight]).

We could easily chalk these rhetorical and stylistic "deviations" up to Farès' longstanding taste for poetic and scriptural experimentation. All of his novels bear the mark of a writing that refuses transparency and defies limitation to a predetermined genre or theme; each text represents a "crossing," moving among the most diversified genres of writing possible. Faced with such a diversity of tone and style, it would be easy to improvise a plausible interpretation of what we are given to read, to "explain it away" as a form of "allegory," or "myth": in short, we could opt for a "symbolic" reading in the most banal sense of the word. Thus the dialogue between the Earth and Dusk that closes the book could be "read" as a dialogue—or dialectic—between two opposing principles that are supposed to control artistic and literary production: the reality principle and the pleasure principle, or reason and imagination, or materialist (earthly/Tellurian) thought and idealist (ethereal or abstract) thought, and so on.

What complicates the situation is that many passages of the book appear to lend themselves perfectly to a soothing "reading" of this sort. For example, Farès writes:

> Bien sûr je suis un astre, mais, avant tout, *je suis la Terre.* Et si de toutes les connaissances *qui m'expulsent hors de moi, on revient toujours à* ce point crucial de l'univers, c'est que, en dépit des nouvelles géométries qui traversent *l'esprit* des hommes, je suis le point équidistant de toutes les origines et de toutes les formulations. Alors, votre nouvelle

géométrie, est autant que moi, d'origine *terrienne* . . . [*UPO,* 153; my emphasis]

Of course, I am a star, but above all, *I am the earth.* And if, from all the knowledge *that evicts me from myself, there is always a return* to this crucial point of the universe, it is because—in spite of the new geometry that penetrates the *minds* of men—I am the equidistant point of all origins and all formulations. So your new geometry is, as much as I am, of earthly origin . . .

We can interpret this text quite easily as the "return of the repressed" of the poet, who, having ventured too far into speculation and "dream," is called back, back to Earth. It is the voice of a superego or of a self-censure that takes to task the individual who too quickly takes his wishes for realities. The letter from the "friend in purgatory" could support such an interpretation:

Et toi, pauvre petit habitant d'une presqu'île que tu n'as plus, tu voudrais aller à rebours de cette vérité, tu voudrais vivre artistiquement cette vérité artistique que tu crois en oeuvre et qui ne t'appartient même pas. Dans le fond, tu voudrais, en littérateur, être peintre, élaborer par petites touches un univers. Ce qui, ma foi, est un désir légitime, mais tout à fait farfelu. [*UPO,* 134]

And you, poor little inhabitant of a peninsula that you no longer possess, you would like to go against this reality, you would like to live this artistic truth, that you believe to exist, and that does not even belong to you, artistically. Deep down, as a literary man, you would really like to be a painter, elaborating a whole universe with tiny brushstrokes. This is, by God, a legitimate yet totally lunatic desire.

(One can almost hear the voice of the Commandatore of Mozart's *Don Giovanni:* "*respondi me!*")

This "reading" would be possible if Farès had not taken pains to warn us many times against any temptation to reduce the reality principle—and materialism into the bargain—to the most banal sort of realism, and if he had not expressly associated the "paralyzed consciousness" of realism in the domain of art and poetry with the "States that impose a complete lack of culture":

Conscience méduse, ou conscience médusée, sont les deux formes de l'expression réaliste. A elles deux, elles constituent l'idéologie artistique la plus réactionnaire qui soit: l'idéologie réaliste. C'est pourquoi, les politiques réactionnaires auront toujours en leur possession des valets du réalisme. [*UPO*, 36]

Paralyzing or paralyzed consciousness are the two forms of realist expression. The two of them constitute the most reactionary artistic ideology that exists: realist ideology. That is why reactionary politics will always have lackeys of realism in their service.

We have been put on notice: interpreting the reality of modern Algeria—and, as we shall see, that of the Mediterranean world, the Maghreb included—in allegorical terms means falling into one trap or another: mistaking straw for gold, or the fool's gold of allegory (if not an idealist phantasmagoria) for a reality:

Voilà pourquoi nous assisterons (nous les habitants de la presqu'île) au *passage d'une réalité allégorique à une allégorie devenue réalité*. D'où cet espoir DÉMESURÉ que nous avons: voir l'expression artistique offrir à la réalité une densité qu'elle n'a pas encore obtenue. [*UPO*, 37; my emphasis, Farès' capitals]

This is why we (the inhabitants of the peninsula) are present at the *passage from an allegorical reality to an allegory that has become reality*. Whence our inordinate hope: to see artistic expression giving reality a density that it has not yet attained.

Under certain historical and political conditions, it falls to artistic expression to sustain the world, rather than to the world to be expressed, represented by reflection in the work of art. It seems to me that, given Farès' allegory of his own devising, we must seek other ways of taking seriously what he offers for our consideration: not by "reducing" the contribution of any given element to another, but by understanding *literally (and in all senses)* the *real* meaning of the allegories that are left to us to decipher. Thus, the dialogue between Earth and Dusk is not to be interpreted as allegory—a transposed or transcoded teleological narrative—of what Farès "means," but as a *becoming-imperceptible*, or a *becoming-aerial* that is to be taken at its word. Similarly, references in Farès' book to the work of James Baldwin are to be interpreted not allegorically or symbolically, nor solely as a text of militant demands or a "Defense and Illustration" of Berber culture and its cause, but (also) as a *pact of alliance* that occasions a reevaluation of the nature of heterogeneity among Mediterranean peoples and cultures.

I am not unmindful of the risks I take in proposing such a shift in the reading of this text. In seeking at all costs to avoid the aforementioned "reduction reflex," one may in turn be in danger of reducing or taming/blunting the directly political thrust of this text. It should be more clearly stated that, although the first inspiration of Farès' text may stem directly from a scrupulous presentation of the Berber cause in Algeria, this is by far not the only impetus behind his effort.

What could be more tempting than to interpret Farès' use of James Baldwin's work as a foil for the depiction of the Kabyle community's status in postcolonial Algeria? In particular, how can we resist the temptation to transpose the crucial message of *The Fire Next Time*— the imperative that the United States recognize its racially mixed identity—[5] as the rallying cry of a new crusade launched against the power that, after Algerian independence, attempted to suppress the "hybridism" of modern Algeria? This power—the State—blindly refused to admit that there is no salvation without an affirmation of the multiple ethnicities, mores, and languages that make up Algeria. Stubborn insistence upon flatly "translating"—and thereby betraying— this text would lead to the following formula: it is imperative that Algeria (in the literal sense of its Arabic name, El-Djazaïr: "the islands")—the powers that currently govern Algeria—accept that it is a racially mixed nation.

This radical "formula," found throughout Farès' book, is reinforced by a series of notations that, whether they come from a reinterpretation of the "official" history of Algeria or whether they take on the more direct appearance of a solemn declaration, leave no doubt as to the intentions and ultimate aims of the author. Here is an example:

> it is a reality, la Petite Kabylie, a reality in continual agitation, even
> though the Petits Kabyles have never wanted power for the good (the
> only, the true) reason that it has always been taken away from them,
> they (the Petits Kabyles) have never wanted power. as for the Grands
> Kabyles, their power ends at the edge of the Azazga Forest, or in the
> meadow of Lake Fadou. everything else belongs to the invaders from
> the plains.[6]

5. "What it comes to is that if we, who can scarcely be considered a white nation, persist in thinking of ourselves as one, we condemn ourselves, with the truly white nations, to sterility and decay, whereas if we could accept ourselves *as we are*, we might bring new life to the Western achievements, and transform them." James Baldwin, *The Fire Next Time* (New York: Dell/Laurel, 1985), 126.
6. "Kabylie" refers to a specific mountainous region in Algeria. The *Kabyles* are the inhabitants of this region, within which a distinction is made between the Kabylie of the *Djurdjura*, or "Grande Kabylie" (to the east of the national capital Algiers), and "Petite

Further on, among other "meaningful" observations, Farès unambiguously emphasizes (again going so far as to put the entire passage in italics) that:

> *Algeria came after Kabylia. this is a fact. for Algeria is a recent creation of the right of peoples to determine themselves. and if the peoples have the right to determine themselves, we, the inhabitants of the peninsula, do not understand why the inhabitants of these people* [sic] *should not determine themselves. "I am Kabyle" does not mean that "I am not Algerian," but simply that as an Algerian, I am first of all a Kabyle. this really shouldn't be upsetting.* [UPO, 32–33; Farès' emphasis and punctuation.]

On the surface, then, there is no doubt about the meaning to assign to the general trajectory of Farès' book. Its intention is no less, and no more, than to stigmatize the aberrations practiced by the powers that rule Algeria. Within a framework of cultural void and blindness, they attempt to "reduce" contemporary Algeria to the sacrosanct triad of one race, one language, and one faith. While Farès is neither a separatist nor an advocate of the independence of Kabylia in the strict sense, he appears to be the militant voice of a minority that seeks to be recognized *hic et nunc.* Failing such recognition—*the fire next time!*: the autobiography becomes simply a political pamphlet or manifesto bearing an apocalyptic warning.

One might also invoke numerous other passages where Farès seems to militate in this very direction; these sections make it difficult not to read the book as a political pamphlet or manifesto. Once again, we may see it as a "Defense and Illustration" of Kabyle culture as a specific component of Algeria. It is a "fact," Farès would say, that there is a Kabyle "problem" in Algeria. But it is also a historical fact that Algeria is a multilingual, multiethnic, multitribal, multisectarian country resting on a foundation of irreducible ancestral paganism; it is also true that any failure to recognize this "fact" risks igniting the powder keg of national tension. It is not my intention, therefore, to suppress this aspect of grievance and denunciation in Farès' work; on the contrary, I believe that it is necessary as a first step to acknowledge the importance of this posture of protest and to bestow upon it the serious consideration that it merits.

Kabylie." Also called *Berbers,* the Kabyles have a specific language ("Berber" or "Kabyle") and a culture of their own. They represent one of Algeria's ethnic and cultural minorities, another being the Tuaregs—men and women of the Sahara and the south of the nation. *UPO,* 31; Farès' emphasis and punctuation.

Yet at the same time, I claim (for reasons that I shall put forward more precisely) that this grievance absolutely does not circumscribe the book adequately or definitively. Limiting oneself to this vector would reduce the book's scope considerably. If Farès' ultimate intent were to write a political pamphlet or manifesto, what perverse pleasure or "logic" would lead him to scramble his signals so studiously? Why would he end the book with a text that is, to say the least, a far cry from any single political platform pointing the way to concrete political action? Why such an obscure "end(ing)" to a work intended to serve a single *cause?*

Moreover, if Farès' (political or ideological) objective were to serve as an intermediary for the claims of the Berber community as an already *constituted* entity, we would be hard pressed to understand the vehemence with which he hastens to denounce any reduction of his position to a purely reactive or demanding attitude. Interpreting the book from a *strictly* political angle would render incomprehensible the very firm declaration of intent to be found in Farès' explanation of the difficulties of his position, when he reveals some of the "cards" in his hand: "J'ai bien la carte bleue des résidents algériens de Paris, mais elle me laisse encore en état de perpétuelle jonglerie" (*UPO*, 60) [I do have the "green card" required of Algerian residents of Paris, but it always leaves me feeling like an impostor"]. He continues:

> Si je n'ai jamais *biaisé* avec *les réalités* nationales, j'ai toujours eu des *tentations d'évitement.*
>
> Ce qui ne m'a nullement empêché de participer (modestement, mais activement), à l'élaboration d'une nouvelle nationalité (j'étais jeune, il est vrai), *au temps où, précisément, cette nationalité était refusée.* Car, ce qui m'avait attiré alors (du moins c'est ce que je me dis actuellement), *c'était de vivre contre le refus.* Non pas *dans* le refus, mais *contre* le refus. [*UPO*, 60–61; my emphasis]
>
> Although I have never *shied away* from confronting national *realities,* I have always been *tempted to avoid them.*
>
> This has not in any way prevented me from participating (modestly yet actively) in the development of a new nationality (it is true that I was young) *at the exact moment when this nationality was denied.* For what had then appealed to me (at least, this is what I tell myself now) was *living against refusal.* Not *in* refusal, but *against* it.

Living not IN but AGAINST refusal: if we really *read* what he *writes* here, it appears clearly that, for Farès, living *in* refusal—which is a reactive attitude—is not the same thing as living *against* refusal. The first "posture" is the relatively comfortable "position" of the person who, according to Farès, holds in good faith that something already belonging to him, already *constituted* (granted) as his own, has been taken away. The second is the "desperate" position of the person who refuses the dangers (or as Farès puts it better, the "mystifications") of false dialectics—consisting here very simply of countering refusal with a refusal *of the same type.* One may discern a Spinozian reasoning in Farès: an aversion to negation, to the dialectics of negation, and a taste for *"univocity."* Therefore, instead of simple oppositions (even contradictions) between Master and Slave, Majority and Minority, National and International, National and Regional, we find in his work an attraction for the middle ground, the gray areas between these poles. Farès explores the gradations, degrees of intensity, the events and accidents that compose metastable singular individuations. Out of this attraction arises his interest in the work of Baldwin, Faulkner, Memmi, Fanon, Feraoun, or even Camus—any writer who is preoccupied with *minority*—as well as something else: the appeal the Neutral holds for him.

By the Neutral, we mean not *neutrality,* a quaint and timid attitude that hesitates between two polar opposites, but rather a position that calls into question the forces that lock Master and Slave into a fight to the death. It is also a position that keeps a certain "distance" from everything that tends to characterize protagonists rigidly and definitively as "adversaries" or predetermined subjects in opposition: Algerian vs. Kabyle; European vs. "oriental," man vs. woman, Self vs. Other, and so forth. According to Farès, writers—like Lacanian analysts—are utterly defenseless in confronting the dialectics of adversity, precisely because they are "neutral": NE UTER, "neither one nor the other," as Catherine Clément reminds us.[7] "Neuter" is *not*

> like diplomatic mediation, Swiss style, but a *proper* distance between *proffered passivity* and *interventional activity.* A "non-actor" is he who is capable of acting, but does not exercise this ability. He can show action by simply holding back; contrary to the shaman, he lets the patient act, unfettered. This is the power of the *neutral.* [141–42]

7. Catherine Clément, *Vies et légendes de Jacques Lacan* (Paris: Grasset et Fasquelle, 1981), 141.

This seems to be Farès' position in this multilayered book: he does not choose one position over another, since this would strengthen exclusionary forces; instead, he delineates lines of flight (*lignes de fuite*), traces drifting movements, effectively keeping his "proper distance between proffered passivity and interventional activity." In a striking passage, Farès writes:

> Car si, dans ces moments *romancériens*, j'apparais comme un zéro qui vadrouille, je dois dire que la vadrouille de ce zéro semble *mystérieusement active*. Il suffirait qu'un événement provoque *l'activité* de ce zéro pour que, immédiatement, surgisse la *multiplication des capacités du zéro*. [*UPO*, 59; my emphasis]

> If in these flights of *romancerian*[8] fancy I appear to be a wandering zero, I must say that the wanderings of this zero seem *mysteriously active*. A single event is enough to provoke this zero into *activity*, immediately *multiplying the zero's capacity*.

That Farès is well aware of the difficulty his position implies is also evident in the following passage describing the passivity of the *"Benni-Oui-Oui"*:

> Ce type d'être qui, en Algérie, fut nommé "fils de Oui-Oui" (Benni Oui-Oui) reste pour bien longtemps encore *à l'état structural* dans pas mal de sociétés. Aussi, *à vivre dans l'antithèse du refus*, on garde, à portée de soi, des nostalgies d'insurrection.
> Jusqu'à présent, cette position, bien que *désespérante*, m'a évité beaucoup de mystifications.
> *Accepter de refuser le refus de l'autre:* telle est la devise d'une position en catastrophe.
> Je risque gros. Mais, ce risque est mesure de ma passion d'existence, et ce risque, ce soir-là, je l'ai pris avec Conchita.
> Comment parler de ce risque? C'est une question à laquelle je vais m'efforcer de répondre. [*UPO*, 61; my emphasis]

> In Algeria, the type of yes-man referred to as *Benni Oui-Oui* (literally "son of yes-yes") has long been an integral part of the structure of quite a number of societies. Thus, by *living in the antithesis of refusal*, one keeps within reach nostalgic desires for insurrection.
> Until now, this position, although maddening, has been fairly un-

---

8. *Romancerian* plays on *La Romance*, the name of a bar frequented by Farès' narrator, as well as on the words *roman*, [novel] and *romancier* [novelist].

complicated to me: *agreeing to refuse the refusal of the Other*: this is the motto of catastrophe.

I have staked a lot on this, but this risk is a measure of my passion for existence; this evening, I took this risk with Conchita.

How can one speak of this risk? I must force myself to answer this question.

Farès' position is not really one of refusal, but neither is it the paranoid stance of a "paralyzed conscience" or, in other words, an Ego that is perpetually subject to the values and desires of the Other—the Adversary, the Castrating Father, the Colonialist, the Frenchman, and so on. Farès takes another tack: slipping imperceptibly towards the "Neutral," in a twilight or disappearance that is also a new birth. What interests Farès is not belonging to a minority whose values, cultural patrimony, and political interests he ardently defends (this agenda is the legitimate aim of writers such as Mammeri, Feraoun or Memmi) but rather using this minority status as a pretext for setting in motion a "war machine."[9] In radical opposition to the "minority" as an already constituted *ensemble* or *State*, this "war machine" (inseparable from a "writing machine") unleashes the "minoritarian" as a *becoming* or a *process*. Here, in this sort of imperceptible dehiscence, lie the strength and the genius of Nabile Farès' work—his discovery of a new world. "Un air doux Souple Qui ouvre les Mains du Monde les pose là Sur le Ciel pour l'Eloigner de la Terre Car la Terre doit respirer Profondément Nouvellement Avant de s'Elancer dans l'étroit défilé de sa Mort et Naissance" (*L'Exil*, 19; Farès' capitalization). [A balmy Pliant air Which opens the Hands of the World places them there On the Sky to Separate the Earth For the Earth must breathe Deeply Newly Before Hurling itself into the narrow straits of its Death and Birth].

Indeed, in this incandescent book Farès attempts to make plain that while minorities incontrovertibly exist throughout the world, and

9. I shall elaborate on the pertinence of Deleuze and Guattari's notion of the "war machine" below. Cf., *Mille Plateaux*, chapter 12, "1227 - Traité de nomadologie: La machine de guerre," 434 ff., and in particular the following: "Is it by chance that whenever a "thinker" shoots an arrow, there is a man of the State, a shadow or an image of a man of the State, that counsels and admonishes him, and wants to assign him a target or 'aim'?" (*TP*, 378). The "arrow"—i.e., the *becoming*—that Farès wants to shoot or set in motion has no "aim," strictly speaking, but rather an "objective": that of discovering a new political "plane of consistency," new relations of movement and rest, as well as new relations of power and of affect in "ce pays qui est le nôtre" (*L'Exil*, 19). "Entre la vérité, et la foi, le passage reste obscur, même si l'Archer est là, parmi les espoirs et les rêves, pour désigner les pistes" (*L'Exil*, 69).

while it is true that a minority is in essence a community that is always—actually or potentially—subject to repression, despoilment, relegation to an inferior status, still it does not follow from these undeniable circumstances that the best reply is a maniacal self-defense and withdrawal into oneself. Insistence on only *my* language, *my* region, *my* village, *my* history, *my* tribe, *my* craft, is a *molar reflex*[10]—or as Farès would say, a *"mullah reflex"*—that can appear necessary and legitimate only in the context of reassuring the Other. This reassurance, a specular movement that merely reproduces and idealizes the principal images of its refusal, also reflects the individual hope of holding the majoritarian position with one language, one race, one religion, one territory—in sum, by positing another "State" or "stasis." Countering one "state" or "substance" with another is always to second wholeheartedly the political and religious ideology of the Other, and unconsciously to reinforce its values in blind pursuit of the very same "ideals." What appears very clearly in every attitude rooted in refusal is that the individual desires *Stasis* for himself, the majoritarian power of the State—leading, in a paradoxical self-sabotage, to his own annihilation as a minority. This, most emphatically, is not what Farès envisions for Kabylia—*nor for Algeria itself!*[11]

VOIRIE (voi-rie), s.f. * 1. Partie de l'administration publique qui a pour objet la police des rues, des chemins, l'alignement et la solidité des édifices, etc. * Grande voirie, celle qui s'occupe des grandes voies de communication. * Terme de féodalité. Charge héréditaire de certains fonctionnaires qui devaient veiller à la sûreté des routes. * 2. En administration et en hygiène, dépôt des débris que fournissent les villes . . .

"L'ordure et la voirie du monde," Charron *Sagesse,* 562, dans La-

10. Deleuze and Guattari oppose the majoritarian tendency of the *molaire* ["molar," a term borrowed from chemical terminology] to the minoritarian impulse of the *moléculaire* [molecular]: ["man is the molar entity par excellence, whereas becomings are molecular," *TP,* 292].

11. In this respect, Farès' work is very close to the work of an Irish writer such as James Clarence Mangan, as masterfully analyzed by David Lloyd in a book I came across while rewriting this article, *Nationalism and Minor Literature: James Clarence Mangan and the Emergence of Irish Cultural Nationalism* (Berkeley: University of California Press, 1987). See chapter 7, "The Ends of Mangan," and particularly the following. "In his resistance to the identifying drive of the aesthetic, Mangan [and this would apply to Farès as well] prevents the logic of our own desire to *force some neatness of identification upon him by suggesting that he is the ironic type or representative of an Ireland [Algeria], or by extension of any colony or ex-colony, that, precisely by seeking its authentic identity and declaring its opposition to imperial power through the constitution of a democratic state, perpetuates its own dependence . . .* " (210; my emphasis).

curne. "Les seigneurs ayant seulement basse justice et simple voirie qui est tout un," *Coust. gén.* t. 2, 118. [Dictionnaire Littré, article "Voirie"]

VOIRIE (voi-rie), * 1. Section of public administration that has as its task the maintenance of streets and highways, the placement and the durability of buildings, etc. * "Grande voirie," *responsible for maintaining major* connecting arteries. * Feudal term. A hereditary responsibility of certain functionaries responsible for overseeing the safety of the roads. * 2. In public works and hygiene, the disposal of debris created by towns and cities . . .

Farès writes:

Il n'est pas étonnant que, souvent, dans la littérature algérienne n'appraissent que des considérations "tribales," fraternelles (style *"les barbelés de l'existence"*[12] feuilleton du quotidien du peuple), ou catastrophiques.
    Qui croire?
    La réponse la plus simple serait: les Puits de Pétrole, car eux, on les voit. [*UPO*, 76]

It is not surprising that often in Algerian literature only "tribal" elements are considered. These may be fraternal (as characterized by comic strips in the daily papers), or catastrophic.
    Whom to believe?
    The simplest answer would be the *Oil Wells*—these we can see.

Farès may be seen to hold fast to one boundary. On one side of this clear demarcation is the space created by the stratifications (of territory) and manipulations (of history, of the past, of social contradictions as well as of sociocultural forces) used by a given State in order to achieve certain political ends or to confer a certain efficacy and legitimacy on itself.

    "There is no country that is not nationalistic. Nor any government, once it is "installed," that is not predisposed to narcissism. So?"
    "So? Nothing. I don't know. First to understand what is happening to me. . . . To understand: yes: understand." [*L'Exil*, 18]

---

12. Farès is referring to a popular daily comic strip that features ironic commentary on politicians, bureaucrats and intellectuals (somewhat in the style of *Doonesbury*).

On the other side of this boundary we find the "reality" of heterogeneous social, political, and cultural elements that are constantly
working covertly upon the fixtures of sovereignty and domination that
are the underpinnings of majority principles, or, in Farès' terms, principles of nondifferentiation. Farès' notions recall the remarks made by
Deleuze and Guattari at the outset of their discussion of the "logic" of
minority emergence.

> Pourquoi y a-t-il tant de *devenirs de l'homme,* mais pas de *devenir-*
> *homme?* C'est d'abord parce que l'homme est majoritaire par excel-
> lence, tandis que les devenirs sont minoritaires, tout devenir est un
> devenir-minoritaire . . . [*MP,* 356]

> Why are there so many becomings of man, but no becoming-man? First
> because man is majoriterian par excellence, whereas becomings are
> minoritarian; all becoming is a becoming-minoritarian. [*TP,* 291]

Transposing and adapting this observation for the purposes of the present discussion, I would say that one of Nabile Farès' major concerns is
not to resolve a contradiction, but to formulate a paradox, to wit: Why
do countries that have derived their power from their minoritarian
position aspire so ardently to join forces with the majority camp?
Asked in another way: what makes the active presence of minorities so
dangerous in newly formed nations?[13]

Paul Virilio writes: "Le pouvoir politique de l'État est *polis,* police,
c'est à dire voirie" [The political power of the State is *polis,* police, that
is, management of the public ways"].[14] From a certain perspective, this
is the "lesson" Farès draws in his book, taking up the cause of the
minority to which he belongs as a case in point. Although one could
have hoped that an independent Algeria would have been aware from
the outset of the dangers entailed by the assimilation of the category
"man" into a standard "par rapport auquel les hommes forment néces-
sairement (analytiquement) une majorité" (*MP,* 356) [in relation to
which men necessarily (analytically) form a majority] (*TP,* 291), it was
sadly the case that Algeria aligned itself with the levelling forces of
majoritarian formations. Under the pretext of promoting national
unity—an entirely legitimate worry—Algeria was at a loss to realize
the extraordinary potential of its ethnic, social, and cultural diversity,

---

13. See again David Lloyd's *Nationalism and Minor Literature.* I direct the reader
in particular to pages 49–59 in chapter 2, entitled "The Spirit of the Nation."

14. Paul Virilio, *Vitesse et politique* (Paris: Editions Galilée), as cited and discussed
by Deleuze and Guattari (*MP,* 479; *TP,* 386).

the legacy of its history. Instead of affirming the existence of minorities as a cultural and political asset fostering pluralism, instead of defining itself as a minority, a *becoming-minoritarian*, Algeria "chose" to try to reduce to a single unity the multiplicities that make up its depth and breadth. The One (the majority) is "inside"; the Others (the minorities) are always on the "outside." Farès brilliantly demonstrates that such a "dialectic" could only damage Algeria and all other nations suffering from the dangerous notion of the majoritarian principle, which excludes them precisely by making them into minorities.

At this point, we may better understand the explosive influence exerted by the work of James Baldwin upon Farès' book. Baldwin's presence recalls *in practical terms* the urgent necessity of breaking with these "dialectics" that leads to *inventing a majoritarian* past rather than accepting the past and putting it to good use. Farès quotes from Baldwin's essay "Down at the Cross: Letter from a Region in My Mind" that appears in *The Fire Next Time.*

> To accept one's past—one's history—is not the same thing as drowning in it; it means learning how to use it. An invented past can never be used; it cracks and crumbles under the pressures of life like clay in a season of drought. How can the American Negro's past be used? The unprecedented price demanded—and at this embattled hour of the world's history—is the transcendence of the realities of color, of nations, and of altars. [*Fire*, 128; quoted by Farès, *UPO*, 46]

There it is a great temptation in reading these lines to "translate" these concerns automatically into questions on how best to use the Kabyle past—or that of the Tuaregs, or the Turks in Algeria. Although it is undeniable that Farès is resolutely committed to posing this question, it does not limit the scope of his enterprise. Let us return to the opening chapters of *Un Passager de l'Occident*, entitled "Paris-New York" and "New York-Paris." In rereading these chapters, we perceive that what engages Farès' attention above all is not the accession of a given minority to majority status, but rather the potential eruption of white America—majoritarian America—from the internal pressures of *becoming-minoritarian*. This eruption will bring forth not chaos, but a redistribution of priorities and defining features (ethnic, cultural, or linguistic) that make up present-day America. It is never a question of returning to *what one is*, but a matter of freeing up the potentialities of *what one is becoming*, by adopting an itinerary that owes nothing to the ambitions of the *Etat-Voirie:*

Bien sûr, je ne veux pas dire qu'il faille être reconnaissant d'être ce qu'on est (quelle blague!). Ce que je veux dire, c'est que *la force de la réalité noire* a éclaté les Etats-Unis, et que cet éclatement a provoqué chez les auteurs américains blancs des fuites dans tous les sens.

Ce que j'admire en Baldwin, c'est qu'il a gardé une présence aiguë de cet éclatement. Cette fois, *non seulement chez l'homme blanc, mais aussi chez l'homme noir.* Avec cette différence que l'éclatement chez l'homme blanc est plus meurtrier que l'éclatement de l'homme noir . . . [*UPO,* 19]

Of course, I do not mean to say that one must be grateful for what one is—what a bad joke. What I do mean to say is that *the force of black reality* has shattered the United States and that this explosion has, in white writers, caused flight in all directions.

I really admire Baldwin for his ability to retain a sharp presence of this explosion in his work. In this instance, *it is happening not only to the white man, but to the black man as well.* Yet—there is a difference; this explosion is much more lethal in the white man than in the black man.

A word to the wise . . . The warning words of the slave song quoted by Baldwin achieve a stunning clarity: "God gave Noah the rainbow sign / No more water, the fire next time." Fire, if we repeat the "mistake" that we are all too ready to pounce upon in others but to which, para- doxically, we remain blind in ourselves as long as our narrow vision consigns everyone who is not the "standard man"—the "Algerian-in- general—to the category of the "other": foreigner, immigrant, *beurs.*[15] These pages tell us that any group (blacks, Gypsies, Kabyles, Jews, etc.) can, under the right political or historical circumstances, form a mi- nority; they also tell us that this is not enough to make them into a *becoming* or, in other words, into active principles of revolutionary transformation. Setting aslant Baldwin's passionate work, Farès shows that simply *belonging* to a minority is not sufficient to escape the ever- present menace of *stasis,* nor does it eliminate the taste for *conquest.* Farès does not limit himself to putting this minority in opposition to that majority, or to the majority in general; rather, he consistently portrays the *becoming-minoritarian* (the minority as *process*) con- fronting the majority in which the minority-as-process is necessarily inscribed. Farès' approach converges with that of Deleuze and Guat- tari: "On se reterritorialise, on se laisse reterritorialiser sur une minor- ité *comme état;* mais on se déterritorialise *dans un devenir*" (*MP,* 357;

15. The term *beur* refers to a child born in France to parents who are immigrants.

my emphasis] [One reterritorializes, or allows oneself to be reter-ritorialized, on a minority *as a state; but in a becoming,* one is deter-ritorialized *(TP,* 291)]. All of Farès' reflections on paganism serve the objective of rediscovering a real "political fervor" while avoiding the trap of reducing the history of Algeria to a single dimension that ne-glects the country's pervasive multiplicities:

> La vraie patrie de l'Algérie est son passé le plus ancien, et le passé le plus ancien de l'Algérie—ESTHETIQUEMENT PARLANT—est le paga-nisme. Que l'expression révolutionnaire rencontre l'expression païenne et le moment de vie que traverse le pays se multipliera de ferveur politique. De cette manière, la pensée païenne vaincra la bu-reaucratie et la technocratie actuelles. De cette manière, la pensée païenne *activera la critique révolutionnaire d'une idéologie essen-tiellement étatique.* Ainsi apparaîtra, *dans l'authenticité de son de-venir,* une histoire *algérienne libérée* de toutes les conquêtes qu'elle a connues." [*UPO,* 74; my emphasis, Farès' capitals]

> The true homeland of Algeria is its most ancient past, and Algeria's most ancient past—AESTHETICALLY SPEAKING—is paganism. Let the revolutionary and pagan expression meet and join; and this mo-ment of life that flows through the land will grow into political fervor. In this way, pagan thought will defeat present-day bureaucracy and technocracy. In this way, pagan thought will activate revolutionary crit-icism by means of a statist ideology. In this way will appear in its full authenticity, an *Algerian history,* liberated from all the conquests it has known.

It is clear that what interests Farès is not the Kabyle minority as a determined entity or subject whose primary hypostatic integrity must be restored, but rather Berbers as a becoming-minoritarian. Farès has clearly understood how, "d'une certaine manière, c'est toujours 'homme' qui est le sujet d'un devenir" (*MP,* 257) [in a way, the subject in a becoming is always man *(TP,* 291)]—whether it is black Americans, Jews, Gypsies, Kabyles, or Algerians. Farès' unique contribution in this powerful "novel" is to make us see that these men—African-Ameri-cans, Kabyles, Sahraouis, Mexican-Americans, Puerto-Rican Ameri-cans, Algerians—become the subject of becoming only by "entering into a becoming-minoritarian *that tears them away from their major-ity identity.*" Farès has but one goal, one objective: separating Al-geria—and the entire Maghreb—from its "major identity," which for him is but a borrowed identity, a treacherous fabrication cut of whole cloth, one which does harm to Algeria and the Maghreb.

Thus, for Farès, being Kabyle means not only belonging to a minority, but above all being part of, or rather taking part in, a gathering force, a *becoming-minoritarian* that infects both Kabylia and the wider community to which it rightfully belongs. In this sense, in the same way that *becoming-black affects whites as much as it does blacks*, as Farès himself says, *becoming-Kabyle necessarily affects non-Kabyles as much as it does Kabyles.* Becoming-minoritarian is not and cannot be a *state*, a station, but must be a *process* that leaves nothing intact in its wake. In Kantian terms, we could say that it is a "negative magnitude": not a negation of the state (an-archy), but rather, the negative (or the "neutral") dimension of the state, of stasis. In other words, becoming-Kabyle is a true nomad "war machine."[16] This sums up the primary aspect of Farès' oblique project in *Un Passager de l'Occident.*

Yet we should constantly keep in mind that if the Kabyles must themselves experience their own *becoming,* it is only "dans la mesure où *seule une minorité* peut *servir de médium actif au devenir*" (*MP,* 357; my emphasis) [because *only a minority* is capable of serving as the active medium of becoming (*TP,* 291; my emphasis)] and this process occurs only "dans des conditions telles qu'elle *cesse à son tour d'être un ensemble définissable par rapport à une majorité*" (*MP,* 357; my emphasis) [under such conditions that it *ceases to be a definable aggregate in relation to the majority* (*TP,* 291; my emphasis)]. Like becoming-black as presented to us by writers such as Baldwin, becom-

16. Once again, I turn to *Mille plateaux* for invaluable insights into the relationship between this nomad "war machine" and the State. In particular, the sections that beautifully analyze the status of nomads as compared to migrants and settlers are noteworthy. I call special attention to the following passage: "It is in this sense that nomads have no points, paths, or land, even though they do by all appearances. If the nomad can be called the Deterritorialized par excellence, it is precisely because there is no reterritorialization *afterward* as with the migrant, or upon *something else* as with the sedentary. . . . With the nomad, on the contrary, it is deterritorialization that constitutes the relation to the earth, to such a degree that the nomad reterritorializes on deterritorialization itself" (*TP,* 380–81).

This "transporting" movement that runs through all of Farès' work is doubled by a movement of "translation" or—in the sense in which Roland Barthes uses this term—"deporting." Instead of the "dialectique à deux termes," the "dialectique binaire," Barthes writes with respect to his own practice: "In him, another dialectic appears, trying to find expression: the contradiction of the terms is succeeded by the discovery of a third term, which is not a synthesis but a *translation:* everything comes back, but it comes back as Fiction, i.e., at another turn of the spiral." From "Dialectics," in *Roland Barthes by Roland Barthes,* trans. Richard Howard (New York: Hill and Wang, 1977) 68–69. See also the fragment entitled "Comparaison est raison" (62) ["Comparison is motive," 58].

ing-Kabyle "implique donc *la simultanéité d'un double mouvement,* l'un par lequel un terme (le sujet) se soustrait à la majorité, et l'autre, par lequel un terme (le médium ou l'agent) sort de la minorité" (*MP,* 357) [*implies two simultaneous movements,* one by which a term (the subject) is withdrawn from the majority, and another by which a term (the medium or agent) rises up from the minority (*TP,* 291)]. This seems to me to be precisely the impetus behind *Un Passager de l'Occident.*

On the one hand, in solidarity with his community of origin, Farès (alias Ali-Saïd) appears to withdraw from the majority to which he belongs as an Algerian "subject." This sheds light on passages such as the following:

> *si vous dites, au-delà de la presqu'île, à l'Algérien que vous rencontrez:* "je suis Kabyle," *que croyez-vous qu'il vous réprondra?* . . . *il vous dira:* "c'est faux, tu es Algérien avant d'être Kabyle," *ce qui pour nous est impensable historiquement.*" [*UPO,* 32; Farès' emphasis]

> *if, somewhere outside the confines of the peninsula, you say to an Algerian you happen to meet:* "I am a Kabyle," *how do you think he will answer you?* . . . *He will tell you:* "That's not true! You are an Algerian first and a Kabyle second." *For us, this is a historically inconceivable notion.*

Or again: "Je dois dire aussi, que par rapport à la vivacité que je connus, je suis un être en recul, *en recul de soi et des autres,* et dont le maintien vital ne peut provenir que d'une croyance très ancienne envers et contre tout (*UPO,* 73) [I must also say that when considering the passion for living I once knew, I am now a being *retreating from himself and from others,* and a someone whose life force can only come from an extremely ancient belief in and against everything].

Moreover, insofar as Farès opts for the becoming that is in process within every authentic minority, he comes out of the minority by constituting an asymmetrical "bloc d'alliance" (*MP,* 357) [block of alliance, *TP,* 291] with other minorities and minority movements, such as those of black Americans, Sahraouis, opponents of Franco, Algerian *émigrés,* Palestinians, and so forth. To Farès, being "Algerian" means being able to play it both ways, at the same time playing each side off against the other. This movement seems to me to explain the reference to James Baldwin as well as Farès' recourse to various pseudonyms such as Ali-Saïd and Brandy Fax.

The former appears when it is a question of withdrawing from the majority as a "détermination d'un état ou d'un étalon par rapport auquel les quantités plus grandes aussi bien que les plus petites seront dites minoritaires" (*MP*, 356) [determination of a state or standard in relation to which larger quantities, as well as the smallest, can be said to be minoritarian (*TP*, 291)]: Algerian in relation to Kabyle, French in relation to Algerian, white American in relation to black American or to Mexican-American, to name only a few.

The pseudonym Brandy Fax appears when, on the contrary, it is a matter of leaving the sphere of influence of a minority that is in constant danger of being reterritorialized or "coopted" in a statist dimension. Farès illustrates clearly how the "essence" of the minoritarian is not merely in becoming but also in casting off (from) any and all *genetic* or *racial* filiation—and perhaps even historical or geographical filiations as well: in this sense there is more "kinship" among African-Americans, Saharaouis, Palestinians, and Algerian *émigrés* (Kabyles or non-Kabyle in this case!) than there is between the French and either the Algerians or the Americans.

As we can well see, it is not for lack of affinity, or because of temperamental incompatibility, that filiation is at times rejected in favor of an *alliance*; rather, it is because of a series of pragmatic and practical (ethical and political) characteristics that the itinerary of a black American writer is "closer" or speaks more directly than a French writer can to a (Kabyle) Algerian. We may now better understand why such an atopical decentering operation (for there is no ideal topography; we are not in a *topos*), while addressed to Algerians (or Maghrebians) had to go through an agent who himself belongs to another minority. This necessity brings to mind the French proverb, "*Qui trop embrasse mal étreint.*" The "proper distance" must always be maintained from the nationality, race, and history to which one belongs, and the appropriate position, speed, and slowness.

I stated earlier that according to Farès the Kabyle must experience a *becoming*-Kabyle within the larger context of a *becoming-Algerian*; but at the same time, an Algerian must in turn experience a *becoming-Algerian* within the becoming-Algerian of the non-Algerian. This is Farès' utopia. The same movement of deterritorialization is operative: a Kabyle *becomes* a Kabyle, but in a *becoming-Kabyle of the non-Kabyle*; and likewise with black Americans, Sahraoui,or Palestinian insurgents, and so forth. Farès' extravagant, even *outlandish*, ambition—which in some ways follows the "model" of James Baldwin—is therefore not to set Kabyle demands against Algerians as a *homogeneous* block, as the values of an "endangered" or "dispossessed" minority, but rather to involve Algerians in a *becoming-minoritarian* that, according to Farès, actually corresponds far better to their own historical "reality."

Farès would provoke us to consider that the constitution of Algeria as a majoritarian entity—its reduction by an all-powerful State [Tout-Etat-Voirie] to a monolithically Arabic-speaking and Islamic territory and the constitution of the Algerian as a determined subject, is in the best interest neither of Algeria nor of the Algerian. According to Farès, Algeria's pagan origin initially destined it to a cultural and linguistic multiplicity, a crazy-quilt pluralism of civilizations—in short, to an irreducible becoming-minoritarian. To put it another way: the "dialectics" that brought Algeria into a majority camp can be seen as the adoption, by independent Algeria's governing powers, of a majoritarian "ideal" that could in no way serve the country's true interests. The desire to join the majority camp betrays continuing "victimization" by an imperialist ideal. To return to a point I have already touched upon briefly, it is clear that Algeria embraced this tantalizing illusion: rather than affirming its identity as a resolutely multiracial and multicultural nation, it *spontaneously*—oblivious to the dangers implied by this choice—opted for conquest by and of a "transcendent" majority, thus producing a mirror image of the former colonial power's theocentric and centralist "ideal."

Farès' strategies and the stakes involved emerge clearly from this pseudoautobiography. At first, by siding with the minority in his particular way—that is, "against refusal"—he demonstrates the potential power that the becoming-minoritarian of the Algerian "subject" derives as a "deterritorialized variable of the [Algerian] majority" (*MP*, 357; *TP*, 292). However, by adhering to this minority only via a series of mediations (by turns historical, literary, and linguistic) by "other" minorities, he transforms or transmutes this very "belonging" into none other than a "deterritorializing variable" of the minority itself! In the process the "minor" being is himself de-stabilized and can no longer act as a "refuge-value," to borrow the term used by Albert Memmi in *Portrait d'un colonisé*.[17]

It becomes easier to see how this precarious "position" can be deemed at once "desperate" and full of hope, and how as the "agent" of this operation our narrator-essayist necessarily becomes an enemy of

17. Albert Memmi, *Portrait du colonisé*, précédé du *Portrait du colonisateur* et d'une préface de Jean-Paul Sartre (Paris: NRF Gallimard, 1985). *The Colonized and the Colonizer*, trans. Howard Greensfield (Boston: Beacon, 1967).

"realism." *Realpolitik* seems to have merely recycled schemes that have historically transformed countries such as Algeria into "allegorical realities"—when the true imperatives were creating new realities and reversing alienated mentalities. Farès explains:

> Cet espoir que nous avons (nous les habitants de la presqu'île) est la réalité à laquelle nous destinons tous les valets du réalisme. La réalité de cet espoir étant le prochain départ de l'allégorique radeau de la Méduse via l'éternité! Il appartiendra ainsi, au symboliste Géricault, d'être l'initiateur d'un très vaste mouvement allant de l'allégorie à la réalité . . . [*UPO*, 37–38]

> This hope that we, the inhabitants of the peninsula, have is the reality to which we condemn all the lackeys of realism. The reality of this hope is the imminent departure of the allegorical raft of the Medusa into eternity! It thus falls to the symbolist Géricault to initiate a vast movement springing from allegory into reality.

It falls to Farès as well to instigate the vast movement that indeed bridges the gap between allegory—as seen in the transformation of Algeria into a two-dimensional cliché, or in a public-relations campaign carried out by the *Etat-Voirie*—and "reality": that is, Algeria as

> [u]n pays où on pourrait clairement vivre, aller au café, boire un coup, draguer les filles, faire des études, danser le soir, et travailler quinze heures par jour, la cigarette au bec. . . .
> Un pays, en somme, au niveau de sa réalité politique. Un pays, en somme, réellement politique. [*UPO*, 77]

> [a] country where you could simply and clearly live, go to cafés, have a drink, chase girls, study, go out dancing at night, work fifteen hours a day, cigarette in mouth. . . .
> A country, in short, that is at the level of its political reality. A country, in short, that is really political.

However "utopian" or "idealistic" this "program" may appear, we must not be misled; Farès never intends to play the role of reformer or moralizer. If at times the narrator—Brandy Fax? Ali-Saïd? Nabile Farès "himself"?—seems to harp on the same message, the general economy of the book does not allow us to consider these recurring refrains in revisionist or reformist terms, as objectives to be obtained *hic et nunc!* As I have attempted to show, Farès is bent on identifying, indeed on mapping the disjunctions or dehiscences that separate (for example) the political discourses of power from the "reality" of linguistic practices, as well as from the *ethos* that they constitute. Already in *L'Exil et le désarroi,* Farès had staked out the political terrain for us, as in this warning:

> . . . a word about revolution: the good word . . .
>
> It does exist, along with many other things that, beyond declarations handed down from the lofty spheres of politics, show us *a sort of funny gap* between words of Power and communal realities. There exists a certain indifferent irony between Powers and Realities, which, casually disregarding our principal beliefs, amuses itself by erecting divisions, connections, collisions, illusions. [*Exil,* 14–15; my emphasis]

Farès' aim—his always, but never merely, *political* aim—is far more ambitious and his tactics ("tactics without strategy," Barthes might have said)[18]—are far more incisive than we might have imagined at first glance. Amidst the decentering and the false majoritarian transparency of a country such as Algeria, Farès keeps his sights trained on bringing the entire Maghreb, along with all the other countries of the Mediterranean rim, into this atopical movement of deterritorialization by opening up the metastable—even *meta-statist*—space of becoming-minoritarian, into which these nations are propelled despite themselves, perhaps even in their own absence. "Le pays avait même fait une terrible erreur: celle de ne pas *ouvrir le territoire à* l'ensemble de la terre, mais à une partie seulement, celle qui n'était que reflet inconsistant de son égoïsme" (*Exil* 58; my emphasis) [The country had even made a terrible mistake, in *opening up its territory* not to the whole earth, but only to a fraction of it, the part that is but the wavering reflection of its selfishness].

And in fact, when a country such as Algeria becomes the object of a becoming-minoritarian that sabotages its own pretensions to the alienating majority that surrounds it, there is no longer any important reason to stop the process, now so well under way. Henceforth all Algeria need do in order to serve actively as a medium for the collective becoming of the Mediterranean countries is to open itself up to the

---

18. From the fragment entitled "Tactique/Stratégie," in *Roland Barthes par Roland Barthes* (Paris: Seuil, Ecrivains de toujours, 1975), 175 (my emphasis, except for last). "The movement of his work is tactical: it is a matter of displacing himself, of obstructing, as with bars, *but not of conquering.* . . . It is only a little *machine for making war* against philological law, the academic tyranny of correct meaning. This work would therefore be defined as: *a tactics without strategy.*" From "Tactics/Strategy," in *Roland Barthes by Roland Barthes,* trans. Richard Howard (New York: Hill and Wang, 1977), 172.

becoming-minoritarian that has been working on it underground. Rather than establishing a new majority or a new majoritarian "alliance" of "States," such a process would lead to a "transversal"—or, to borrow Blanchot's term, "unavowable"—community.

In this way, by a heretofore utterly unknown phenomenon that I will call "transversal contamination," not only Algeria but the entire Mediterranean would be contagiously caught up in a movement whose "territory" would extend to the whole world.

> (A ces dernières paroles de Terre, un rire d'étoiles parcourt Crépuscule) (et Crépuscule ne peut s'empêcher de dire) (Belle Femme de la Terre, quel plaisir de vous boire si entière) (et Crépuscule disparut dans la boisson de Terre.) [*UPO*, 153]

> (To these last words of Earth, a star-laugh runs through Twilight) (and Twilight cannot keep from saying) (Lovely Earth Woman, what a pleasure to drink you so whole) (and Twilight disappeared in Earth's drink).

The Mediterranean would no longer be thought of as a homogeneous entity made up of States and Subjects that are determined once and for all; it would be conceived as a "boundary/liminal phenomenon" that makes it possible to "couple" or *bring into phase* communities in the process of becoming, of creating a *media-terranée* or, in Deleuzian terms, a "multiplicity."[19] This explains why, when Farès speaks of the *Maghreb*, it is never in terms of the geographical "elements" that make up its *extension*—Tunisia, Algeria, Morocco—nor in terms of the elements that comprise its ethnic or cultural *comprehension*—Arabs, Berbers, Turks, Tuaregs, Moslems, Christians, Jews. Rather, he always invokes it in relation to the [multiple] *"dimen-*

---

19. In order to give the utmost coherence to the problematic I have formulated, I have used the word "multiplicity" as Deleuze and Guattari have defined it in the chapter entitled "Rhizome" in *Mille plateaux*: "A multiplicity has neither subject nor object, but only determinations, magnitudes, and dimensions that cannot increase in number without the multiplicity changing in nature. . . . All multiplicities are flat, in the sense that they fill or occupy all of their dimensions: we will therefore speak of a *plane of consistency* of multiplicities, even though the dimensions of this "plane" increase with the number of connections that are made on it. Multiplicities are defined by the outside: by the abstract line, the line of flight or deterritorialization according to which they change in nature and connect with other multiplicities. The plane of consistency (grid) is the outside of all multiplicities" (*TP* 8–9). It is clear that Farès' ideal would be to display everything on just such a plane: lived events, historical determinations, individuals, social groups or formations, envisaging the goal of redrawing the political-ideological map of the Maghreb/West.

sions" *embraced in its intention*, that is, in relation to the minorities that compose its surface.

In Arabic, *Maghreb* means "West." But Farès shows us that through an inverse (but not at all symmetrical) operation, "West" may in turn come to signify something other than the supremacy of majoritarian man. There will no longer be alignment along the poles of "minorities" or "States," nor will there be simple polarizations such as the one opposing French-white-civilized-adult to Algerian-Arabic-Muslim or to White-Anglo-Saxon-Protestant. Analyzed in terms of its margins and its lines of flight—its minorities and its becomings—the Maghreb and/or the West (the ambiguity is richly suggestive) will itself be caught up in a movement of "translation" or "deporting"[20] whereby it will succeed at last in freeing itself of the restrictive majority. It will become an instrument for challenging the majoritarian "good conscience" (majoritarian) of the West as a whole. Thus, for Farès, if the Maghreb wishes to break away, once and for all, from the "logic" that has made it a nation of exiles, it must sooner or later come to grips with what splits it into East and West, Majority and Minority, Inside and Outside. In this notion we may discern Farès' kinship with another exile, the filmmaker Andrei Tarkovski, particularly in his films *Solaris* and *Stalker*.[21] Both artists are *stalkers* of those intermediate zones, the "inter-mediate" ideas that are the "homeland" of the exiled:

> Autour, existe ce vaste pays que les constructions les plus vastes, et, les plus digestives, ne peuvent masquer, ce vaste pays où le ciel trace des auréoles de bonheur, et, de vie, au-dessus du souffle miraculeux de la mer, et, du vent." [*Exil* 17; Farès' punctuation]

> All around lies this vast country that the most grandiose constructions, the most devouring structures, can never hide, this vast land where the skies bear the glowing traces of happiness, and of life, above the miraculous breath of the sea, and the wind.

The West/Maghreb will be conceived—or rather, *lived*, experienced—as a "block of coexistence" (*MP*, 358), a zone of intensive proximity or copresence: of minorities in a perpetual state of becoming and movement. Its "objective" will most assuredly no longer be conquest of, or by, an imperial (imperious) Majority, but rather to set up a "plane

20. The reader is referred to note 16 above for a discussion of Barthes's term *"déport."*

21. *Solaris* (USSR, 1972); *Stalker* (USSR, 1975).

of consistency" that will privilege not the development of determined cultural or political forms, but instead the relations of movement and rest, of rapidity and slowness—relationships among unformed, or *relatively* unformed, elements. There will be circulation, passage, not from one culture or country to another, but from one margin to another, from border to border, edge to edge: never "in," but always "in between." Farès calls this circulation *"les cavales frontalières"* (*UPO*, 158) of the nomad, the "border evasions" whose movement "breaks (up)" the earth.

The nomad and the exile had appeared to be each other's double, but Michel Serres—another nomad—finds them to be

> triple ou tiers, habitant les deux rives et hantant le milieu où convergent les deux sens, plus le sens du fleuve coulant, plus celui de vent, plus les inclinaisons inquiètes de la nage, les intentions nombreuses produisant les décisions.[22]

> threefold or triple, inhabiting both banks and haunting the middle ground where the two *sens*[23] converge, along with the *sens* of the river, and also the wind's, and with the turbulent inclinations of the swimming waters, a plethora of intentions bringing forth decisions.

Triple, only?

> Vous vous méprenez encore, le voilà multiple. Source ou échangeur de sens, relativisant à jamais la gauche, la droite et la terre d'où sortent les directions, il a intégré un compas dans son corps liquide. Le pensiez-vous converti, inversé, bouleversé? Certes. Plus encore: universel. Sur l'axe mobile du fleuve et du corps frissonne, émue, la source du sens. [Serres, 27]

> You are mistaken again, for it is multiple. Source or transformer of *sens*, forever relativizing the right, the left, and the earth whence these directions spring, it has fused a compass into its liquid body. Did you believe it to be converted, inverted, overturned? Quite so. But even more: universal. Along the mobile axis of the river and the body shivers, stirred, the source of *sens*.

—Translated by Jennifer Curtiss Gage

22. Michel Serres, *Le Tiers-instruit* (Paris: Editions François Burin, 1991), 26.
23. *I have kept the French word* sens *because of the polysemy of this word, which means* "direction," "meaning," *and (sensory)* "sense."—Translator's note.

H. ADLAI MURDOCH

Rewriting Writing: Identity, Exile and Renewal in Assia Djebar's *L'Amour, la fantasia*

I

The invasion and conquest of Algeria by the French in 1830 provided an enabling context not only for the development of a multilayered system of repression on the part of the colonizing power, but also for the elaboration by the colonized of patterns of resistance which arose as a reciprocal response to this subjection. The cultural and subjective duality which are the primary manifestations of the colonial encounter—the product of simultaneous processes of cultural subordination and assimilation whose displacements render both colonizer and colonized subject to the colonizing process—tends to inscribe postcolonial literary discourse within a context of alienation and dislocation, as the authors seek to devise strategies which will mediate the demands of a colonial legacy which, *inter alia*, compels them to inscribe subjectivity in the language of the colonizer.

The effect of colonial domination on the literary production of the colonized is thus of a plural nature. Further, the problems implicit in the (re)construction of identity through writing raise questions of discourse and signification germane to the production of autobiography, where identity itself may be read as a construct subject to external patterns of connotation. The result of this desire for discursive identity is the adoption of narrative forms which tend to displace and subvert the norms imposed by the colonizer upon the colonized; the divisions and pluralities of the colonial heritage are subsumed into the narrative matrix and turned to the determination of a postcolonial identity-

YFS 83, *Post/Colonial Conditions,* ed. Lionnet & Scharfman, © 1993 by Yale University.

structure which adopts fragmentation and displacement as its primary discursive strategy. What interests me, then, in the case of minority or marginalized literatures, is the process whereby the trajectory of the experience of exile and subjection tends to lead to the elaboration of discursive codes of resistance as a means toward the construction of a culturally specific identity paradigm. The inscription of such a counterdiscourse is exacerbated by the particular configuration which the colonial dialectic and its neocolonial traces impose upon desire; defined by Lacan as that which is never satisfied, desire and its corollary, recognition, may ultimately be read as the overriding tropes of the entire colonial undertaking, figuring colonizer and colonized through a self-perpetuating web of fragmentation, lack, and demand. A prime example of the working-through of these dichotomies may be encountered in the work of the Algerian writer Assia Djebar. By examining her attempt to recodify colonial history and its subjective corollaries in her novel of the French invasion entitled *L'Amour, la fantasia,* I show how the multiplicity of issues inherent in the inscription of biculturalism informs the critical role played by displacement in the elaboration of postcolonial identity.

Djebar's work in both novel and film is emblematic of the paradoxical ambiguities of the colonial paradigm. Born in Algiers, she seeks in her work to come to terms with the legacies and implications of the French colonial presence in Algeria. To do this, she confronts the history of Algeria written by the French; signification and self-affirmation imply the displacement of the colonizer's discourse and its replacement by the discourse of the Other. Yet the overarching paradox of this process remains the legacy of division which is the heritage of the colonized; negotiating the cultural codes of *métissage* is what ultimately lies at the heart of this postcolonial paradigm. Given her position as a bicultural, postcolonial subject, Djebar undoes centuries of overdetermination, while at the same time putting into place a self which draws on the complicitous dialectic of the colonial encounter in order to express the multivalency of its subjective codes. Before proceeding to a detailed reading of the text, however, let us elaborate further some of the bases which will allow subjectivity and desire to be written within a colonial framework.

II

The primary issue faced by postcolonial novelists, that of writing the subject into being through fictive discourse, makes the colonial subject doubly subject to the writing act, since the erasure of identity which is the primary product of subjection to the colonizer's discourse is eventually countered by the effort to rewrite and to recodify historical experience on its own terms. Yet such a process tends to reinforce the issues of alienation and duality which seem to be an attendant part of the production of subjectivity through writing. David Lloyd, in his reading of the role of autobiography in the production of minor literature, puts this issue well: "A perpetual tension subsists between the desire for self-origination, to produce oneself as if without a father, and the awkward knowledge of indebtedness to what precedes and influences the subject."[1] However, the recognition, and, indeed, the tacit acknowledgment of the existence of any kind of cultural or psychological precursor appears inevitably to reinscribe for the subject its inescapable overdetermination by the figure Lloyd terms the "metafather." A further process aimed at internalizing this figure results in the subject's identification with what Lloyd terms "the nation's transcendental paternity," permitting a certain reciprocal signification between the subject and the group in whose name it purports to speak, to write into being (Lloyd, 163). At the same time, however, the elaboration of this problematic inscribes the presence within the determining matrix of a cultural and psychological Other, a figure in whom the postcolonial subject perceives both its progeniture and the field of its defining alterity.

This continuing dialectic between the colonized self and the colonizing other is given succor by the suppression of the colonial identity and culture, where, as Abdul JanMohamed puts it, the colonialist "destroys without any significant qualms the effectiveness of indigenous economic, social, political, legal, and moral systems and imposes its own versions of these structures on the Other."[2] One eventual consequence of this activity of negation and appropriation is the production of a paradoxically mimetic sense of alterity on the part of the colonized subject, manifest in her tendency not only to see herself through the

---

1. David Lloyd, *Nationalism and Minor Literature: James Clarence Mangan and the Emergence of Irish Cultural Nationalism* (Berkeley: University of California Press, 1987), 162. See especially Chapter 6, *The Autobiographies,* for a discussion of these and other related issues.

2. Abdul R. JanMohamed, "The Economy of Manichean Allegory: The Function of Racial Difference in Colonialist Literature," *Race, Writing and Difference.* Henry Louis Gates, Jr., ed. (Chicago: University of Chicago Press, 1986), 78–106, see 85.

eyes of the Other, but to draw on aspects of the colonizer's model in order to elaborate her own sense of subjectivity.

A psychoanalytic approach which embodies the desire for recognition in a postcolonial context suggests itself here as providing an effective enabling matrix which will illuminate the problematic of subjectivity. In this context, the constitution of the subject places him or her as secondary in relation to the signifier, which then imposes its laws on the subject, turning it, in effect, into a signifier which will then possess constituted meaning only in relation to another signifier. In the colonial context, then, this subject may be said to await approval and approbation from the colonizer, while, at the same time, she becomes an object of this Other's discourse through being defined by him, being spoken for, as well as by being forced to express her quest for identity in the colonizer's language. As Danielle Marx-Scouras points out: "As for the Maghrebine Francophone writer who appropriates the language of his adversary, he occupies an untenable site . . . Hence a profound sentiment of intrusion, non-belonging and alterity on the part of the writing subject who alienates himself in the language of the Other."[3] Issues of language and difference thus assume paramount importance in the double gesture constituting the (re)construction of a feminine identity within a postcolonial context. For if, as Nancy Miller points out, the question of subjective identity within a textual context "is irreducibly complicated by the historical, political, and figurative body of the woman writer,"[4] then such complications are even further exacerbated by a discursive history of conquest and subjection, racism and erasure written upon the figure of the colonized feminine body itself. The initiatory movement of any recodification must be to incorporate figures of race and conquest in the inscription of Algerian subjectivity. Negotiation of these barriers and absences will involve "a radical subversion of the meanings of the master's tongue,"[5] a rewriting of established codes of self and Other, subject and object, of discourse previously employed as a means of subjection.

3. Danielle Marx-Scouras, "The Poetics of Maghrebine Illegitimacy." In *L'Esprit Créateur*, (Spring 1986), vol. 26, no. 1: 3–10, see 3.

4. Nancy K. Miller, "Changing the Subject: Authorship, Writing, and the Reader," *Feminist Studies/Critical Studies*, Teresa de Lauretis, ed. (Bloomington: University of Indiana Press, 1986), 102–20, see 107.

5. Bill Ashcroft, Gareth Griffiths, and Helen Tiffin, *The Empire Writes Back: Theory and Practice in Post-Colonial Literatures* (New York: Routledge, 1989), 146.

III

Assia Djebar's *L'Amour, la fantasia*[6] is paradigmatic of the textual confluence of issues of decolonization, desire, and alienation as specific themes in Francophone North African literature. Published in 1985, Djebar's text takes as its point of reference the French invasion and conquest of Algeria in 1830. Through the figuring of Algeria itself as an object of desire for the pillaging French troops, Djebar is able to examine the process of colonization from the novel approach of territorial conquest as a trope of human cultural and political relations. With the narrative strategy aimed at evoking the anguish and ambiguity of the colonized subject as desired object, and as desiring subject, the dislocation generated by the use of the colonizer's language on the part of the speaking subject, and the historical, cultural, and textual interrelation between desire, the body, and writing, become the means by which Djebar's text eventually inscribes the code of its own affirmation. Crucial here will be the evolving dialectical relationship between writing and desire, in which writing will become inextricably bound to the unveiling and implementation of desire, the obscene imposition of the colonial undertaking, the double quest for recognition, and the integration of a valorized, decolonized self into the historical and cultural continuum.

Djebar's initial approach to the text will be that of problematizing writing itself. Her task will be to take on the "official" record of the French colonial conquest of Algeria, itself a rewriting of historical fact, and to rewrite this rewriting from the perspective of the colonized subject. With Algeria as the body upon which the history of this subject has been inscribed by the Other, this inscription has assumed, over time, the force of unassailable truth. Djebar will thus approach writing as a means toward subjective signification, drawing on the ambiguity and impossibility of consonance inherent in the discursive in order to reflect the colonial paradox and subvert the already written text of the colonizer. Djebar writes woman as object of desire into woman as desiring subject, drawing on the alienation and desire for recognition which are the legacies of a colonialist discourse.

Appropriately, duality is inscribed as a permanent condition of

6. Assia Djebar, *L'Amour, la fantasia.* (Paris: J. C Lattès, 1985). English edition translated as *Fantasia: An Algerian Cavalcade*, by Dorothy S. Blair (London: Quartet, 1989). All quotations are drawn from this edition; page references are to the French and then to the English editions.

Djebar's (re)codification of Algerian subjectivity. The ambiguity that the colonial process has inscribed upon the colonized subject, as it alternates between the erasure of its own culture, and the desire to assume that of the Other, is refigured through the narrative's constant alternation between the presentation of the events of the 1830 invasion and the presence of writing as autobiography, as the female subject awakening to desire seeks to chronicle the constitution of her own subjectivity in the face of patriarchal domination. Djebar's text is thus structurally reflective of its own discursive quest, as it puts into place alternative writing strategies which figure the oppositional relationship to selfhood that colonialism institutes. Indeed, this ongoing ambiguity becomes prefigurative of the crisis of cultural integrity towards which the narrative inexorably leads the protagonist.

The novel in fact tacitly states this crucial disjunction in its very title. Between the implied integrity of *l'amour* and the binary encoding of *la fantasia*, whose duality mediates not only a musical fragment within Western culture, but also an equestrian display germane to the Arab region which traverses the domains both of the wargame and of the cultural festival, there lies the crux of the dilemma that this text attempts to address. The interpenetration of the formal latitude and freedom to improvise symbolized by the musical figure, on the one hand, and the violence necessary to cultural affirmation symbolized by the equestrian exhibition of the noble warrior, on the other, this interpretation subsumes the contradictions which underlie the colonial undertaking, inscribing through the double reading of the *fantasia* not only the opposition between cultures, but also the desire for autonomy as well as the very paradox of love as forcible appropriation whose intricacy the text will seek to explore. Indeed, the very tendency of the colonial paradigm to reduce the colonial identity by inverting traditional forms draws on the *fantasia* itself as a figure for this elemental conflict, appropriating and debilitating even cultural forms of self-affirmation as a means of colonial control, as Albert Memmi has indicated: "The Arab *fantasia* has become nothing more than the act of a trained animal which is asked to roar, as he used to, to frighten the guests."[7] The narrative will persistently work through this duality, beginning with the title and subtitle of Part I, *La Prise de la ville* ou

---

7. Albert Memmi, *The Colonizer and the Colonized*. Trans. Howard Greenfeld (Boston: Beacon Press, 1967), 93–94.

L'Amour s'écrit, which establish the reciprocity between conquest and desire that the text will explore. The alienation of the subject is put into place on the very first page, through the narrator's objective perspective. The somewhat enigmatic statement that "Toute vierge savante saura écrire, écrira à coup sûr 'la' lettre" [Any girl who has had some schooling will have learned to write, and will without a doubt write that fatal letter] links conquest to writing, and the duality of this inscription is further contextualized by the one that follows: "Viendra l'heure pour elle où l'amour qui s'écrit est plus dangereux que l'amour séquestré" [For her the time will come when there will be more danger in love that is committed to paper than love that languishes behind enclosing walls] (11; 3). Here, the double reading possible in "s'écrit" (ses cris) [writes/its cries] is directly linked to the preceding figural elements "vierge" and "écrire," effecting a double codification of subjectivity both as a product of the discourse of the Other and as the cry of anguish generated by colonial subjection.

As the third-person references to the protagonist give way to the first person, the patriarch simultaneously makes his appearance, linked to the plot by the insistence of the discursive: "A dix-sept ans, j'entre dans l'histoire d'amour à cause d'une lettre. Un inconnu m'a écrit . . . Le père, secoué d'une rage sans éclats, a déchiré devant moi la missive." [At seventeen, I am introduced to my first experience of love through a letter written by a boy, a stranger . . . My father, in a fit of silent fury, tears up the letter before my eyes . . .] (12; 4). The inevitability of conflict and the contours of a burgeoning subjectivity begin to assume their form: "L'adolescente . . . a reconstitué la lettre qui a suscité la colère paternelle . . . Les mots conventionnels et en langue française de l'étudiant en vacances se sont gonflés d'un désir imprévu, hyperbolique, simplement parce que le père a voulu les détruire." [I piece together the letter which has aroused my father's fury . . . Simply because my father wanted to destroy the letter, I interpreted the conventional French wording used by this student on holiday as the cryptic expression of some sudden, desperate passion] (12; 4).

Interestingly, what emerges in this discursive hierarchy are the axes of language and desire, recuperating the invasion matrix and subjecting the protagonist to the effects of a desire which is the product of the imposition of patriarchal law. Ultimately the incident presages the inscription of an ineluctable ambiguity: "ainsi, cette langue que m'a donnée le père me devient entremetteuse et mon initiation, dès lors, se

place sous un signe double, contradictoire . . . " [thus the language
that my father had been at pains for me to learn, serves as a go-between,
and from now on a double, contradictory sign reigns over my initiation . . .] (12; 4). This duality which the subject must undergo stems
directly from the insistence of patriarchal coercion and a falsely constituted desire for alterity through the use of the language of the colonizing Other, symbolized through the duality of the paternal inscription; discursive resistance and female subjectivity are thus linked to
desire and the subversion of patriarchy, the main issues to which the
text addresses itself. What arises from such a collision of thematic
variables is the question of whether language will merely mark desire,
or whether it will mask it as well. In other words, if the colonizer's
language is read as the mark of colonial desire, then its appropriation
by the colonized may undermine the very goal it sets out to achieve,
screening the desire of the colonized subject. For, in situating herself as
a writer who must come to terms with the history of Algeria and with
herself as a postcolonial, Arab, female subject writing in French about
Arab women who do not speak French and cannot speak for themselves, Djebar's narrative will inevitably problematize its own discourse to the point where its own tenuous coherence threatens to
dissolve.

But this is (the) prologue. The first chapter opens by situating the
reader at dawn on the day of the attack, 13 June 1830, just prior to
hostilities; what the narrator calls the "premier face à face" [first con-
frontation]. Following the inscription of the city as female subject—
"La ville . . . surgit dans un rôle d'orientale immobilisée en son mys-
tère" [The city . . . makes her first appearance in the rôle of 'Oriental
Woman', motionless, mysterious] (14; 6)—the very indecipherability
of the respective roles, the inseparability of subject and object, are
integral to the immobility of the scene: "Qui dès lors constitue le
spectacle, de quel côté se trouve vraiment le public? . . . Parmi la première escadre qui glisse insensiblement vers l'ouest, Amable Matterer
regarde la ville qui regarde." [But who are to be the performers? On
which side shall we find the audience? . . . Amable Matterer is at his
post in the first squadron which glides slowly westward; he gazes at the
city which returns his gaze] (14–15; 6–7). The first chronicler, Amable
Matterer, watcher as well as watched, is present, about to write, and
the story again suggests an equivalent relationship between military
conquest and desire, the women a metonymical representation of an
Algeria taken against her will:

En cette aurore de la double découverte, que se disent les femmes de la
ville, quels rêves d'amour s'allument en elles . . . Comme si les envahisseurs allaient être les amants!

As this day dawns when the two sides will come face to face, what are
the women of the town saying to each other? What dreams of romance
are lit in their hearts . . . as if the invaders were coming as lovers! (16;
8).

The suggested equivalence between "envahisseurs" and "amants"
foregrounds the duality inherent in the activities of desire and conquest, linking this equivalence to the dichotomies which ground and
structure the text. Indeed, the suggestion of forcible conquest tends to
foreground the violent nature of colonial appropriation, further problematizing the inscription of this fragmented female voice. We are
witness, shortly thereafter, to the doubling of the axis of writing, of
alterity. A second chronicler makes his appearance, also inscribed under the double sign of love and writing, thus assimilating the inscription of the Other to the workings of desire: "Un second témoin . . . le
baron Barchou de Penhoën . . . rédigera presque à chaud ses impressions de combattant, d'observateur, et même, par éclairs inattendus,
d'amoureux d'une terre qu'il a entrevue sur ses franges enflammées" [A
second eye-witness . . . Baron Barchou de Penhoën . . . still fresh from
the scene, [he] sets down his impressions as a combattant, as an observer and even, with unexpected insight, as one who has fallen in love
with a land of which he has glimpsed the fiery fringes] (26; 16). The
interstices foregrounded between writing, conquest, and desire cause
desire to emerge as the primary mediator of this encounter between
self and Other.

By equating the desire of the French soldiers to take the town of
Algiers with physical desire, the narrator is in effect putting into place
a polyvalent form of desire which knits this web of signification together, and which is equally applicable to the domains of military and
cultural appropriation. Now if as Lacan states, "man's desire finds its
meaning in the desire of the other . . . because the first object of desire
is to be recognized by the other,"[8] then a reasonable inference here is
that this action of physical and cultural appropriation by France
masked, or marked, a desire on its part to be recognized, that is to say,
desired, by its own Other, a cultural opposition symbolically under-

8. Jacques Lacan, *Ecrits*. Trans. Alan Sheridan (New York: Norton, 1967), 58.

taken by Algeria in this particular instance. Conversely, the narrator's ongoing subversion of this patriarchal colonial text signifies her own desire to be recognized in turn by this Other, to reclaim and reconstitute that self which was subverted and devalorized by the original writing and possession. Thus the assertion that "Dès ce heurt entre deux peuples, surgit une sorte d'aporie" [After this first encounter between the two nations, both sides watch and wait] (26; 16). The aporia covers exactly the space of that reversal of desire between these two historically differentiated attempts at inscribing identity out of the discourse of alterity. Repeatedly, writing marks, or masks, desire, and this opposition will continue to figure to a large extent the continuing ambivalence of identity's inscription in the narrative.

But it is the obscenity of colonial desire, with all its myriad implications, that demands emphasis. The narrator asks: "pourquoi . . . cette première campagne d'Algérie fait-elle entendre les bruits d'une copulation obscène?" [why . . . does this first Algerian campaign reverberate with the sounds of an obscene copulation?] (29; 19), marking this colonial effort with the sign of negativity and forced possession: "est-ce le viol, est-ce l'amour non-avoué . . . " [are these the ghosts of the raped . . . ? Is it the spirit of an unacknowledged love . . . ? (26; 16). Here, the overt equivalence between colonial desire and rape bespeaks the violent subjection inherent in the colonial condition, and underscores the brutal force of the colonial desire to which the colonized are traditionally subjected. The unreciprocated nature of this desire nullifies the female voice, foreclosing the context for elaborating its desire and ending the very possibility of establishing a unified identity. The narrative continues to mark the growth in the ambiguity of this colonial desire, as succeeding chapters alternate between the (re)codification of the events of 1830 and the efforts of the protagonist in the present to mediate the opposition between desire and paternal law. Still, an almost inevitable interpenetration of discourses occurs as the concept of the *fantasia* comes to inform the context of the invasion: "Les tribus bédouines sont venues comme à une fantasia de plus où le risque est paré d'insouciance" [The Bedouin tribes arrive as if to participate in yet another *Fantasia*, where the less caution is shown, the more attractive the hazards] (26–27; 16). By putting the figure of the fantasia into place, the narrative extends the inseparability of the subject-object dichotomy to the colonial context itself, as this basic constituent of Arab culture becomes incorporated into the enigmatic indecipherability of the colonial undertaking. The pervasive duality of the discursive operation is thus intrinsic to the process of working through the parameters of desire. Thus the appearance and contribution of a third chronicler, one J. T. Merle, "venu là comme au spectacle" [tantamount to a visit to a theatrical performance] (39; 28), occurs in Chapter III as the progressive overdetermination of the identity of the colonized continues to be subsumed by the discursive matrix constituting the desire of the Other. Indeed, Merle himself, "notre directeur de théâtre qui ne se trouve jamais sur le théâtre des opérations" [our theater manager who is never in the theater of operations] (42; 32), ultimately becomes a figure for the paradoxical absence, the lack which ultimately underlies the entire colonial undertaking. The narcissism and self-absorption which figure his discourse come to stand for the trajectory of precisely that colonial desire which he seeks to describe and to define: "Pourtant ce publiciste . . . ne s'attache qu'à décrire son rôle dérisoire. Il est sans cesse à la traîne du combat décisif; il n'est jamais témoin de l'événement." [However, this publicist . . . is only interested in describing his own ridiculous role. He lags permanently behind any decisive battle; he never witnesses any actual events] (45; 33). This constant slippage which figures the relationship between Merle's presence and the events he seeks to recount marks the entire discursive contextualization of the colonial invasion. The subjective and cultural appropriation that these accounts seek to effect are reflected in the lack of consonance between discursive subject and object, between signifier and signified.

It is the recognition of the impossibility of immediacy, of a subversion of the figural ground which eventually subsumes both subject and object, that has undermined this inscriptive intention and made duality supreme. Such a slippage ultimately renders this writing nothing but an elaborate recuperation and ordering of referential materiality: "Hors combat, toute parole semble gelée et un désert d'ambiguïté s'installe." [Outside of the battlefield, speech is at a standstill and a wilderness of ambiguity sets in] (45; 33). As such, writing itself becomes representative of the objective underlying this colonial desire; as its misreading produces an unnecessary death, it embodies this desire for recognition from the Other, and encodes the ambiguous slippage so injurious to colonial subjectivity: "Toute écriture de l'Autre, transportée, devient fatale, puisque signe de compromission" [Any document written by 'The Other' proves fatal, since it is a sign of compromise] (44; 33). The inherent instability of colonial writing, exacerbated here by the insidious nature of its double task of justifying territorial dispossession and destroying colonial subjectivity, displaces the lack underlying the colonizer's desire onto the alienation and dislocation by which the colonized are figured. And it is this lack which ultimately overdetermines the discourse by which colonial subjectivity is constructed. Such a discourse eventually becomes so pervasive that it is systematically accepted as the final and authoritative definition of the culture in whose name it purports to speak, and which it in effect circumscribes. It is the subversion and reversal of this practice, the putting into place of a new form of writing which will speak to the anguish of alienation and the desire for recognition and identity on the part of the dispossessed, that Djebar attempts to effect here.

Given this importance assumed by discursive representation, it should be no surprise that instances of its occurrence continue to proliferate. Indeed, almost on cue, a fourth chronicler appears in Chapter IV, although, interestingly, this one appears to be an Algerian witness: "Hadj Ahmed Effendi, mufti hanéfite d'Alger . . . nous rapporte le siège en langue turque, plus de vingt ans après et en écrivant de l'étranger, car il s'expatriera." [Hadj Ahmed Effendi, the Hanefite Mufti from Algiers. . . . More than twenty years later he reports the siege for us in the Turkish language, writing his reminiscences . . . from his exile in foreign parts] (50; 39). To the paradox of his nationality, an Algerian recounting the invasion and conquest of his own country by the Other, is added the further paradox of the use of a language not his own, leading to the additional displacement of his place of residence. This doubling of the undecidabilities already inherent in discursive recuperation exacerbates the sense of alterity already attached to the imposition of paternal law through the obscenity of colonial desire; by extending the field of the Other through the use of an alternative language to represent subjective repression, a national subjectivity in danger of being subsumed, Hadj's efforts to work through these ambiguities ultimately symbolize that lack of a stable scriptive ground which figures the colonial subject. The apparent inadequacy of any form of discursive representation to codify fully subjective integrity appears to presage the paradox facing the narrator of having to rewrite the colonial undertaking in the language of the colonizer. This impossibility of consonance between language and the object it seeks to represent makes desire, in language, the ground of subjective definition. Thus the number of representations of this event is itself a recognition of the paradoxical inadequacy of the role of language in the elaboration of the subject and the appropriation of culture: "trente-sept descriptions seront publiées, dont trois seulement du côté des assiégés . . . il reste tout de même trente-deux écrits, en langue fran-çaise, de ce premier acte de l'occupation . . . cette conquête ne se vit plus découverte de l'autre . . . le mot deviendra l'arme par excel-lence . . . " [thirty-seven descriptions will be published, of which only three are from the viewpoint of the besieged . . . there still remain thirty-two chronicles, in French, of this first act of the occupation drama . . . this conquest is no longer seen as the discovery of a strange new world . . . words will become their most effective weapons . . .] (55–56; 44–45). The elaboration of this desire for recognition from the Other through colonial appropriation has metamorphosed into a strug-gle for linguistic mastery, one in which discursive representation ulti-mately overdetermines material referentially: "Toute une pyramide d'écrits amoncelés en apophyse superfétatoire occultera la violence initiale." [The supererogatory protuberances of their publications will form a pyramid to hide the initial violence from view] (56; 45). This double ambiguity, of the discursive and of the colonial subject, is what the protagonist will seek to inscribe as she faces the figure of the familial and the cultural father in the struggle for self-determination.

There is progressively less differentiation between these two scenes of subjective definition, between the discursive recuperation of the colonial desire of 1830, and the linguistic and subjective indeter-minacy figuring the protagonist in the present. Through appropriating and realigning the discourse so as to feminize effectively the figure of invaded Algeria, the narrator is able to instill the beginnings of revolt, of self-affirmation, into the lives of those victimized by historical dis-courses: "Ces lettres parlent, dans le fond, d'une Algérie-femme im-possible à apprivoiser" [between the lines these letters speak of Algeria as a woman whom it is impossible to tame] (69; 57). The resistance on the part of the Algerian woman, both in the plurality of her collective entity and in the singularity of the narrator who speaks for her, engen-ders the resistance which the protagonist will discursively assume in her turn as she seeks to carve subjectivity out of subjection. And in-deed, the importance of recognition in this matrix is critical: "Ne lève pas les yeux pour regarder son vainqueur. Ne le «reconnaît» pas. Ne le nomme pas. Qu'est-ce qu'une victoire si elle n'est pas nommée?" [Does not raise his eyes to gaze on his vanquisher. Does not "recog-nize" him. Does not name him. What is a victory if it is not named?] (69; 56). This repudiation of the Other's desire will determine the appropriation of identity which patriarchy seeks to impose upon the

Other, inscribed diachronically as the female body: "Ce monde étranger, qu'ils pénétraient quasiment sur le mode sexuel, ce monde hurla continûment . . . Y pénètrent comme en une défloration. L'Afrique est prise malgré le refus qu'elle ne peut étouffer" [This alien world, which they penetrated as they would a woman, this world sent up a cry that did not cease . . . Penetrated and deflowered, Africa is taken, in spite of the protesting cries that she cannot stifle] (70; 57). The assimilation of this recognition paradigm to an act of sexual violence serves only to deepen the horror implicit in the colonial encounter.

For in (re)tracing the parameters of this subjective struggle, the protagonist encounters parallel structures of paternal imposition, structures which she must subsume if she is to inscribe any value upon this ambiguity. If the letter which she reconstitutes is read as an attempt to negate colonial subjection and to impose the law of desire, then the continuing elaboration of paternal law must be recodified by this subject for self-assertion to occur: "Chaque mot d'amour, qui me serait destiné, ne pourrait que rencontrer le diktat paternel . . . Mon écriture, en entretenant ce dialogue sous influence, devenait en moi tentative—ou tentation—de délimiter mon propre silence . . . " [Every expression of love that would ever be addressed to me would have to meet my father's approval. . . . By keeping up a dialogue with this presence that haunted me, my writing became an attempt—or a temptation—to set the limits on my own silence . . .] (75; 61). In attempting to surmount the paternal obstacle and to enter into language, the subject in effect seeks the vagaries of signification. This linkage between language and meaning for the subject is a crucial one: ". . . the female subject's linguistic inauguration must be seen as inaugurating her, too, on the side of meaning rather than being."[9] The ultimate goal of elaborating a female postcolonial subject eventuated in discourse will take the very concepts of ambiguity and duality as paradigmatic of the oppositional construct it seeks to define.

So it is that the narrative voice itself becomes plural, fragmented, as the narrator proceeds to write, to speak, in the names of all those women subjected to oppression, and exiled from their heritage; writing and identity become practically interchangeable as past and present meet across the abyss of absence: " . . . soudain la voix explose. Libère

9. Kaja Silverman, *The Subject of Semiotics* (New York: Oxford University Press, 1983), 189.

en flux toutes les scories du passé" [suddenly the voice bursts forth. It drains off all the scoriae of the past . . .] (131; 115). The technique of that which unnames is turned against itself, as alienation and division give way to the quest for voice and presence which will supplant the absence engendered by being spoken for. The one who speaks in the name of all tropes the colonizer's mission in repeating it, while seeking to wrest subjective identity out of objectified nonentity.

Yet the progression of the narrative continues to trace the parallels between past and present, to demonstrate the ineluctable trajectory of the female colonial subject made to undergo the dictates of paternal law. In Part II of the novel, for example, we are witness to the story—which takes place in 1845—of Badra, only daughter of Si Mohamed Ben Kadrouma, who is captured on the eve of her wedding and whose resistance before her captor Mohamed ben Abdallah, a.k.a. Bou Maza, may be read as a model for the maintenance of female subjective integrity in the face of a patriarchal desire for her subjection. Indeed, Badra's refusal to succumb to the desire and will of the male Other implies the effective elaboration of an oppositional discourse, engendering through this process of signification a position of enunciation which negates the ambiguous ground which seeks to define her as a thing to be possessed, a portion of the spoils of war. By encoding and enacting the terms of her resistance to the paternal dictates of the conqueror, Badra nullifies her status as female object, and turns this attempt at an imposition of alterity into a paradigm of postcolonial feminine resistance.

A parallel situation subsequently presents itself for the protagonist with the issue of her own impending marriage and the respective roles of her father and fiancé, suggesting her appropriation of the experience of Badra as paradigmatic of her own dilemma. Here, the protagonist is reduced to the female body across which both father and fiancé vie for supremacy, inscribing her into an economy of exchange which reflects the absence of her grounding as a subject. And it is this lack of grounding that precipitates her inscriptive ambiguity, as she seeks to align herself with an axis which would negate her own burgeoning alterity and produce a means of signification: "C'était vérité: ces deux hommes n'auraient pu s'affronter dans cette ambiguïté, aucun d'eux ne voulant céder le pas à l'autre . . . " [It was true: these two men could not have faced each other in this ambiguous situation, neither of them prepared to give way to the other] (121; 105). As we observe an increasing shift in the discourse toward the autobiographical mode, the attempt to subvert the alienation and dispossession produced by the discursive inscription of the Algerian invasion progressively becomes a struggle to wrest identity out of the vagaries of biculturality and patriarchy, to establish the parameters of female postcolonial subjectivity in a context of shifting, plural codes where even the basic issues of language and culture for this subject hold the possibility of complete subversion of the subjective enterprise.

As Part III of the novel develops, the protagonist states this alienation and displacement implicitly through her oscillation between the first and third persons, giving vent to the division by which she is figured, and which in its turn stems from the presence of an overdetermining colonial discourse. This inability to preserve the first person in fact reveals a subject pervaded with ambiguity, as the impossibility of speaking the self as 'I' marks an identity-structure at odds with its own integrity.[10] This ambiguity to which the protagonist is subjected becomes progressively fixed upon the instability of language, its simultaneous reflection of, and lack of consonance with, the pluralities of postcolonial existence. In this regard, it becomes a perfect figure for her duality, as it represents the basic paradoxes of exile and belonging underlying colonial dispossession: "La langue étrangère me servait, dès l'enfance, d'embrasure pour le spectacle du monde et de ses richesses. Voici qu'en certaines circonstances, elle devenait dard pointé sur ma personne." [Ever since I was a child the foreign language was a casement opening on the spectacle of the world and all its riches. In certain circumstances it became a dagger threatening me] (143; 126). And so it is this double heritage of ambiguity and resistance, traversing the subjection inherent in colonial repression as well as the defiance signified and symbolized by Badra, that overdetermines the protagonist's present-day existence, exacerbates her sense of displacement, and ultimately, as she states, renders it impossible for her to address the exigencies of desire. For in order to do so, she must be able to recognize her own identity, to fix her subjectivity so as to translate it into signification. And here the language of the colonizer proves the ultimate obstacle: "Cette impossibilité en amour, la mémoire de la conquête la renforça . . . J'héritai de cette étanchéité; dès mon adoles-

10. Both Wallace Martin's *Recent Theories of Narrative* (Ithaca: Cornell University Press, 1985), and Shlomith Rimmon-Kenan's *Narrative Fiction: Contemporary Poetics* (New York: Methuen, 1983), discuss at length the discursive implications of the relationship between the speaking subject and the terms of its own enunciation of its identity-structure.

cence, j'expérimentai une sorte d'aphasie amoureuse: les mots écrits, les mots appris, faisaient retrait devant moi . . . " [The impossibility of this love was reinforced by memory of the conquest . . . I had inherited this imperviousness; from the time of my adolescence I experienced a kind of aphasia in matters of love: the written words, the words I had learned, retreated before me . . .] (145; 128). Intangible, fragmented, the essence of this subjectivity remains distanced from itself, caught in the interstices of cultural definition and colonial appropriation. But language, the discursive, appears to lead to betrayal.

One possible way of circumventing the destructive nature of such a paradox is through the incorporation of a form of *métissage*, by attempting to weave together the warp and the woof of conflicting cultural codes rather than remaining subject to the exigencies of their separation. Such a strategy, as Françoise Lionnet points out, works toward a valorization of the pluralities of the postcolonial heritage: "If . . . identity is a strategy, then *métissage* is the fertile ground of our heterogeneous and heteronomous identities as postcolonial subjects."[11] Yet in choosing between two possible formulations of cultural *métissage*, the protagonist simultaneously chooses to place limits upon her own submission, to circumscribe the possibilities for betrayal: as she considers the "seul métissage que la foi ancestrale ne condamne pas: celui de la langue et non celui du sang" [the only *métissage* that ancestral faith does not condemn: that of language and not that of blood] (161), the articulation which she implicitly puts into place acts as a form of cultural affirmation and resistance, delimiting the difference between the adulteration of language and that of identity. This tacit acknowledgement of the continuing inscription of biculturality reinscribes the subject into a field of duality, but one which now incorporates the possibility of discursive signification.

IV

What Djebar confronts here is the ultimate paradox underlying postcolonial identity-construction: the problematic legacy of a bicultural heritage. Such a paradox may have the ultimate effect of negating the entire quest for political and literary liberation. Albert Memmi, for example, in *The Colonizer and the Colonized*, points out that:

11. Françoise Lionnet, *Autobiographical Voices: Race, Gender, Self-Portraiture* (Ithaca: Cornell University Press, 1989), 8.

"current social life . . . the entire bureaucracy . . . uses the colonizer's language . . . *mak[ing] the colonized feel like a foreigner in his own country . . . Possession of the two languages is . . . participation in two psychic and cultural realms. Here, the two worlds symbolized and conveyed by the two tongues are in conflict; they are those of the colonizer and the colonized,"* (Memmi, 106–07, emphasis mine). It is the cultural conflict suggested by this duality, this inability to choose from among discourses reflecting alternative modes of repression, that faces Djebar's discursive reconstruction of a postcolonial Algerian subjectivity at this juncture, threatening this intrinsically ambiguous construct with dissolution.

Such a conflict also presents itself to the narrator, for, having decided to subvert the patriarchal text of her history and her culture by rewriting it from the perspective of its feminine component, she finds herself caught between French and Arabic, between the delimiting impositions of the colonizer on the one hand, and the desire for recognition and affirmation of identity on the other. For her, the issue of language is firmly linked to that of identity; the use of Arabic produces an "instant purificateur comme un frôlement du linge de la mort. L'écriture réintervient et le cercle se referme" [the moment of absolution, like touching the hem of death's garment. Again it is the turn of writing, and the circle is completed] (208; 184). The suggestion of concurrence between signifier and signified which is produced here is immediately placed in contrast to the alienating effects produced by the use of French, and the resulting ambiguities appear to be driving the protagonist to the edge of self-dissolution:

> Quand j'écris et lis la langue étrangère: [mon corps] voyage, il va et vient dans l'espace subversif . . . mes mots ne se chargent pas de réalité charnelle . . . Ces apprentissages simultanés . . . m'installent . . . dans une dichotomie d'espace . . . [la] chance me propulse à la frontière d'une sournoise hystérie.

> When I write and read the foreign language, my body travels far in subversive space . . . the words I use convey no flesh-and-blood reality . . . These two . . . apprenticeships, undertaken simultaneously, land me in a dichotomy of location . . . This stroke of luck brings me to the verge of breakdown. [208; 184–85]

The question of subjective nomadism produced by engagement with the foreign tongue goes to the heart of the dilemma underlying the cultural inscription of identity which the narrative elaborates. The dissonance of the subject to itself is figured by the subversive space of this speech, contextualizing the subject through the division which reflects and recuperates her own discursive dichotomy. Such a dichotomy in language use, the opposition between completion and dislocation, self and other, reduces the speaking subject to a being whose identity-formation is based, and remains, in two separate linguistic and cultural domains, potentially neither one nor the other, broaching that sense of linguistic and cultural dispossession which Memmi has termed "foreignness." The option of *métissage*, whether textual or cultural, suggests the recuperation of the bicultural as a reflection of the extent to which this element has pervaded the discursive space.

At this juncture, however, a second discursive paradigm suggests itself. It is equally possible to postulate the thesis that the paradox of having to write in the colonizer's language—since it is, so to speak, imposed from the outside through the dominant forces of assimilation and acculturation—also provides a means for subverting and rewriting the discursive framework of oppression from the very space of its own elaboration. As Marx-Scouras puts it in her gloss on the Maghrebine dilemma: "For if the situation of being outside was initially perceived to be a negative effect of colonialism, today, it constitutes the basis for a writing and aesthetics of difference," (Marx-Scouras, 4). This difference will ultimately be definitive of the process of subjective recodification which the discourse engages. But since language also structures demand, this dichotomy is the result of a demand inherent in the process of colonization as well; since any demand, in Lacanian terms, is addressed to others and marks, at bottom, a demand for recognition, this makes of colonization a process symptomatic of an inherent lack on the part of the colonizer.[12] In this case, the dialectic of subjectivity and colonial desire is exacerbated by biculturality, which not only inhibits the inscription of integrity, but capitalizes on dichotomies of language use in order to generate the pervading sense of ambiguity that underlies the split subject. Djebar's subject, intensely aware of her own existential and discursive situation, attempts to exorcise these thorny issues by addressing them directly:

> Le français m'est langue marâtre. Quelle est ma langue mère disparue, qui m'a abandonnée . . . Sous le poids des tabous que je porte en moi comme héritage, je me retrouve désertée des chants de l'amour

---

12. See J. LaPlanche and J.-B. Pontalis, *The Language of Psychoanalysis*, Trans. Donald Nicholson-Smith (New York: Norton, 1973), 483.

arabe . . . «L'amour, ses cris» («s'écrit») . . . il ne s'agit plus d'écrire que
pour survivre . . . Après plus d'un siècle d'occupation française . . . un
territoire de langue subsiste entre deux peuples, entre deux mémoires;
la langue française, corps et voix, s'installe en moi comme un
orgueilleux préside, tandis que la langue maternelle, toute en ora-
lité . . . résiste et attaque . . . je suis à la fois l'assiégé étranger et l'auto-
chtone partant à la mort par bravade, illusoire effervescence du dire et
de l'écrit.

French is my 'stepmother' tongue. What is my long-lost mother-
tongue, that abandoned me and disappeared? . . . Burdened by my inherited taboos, I discover I have no memory of Arabic love songs . . .
"*L'amour, ses cris (s'écrit)*" . . . it is no longer a question of writing only
to survive . . . After more than a century of French occupation, a similar no-man's-land still exists between the French and the indigenous
languages, between two national memories . . . the French tongue,
with its body and voice, has established a proud *presidio* within me,
while the mother tongue, all oral tradition, resists and attacks . . . I am
alternately the besieged foreigner and the native swaggering off to die,
so there is seemingly endless strife between the spoken and written
word. [240–41; 214–15]

At this juncture, the subject's ambiguity is encoded discursively. The
struggle between the *langue marâtre* and the *langue mère* bespeaks the
cultural dilemma produced by colonial appropriation and the imposition of colonial desire. Splitting off the corporeal, scriptive French
tongue from the nurturing orality of her Arabic heritage renders the
subject both stranger and native, self and Other. With love now overtly
linked to the violent appropriations of the scriptive, the impossible
context of the language of the Other is made even more explicit. Both
the spoken and the written appear, paradoxically, to engender a context
for survival while simultaneously elaborating a reciprocity which de-
centers the subject mediated by both axes.

    This is precisely the dilemma faced by the postcolonial subject
attempting to establish a history and an identity through language.
And this is the form that exile assumes in the text; a separation not
simply from self, from country, but from language itself, from a singular discourse within and through which one can inscribe for the
subject a valid and coherent sense of identity. In a certain sense, this
subject is attempting to establish her right to define the parameters of
her own perception, to prevent the translation or adulteration of her
own essence: " . . . whether implicit or explicit, there appears to have
been a close connection between language and racial, or cultural, iden-

tity . . . The notion of what is human . . . is intimately tied to the question of linguistic difference."[13] At issue, then, is the capacity for self-definition, the inscription of identity as the visible mark of subjectivity, its viability as a sign-system. In elaborating the identity-structure across the gap of cultures, it is a necessary stage in the articulation of the self-determination that the subject seeks. Those who persist, Januslike, in the attempt to narrow this impossible gap will succeed only in widening it, in making division and separation appear to be both culturally and psychologically inescapable.

Neither French nor Arabic, neither literacy nor orality, is sufficient to allow Djebar's narrator—trapped as she is between discourses—to continue, yet she knows that she must: "Est-ce d'avoir été expulsée de ce discours amoureux qui me fait trouver aride le français que j'emploie?" Is it because I was cut off from this impassioned speech that I find the French I use so flat and unprofitable? (240; 214). The rewriting of the colonialist discourse must find a way to forestall its own reappropriation by the negative pluralities that colonialism inherently generates. As a revalorization of a historically determined absence crucial to the selfhood of both the narrator and the elements of the *Algérie-femme* in whose name she speaks, the binarism proposed by the dilemma of language may indeed, in the final analysis, mask desire as it simultaneously marks the implementation of a strategy of self-affirmation.

Writing, then, the very sign and condition of signification, ultimately undermines colonial desire and affirms the validity of the subject by virtue of its very inscription. The postcolonial subject which it constitutes is the embodiment of displacement, and Caren Kaplan points to the postmodernity of this system in "locat[ing] this moment of alienation and exile in language and literature. In one sense, it describes the effects of radical distanciation between signifier and signified. Meaning and utterances become estranged . . . This writing . . . travels, moves between centers and margins . . . [and is] not imperialism but nomadism."[14] Language, reflecting here the dual inscription of the colonized subject, marks the construction of the sub-

13. Eric Cheyfitz, *The Poetics of Imperialism: Translation and Colonization from The Tempest to Tarzan* (New York: Oxford University Press, 1991), 102–103.

14. Caren Kaplan, "Deterritorializations: "The Rewriting of Home and Exile in Western Feminist Discourse," *The Nature and Context of Minority Discourse, Cultural Critique* no. 6, (Spring, 1987), Abdul R. JanMohamed and David Lloyd, ed., 187–98; see 188.

ject through discourse as well as the double bind of cultural alienation. Marginality thus signifies a subjective pluralism which incorporates the ambiguities of historical experience. Ultimately, the dialectic of the colonial encounter informs the perspective of both colonizer and colonized, generating dislocation in each category and rendering them both subject to the dualities inherent in cultural exchange. Within this context of double displacement, the vision of both self and Other undergoes a critical rearticulation.

In a published interview, Djebar herself has addressed her own recognition of and subjugation to this formative cultural and linguistic duality: " . . . j'écris dans une langue étrangère chez moi, bien plus, dans la langue de l'ancien occupant . . . dans la langue que j'appelle la langue *adverse* . . . Donc, pour me résumer, un premier exil s'installe dans une langue qui m'est langue *d'en face* . . . Le français devient la langue de dehors . . . Donc, mon rapport avec la langue arabe est un rapport dualiste" [At home I write in a foreign tongue, in fact in the tongue of the former occupying power . . . in the tongue which I call the *adverse* tongue . . . So, to sum up, the first exile occurs in a tongue which is opposite to me . . . French becomes the public tongue . . . Thus, my relationship with Arabic is a dual one.][15] Language thus becomes the place of inscription of a paradoxical colonial subjectivity: while marking the divided desire of the colonized subject, at the same time writing may be read as signifying a subjection to cultural alienation as well as its eventual subversion and transcendence. Exile and nomadism become figures for the inscription of an identity which ultimately derives its validity from the experience of alienation. It is from its elaboration of elements of textual and cultural *métissage* as figures for the ambiguities and disjunctures of postcolonial subjectivity that this exploration of the implications of the colonial encounter ultimately derives signification.

15. Marguerite Le Clézio, "Assia Djebar: Ecrire dans la langue adverse," *Contemporary French Civilization*, (Spring/Summer 1985), vol. 9, no. 2, 230–44; see pp. 232–234: [translation mine].

HEDI ABDEL-JAOUAD

Isabelle Eberhardt: Portrait
of the Artist as a Young Nomad

Ego in exilio genitus, in exilio natus sum [I was conceived in exile
and born in exile]
—Petrarch

The horseman dressed in *gandouras* and white *burnous*, in a large
veiled turban, wearing at his neck the black beads of Kadriya, his
right hand bound with a red handkerchief to better grip the reins, this
would be Mahmoud Saâdi, adopted son of the great white Sheik . . .
—Isabelle Eberhardt, 1900, Algerian Sahara, self-portrait

Even before her strange death at twenty-seven in a flash flood in Aïn
Séfra, an oasis in the Algerian Sahara, Isabelle Eberhardt (1877–1904)
was a legend. This Rimbaud-type woman repudiated Europe and its
civilization, converted to Islam, dressed as a man, assumed a male
identity, and roamed the Sahara, untrammeled by the constraints of
her youth and sex.[1] This self-willed nomad also had unbounded literary ambitions. In the course of her brief existence, she wrote more than
two thousand pages of notes, articles, and fiction, travelling tirelessly
in the nomadic fashion, on foot, on horseback, alone, and with car-
avans. Her "vagabondage" (one of the many reference terms to her
"errance" and nomadic way of life) was concomitant with her vocation

1. Isabelle-Wilhelmine-Marie Eberhardt was born in Geneva on 17 February 1877,
under the ominous signs of illegitimacy and statelessness, to Mme Nathalie de
Moerder, née Eberhardt, widow of Senator Pavel Karlovitch de Moerder, and an unknown father. In *Un Désir d'Orient* (Paris: Grasset, 1988), Edmonde Charles-Roux,
hereafter Roux, Isabelle's most recent and authoritative biographer, corroborates the
widely accepted thesis that Alexander Trophimowsky, Mme de Moerder's lover and the
tutor of her children, was Isabelle's father. The truth may have been buried with Mme
de Moerder herself. Pierre Arnoult claims in his book *Rimbaud* (Paris: Albin Michel,
1943) that Isabelle is Rimbaud's illegitimate daughter. He bases his thesis on physical
resemblance and a common destiny. In France and in the Maghreb, Isabelle continues
to be canonized unabashedly: "la bonne nomade/l'ardente nomade/l'androgyne du
désert/la soeur de charité de l'Islam/l'Héloïse du désert, Notre Dame du Sahara, the
Passionate Nomad, Isabelle/l'Algérien," etc.

YFS 83, *Post/Colonial Conditions*, ed. Lionnet & Scharfman, © 1993 by Yale
University.

as a writer. Isabelle considered and practiced writing as a form of nomadism, a journey into language.[2] In order to become a nomadic writer she had to lead, as she repeatedly declared in her *Journaliers* (1923, 1987, 1988), "two lives, one that is full of adventure and belongs to the Desert, and one, calm and restful, devoted to thought and far from all that might interfere with it."[3]

If Isabelle's life is hailed by many as exemplary—Isabelle, the woman and the artist, embodies the quintessential rebel figure,—her precociously promising but unfinished work has not received the critical attention it merits. The fact that little has been written about her creative work is mainly due to the dubious authenticity of *Dans l'Ombre chaude de l'Islam*, an anthology of short stories collected, polished, finished, and sometimes rewritten, by her friend and mentor Victor Barrucand, and of which Barrucand claimed—adding insult to injury—coauthorship. Besides the question of "legitimacy," Isabelle's text still wanders between several nationalities: is it Russian, Swiss, French or Maghrebian, or all at once? Little did Isabelle know when she reflected in her *Journaliers* that: "No work of literature is ever finished" (14) that her own "oeuvre" would remain unfinished; little did she suspect that her work, like herself, would posthumously be doomed to suffer the *heimatlose*, the statusless, plight.[4]

"ILLEGITIMATE," "WOMAN," AND *"HEIMATLOSE"*

Isabelle realized early in her life that true freedom could only be attained outside the purported hell of her milieu, that is, outside her

2. Gilles Deleuze and Felix Guattari, *Kafka: Pour une littérature mineure* (Paris: Minuit, 1975), 29–30.

3. Isabelle Eberhardt, *Mes Journaliers* (Paris: La Connaissance, 1923). *Oeuvres complètes*, "Ecrits sur le sable" (Paris: Grasset, 1988), hereafter *Ecrits sur le sable* 1 & 2. We will use Nina de Voogd's translation whenever possible: *The Passionate Nomad* (Boston: Beacon Press, 1987), 11, hereafter *Journaliers*; Isabelle Eberhardt *Trimardeur* (Paris: Fasquelle, 1923), *Vagabond,* trans. Annette Kobak (London: The Hogarth Press, 1988); Isabelle Eberhardt, trans. Paul Bowles, *The Oblivion Seekers* (San Francisco: City Lights, 1972), 85. *Dans l'Ombre chaude de l'Islam* (Paris, Fasquelle, 1906) *Au Pays des sables* (Paris: Sorlot, 1944) *Lettres inédites,* with an introduction "Amazone ou paumée?" and commentary by Jean Duvignaud in *Internationale de l'imaginaire* nos. 67–92 (Winter: 1987–88), hereafter Amazone ou paumée? Isabelle's personal correspondence is collected in a volume *Ecrits intimes* (Paris: Payot, 1991), hereafter *Ecrits intimes,* edited and presented by Marie-Odile Delacour and Jean-René Huleu. For our purpose we use Duvignaud's text because of the Arabic script.

4. Recent research, especially that of Marie-Odile Delacour and René Heuleu (*"Ecrits sur le sable,"* op. cit.), has revealed that Barrucand's "editorializing" was less substantial than presumed.

culture, religion, and language. Her illegitimacy condemned her, from birth, to an endless and illusory quest for a father, and to a life of exile and nomadism in search of a fatherland.[5]

She had to flee the trappings of a stifling bourgeois life and the domestic entrapments of gender in order to seek sustenance for her art. Isabelle the writer, whose mother tongue was Russian, opted for French, a language she would transform to accommodate her adopted Maghrebian identity. As reflected in her correspondence, diary, and fiction, exile was for Isabelle an experience of becoming, a praxis that necessitated ever more evasions.

At the root of Isabelle's exile and subsequent nomadism was an unhappy consciousness. Because she was an illegitimate child, a woman brought up in a country and a century that denied women their elementary rights, and one who lived for the better part of her life as a stateless refugee or *Heimatlose* (Isabelle never felt comfortable with the precarious and demeaning status of *Heimatlose*, especially in Geneva, where every Russian émigré was regarded with suspicion), Isabelle had more than one axe to grind against the society that rejected her. The root of this rejection, however, predates Isabelle's birth and lies in her native Russia where, on account of her illegitimacy, her family was considered *non grata*. Isabelle came to incarnate the family's guilt—a form of psychological exile—and the consummation of their irrevocable separation from the fatherland.[6]

Paradoxically, Isabelle, like every exile, longed for a community, a country, and a people she could call her own. In her life and writing, the inaccessible Russian fatherland is projected onto the Maghreb, first through flights of imagination, but later, once she is there, through its transformations into the theater of her nomadic wanderings and musings, and, as she desired, her last abode. In her *Journaliers*, Isabelle refers to the Maghreb as her "home," and "the country of [her] choice," (86).

5. Isabelle embroidered endlessly and fantastically the myth of her unknown father. She confessed to her Tunisian friend, Ali Abdel Wahab, that Trophimowsky was her father, only to recant this version in favor of a more fantastic one: "I was the wretched outcome of a rape committed by my mother's doctor, now deceased" in "Isabelle Eberhardt: Amazone ou paumée?" op. cit., (Letter of 1 January 1898), my translation. In a letter to the editor of *La Petite Gironde*, she gives yet another version: "My father was a Russian subject of the Moslem faith, and my mother was a Russian catholic." *The Oblivion Seekers*, 85.

6. Isabelle's mother was also born out of wedlock, born Nathalie Eberhardt, illegitimate daughter of Nicolas Korff and Fraulein Eberhardt, whose name she was given.

From her childhood fantasy, the Maghreb grew to be a consummation. By her teens she was *en connaissance de cause,* so to speak, with
the Maghreb before she ever set foot there. In retrospect, her early
fictional creations appear as a grand rehearsal for the real act to follow.

In one such adolescent and premonitory creation, significantly titled "Visions du Moghreb," a short story published under the male
pseudonym of Nicolas Podolinsky in *Nouvelle Revue Moderne,*[7] we
find the early signs of Isabelle's strategy, namely the subversion of
linguistic, sexual, and cultural hegemonies, her future artistic and
literary preoccupations. Significantly, Isabelle refers to North Africa
by its Arabic name, phoneticized here in the Algerian dialect,
"Moghreb." We find as well the configuration of her fictional world and
leitmotifs. In this story, the fictionalized *taleb* (a divinity student) is
the prototype of a series of portraits that the artist, once in the
Maghreb, will depict again upon close observation. Although drawing
on secondhand material relayed to her by her brother Augustin, his
colegionnaire Edouard Vivicorsi, and her penfriend Eugène Letord, Isabelle creates a strikingly vivid and realistic image of the Maghreb and
its people. Her sympathy goes, as a matter of natural course, to a
kindred spirit: the colonized and the underdog. For a writer acquainted
with the Maghreb only through correspondence and books, she dis-
plays remarkable insight and knowledge. Furthermore, the young
taleb of the story, this seeker of arcane, Sufi knowledge, and a staunch
anticolonialist, is a striking prototype of Isabelle's projected future
identity.

THE YEAR OF THE HEJRA

It was only a matter of time before Isabelle gave a concrete shape to her
"Visions du Moghreb." In May 1897, corresponding to 1275 in the
hejra calendar, Isabelle and her mother sailed to Algeria, to Bône/An-
naba, where they embraced Islam. For mother and daughter, this journey to the Maghreb was tantamount to a *hejra.* The Arabic word *hejra,*
(also spelled *hegira* and *hijrah*), refers to the flight of the Prophet
Muhammad from Mecca to Yathrib, which counts as the beginning of

---

7. The fact that she published this story in this journal, in 1896, is quite an
anomaly: especially since she refers to North Africa by its Arabic name, phoneticized
in the Algerian dialect, Moghreb; and also considering that this journal advocated the
French civilizing mission in Algeria with jingoistic enthusiasm.

the Muslim era: 20 June, 622 A.D. Both literally and figuratively, Isabelle's emigration and conversion constitute a *hejra*.[8]

The Islamic tradition consecrates *hejra* as a radical departure from the beliefs of the past, a total submission ("Islam" in Arabic means submission to God) to the new faith and its prescriptions. For Isabelle, this *hejra* signified the beginning of a new calendar and a new life, the end of her exile as a Russian émigrée, of her humiliation as a *Heimatlose*, and, more importantly, of her seeming failure as an artist in Geneva and the West—all obstacles to her intellectual and spiritual growth. In Isabelle's manichean vision of the world, this journey/*hejra* was a flight from a hostile West to more hospitable and congenial African shores, a kind of spiritual *hejra*, as she noted in her *Journaliers*, from the "land of exile [Geneva] so very far away from the other sacred place devoted to eternal repose and everlasting silence" (6).

For her and many of her fictional alter egos, especially her Russian characters, exile, symbolic of the alienating past, gives way to nomadism, an emblem of the future and of emancipation: "Tereneti Antonoff [father of the protagonist in her story "L'Anarchiste"], persecuted in Russia for his libertarian convictions, and about to be exiled, had escaped to Algeria, searching for a new land and a country of his choice where, under a clement sky, men would be less crusted over with routine." (*Au Pays des sables*, 175).

The bliss of the encounter with her newfound fatherland was marred by the sudden death of Fatma-Manoubia, her mother, who was buried in the maritime cemetery in Annaba, according to Muslim rites. This traumatic event was soon followed, upon her return to Geneva, by the suicide of her brother Vladimir, and the demise of "Vava" Trophimowsky. Isabelle was never to receive her mother's legacies.[9]

At the age of twenty-one, Isabelle, alone, destitute and solitary, resembled one of those "Ouled Bab-Allah" (in Arabic: the sons of Allah's gate, that is, vagabonds, wayfarers) she wrote so much about,

---

8. In her text "Silhouettes d'Afrique," Isabelle, who introduces herself as Mahmoud el Mouskoubi [the Muskovite], equates *hejra*, which she phoneticizes in the Algerian dialect, *Hedjira*, with the glorious days of Islam before the advent of Western civilization: "May our Islam, instead of assimilating the lies and impure posture of the West, return to its purity of the first centuries of the *Hedjira*, especially in its original simplicity," *Ecrits sur le sable* 2, op. cit., 66.

9. In a letter to her friend Al Abdel Wahab, she explains that "In Russia, being able to inherit, especially overseas, takes years and years. . . . And my mother left no cash" "Isabelle Eberhardt: Amazone ou paumée," op. cit., 4. My translation.

who roamed aimlessly and lived from hand to mouth, unburdened by past, family, or possessions, and who stood on the margins of society—outsiders, pariahs, and outcasts—as symbols of fierce independence and absolute freedom: "When he [the wayfarer] comes to a farm or a hut, he stops and pounds the earth with his long staff of wild olive wood. His raucous voice breaks the silence of the countryside as he asks for Allah's bread. And he is right, the sad-faced wanderer. The sacred bread he demands, without begging for it, is his by right, and the giving of it is only a feeble compensation, a recognizing of the injustice that is in the world" (*The Oblivion Seekers*, 20).

Although Isabelle never dwelled on exile or the past, she was none-theless obsessed by what she had not known: the nostalgia of Algeria before colonization, the purity of a land which in her fantasy re-sembled the Russia before her birth. For Isabelle, the South and the Sahara, particularly the Souf region and the little oasis of El Oued, as the only spots that remained uncontaminated by the "French civiliz-ing mission," represented the inner geography of her lost fatherland, her kingdom of innocence. The spiritual configuration of this new-found land was essentially Islamic. In Dar-el-Islam, Isabelle found a spiritual community and an ultimate refuge from her past.

By reterritorializing herself and her Russian characters in the Maghreb, Isabelle sought to link, both in her life and fiction, the two poles of her Orient: Russia and the Maghreb. This dual ancestry is exemplified by her alter ego Mahmoud el Mouskoubi [the Moscovite] who, as illustrated in "Silhouettes d'Afrique," has found in "Dar el-Islam the fatherland which [she] so desperately desired" as a replace-ment for the "Slav country which [she] was never to see" (*Ecrits sur le Sable 2*, 58). In this regard, Isabelle's search for the lost fatherland was a form of repatriation. Hers was a yearning for the Orient of her an-cestors. Like Mahoud el-Mouskoubi, Orschanow, the protagonist of her novel *Trimardeur*, is haunted by his dual heritage: "Ever since he sat daydreaming on the quay of La Joliette, watching the Saint-Augustin leave for Oran, he had been haunted by the idea of Africa, and above all of Muslim Africa. He thought of all his own atavistic links to Islam through his maternal side, Tartar and nomadic."[10] Her Oriental hankering was also exacerbated by the xenophobia of the Swiss who

10. *Trimardeur* [*Vagabond*], 87–88. Orschanow's life and itinerary closely mirror Isabelle's. Isabelle claims she is a Russian Muslim through her paternal side, see also note 5.

never missed a chance, as Isabelle often remarked in her correspondence and diaries, to remind Russian émigrés that they were Orientals.

In her unabashed attempt to bridge the gap between the Russian and the Arab, one clearly recognizes some degree of projection on Isabelle's part. In her novel *Trimardeur*, the Arab and the Russian, the Fellah and the Mujik, seem to be brothers made of the same clay, strikingly similar in attitudes and destiny: "Like the Russian people, the Arab races survived by the force of an almost unchangeable inertia. Like them, they suffered in silence, bringing the same resignation, the same submission, the same tacit reproval of injustice to any dealings they had with the authorities. . . . In addition, like the ordinary Slavs, they were sociable and egalitarian, and showed no disdain for the poor. The rich and the lettered would sit side by side with the most wretched, in the great brotherhood of Islam" (138). Furthermore, a sense of fatality or *Mektoub*, a recurrent term in her writings, pervades every aspect of her life and characters, so much so that she sees in every displaced person, especially Russians, a potential Muslim.

With equal unabashedness, Isabelle strove to transform the despised status of *Heimatlose*, which was at the root of the matrix of exile and nomadism, into a triumph over bourgeois self-complacency: "Not for me," she wrote in her *Journaliers*, "those who feel smug, happy with themselves and their lot, content with the state of their heart. Not for me those boastful bourgeois who are deaf, dumb, and blind, and never admit a mistake" (9). Instead, she longed to experience "the strangely sad and voluptuous well-being of the *Heimatlose*" (154).

Thus, the initial stigma of *Heimatlose* would later be embraced by Isabelle as a form of redemption and martyrdom. The final sentence in her novel *Trimardeur* reads like an ode to the romantic *Heimatlose's* lifestyle, a legitimizing gesture: "He [Dmitri Orshanow] had come back to the Legion with only one desire: to stay forever, and one day to sleep in the corner reserved for the *Heimatlose* in the cemetery in Saïda" (160).

In this projected fatherland Isabelle passionately sought, as she confided in her *Journaliers*, to fulfill her literary as well as her spiritual aspirations, for her secret ambitions were to become a writer and *marcboute*: "Two things are holding my attention at the moment: first my need for progress in the intellectual domain. . . . The other question on my mind is of a very different order, one I would not dare come out with, except when talking to Slimène [her Algerian husband], for he will be the *only one to understand* and go along with it; and that is the question of becoming a *maraboute* [a saint]" (66).

But above all, Isabelle saw herself, as she confided in her *Journaliers*, as a struggling artist in the "burnous," so to speak, of the nomad, untrammeled by routine and material possessions: "A symbol of what my life is now all about, and probably always will be, is that sign saying *'Room for rent'* by the window of the seedy room I am living in, with a camp bed in it, some papers and, my handful of books" (9). Like any artist who chose the nomadic life, Isabelle was compelled—she referred to this compulsion as an act of fate, *Mektoub*—to reproduce her "vagabondage" and restlessness in her own writing, to the point that nomadism may have become the sole focus of her writing: "A subject," she mused in her *Pencilled Notes*, "to which intellectuals never give a thought is the right to be vagrant, the freedom to wander. Yet vagrancy is deliverance, and life on the open road is the essence of freedom" (*The Oblivion Seekers*, 68).

Isabelle's writing dramatizes the fugitive and *Heimatlose* element in her life. She sought to become, like Stephen Hero, the "artificer of [her] own style of life."[11] Isabelle escaped into her new male and Arab identity so as to let live and flourish, in perfect androgyny, the artist in her/him. Isabelle/Mahmoud will henceforth embody the mendicant Sufi as an artist: "Go, Mahmoud, and do great, magnificent deeds. . . . Be a hero . . . " (*Journaliers*, 8). The realization of the dual self—Isabelle/Mahmoud, the artist/the nomad, the illegitimate/the maraboute—will develop into a polysemic archetype.

ISABELLE/MAHMOUD: THE ARTIST AS A NOMAD

Isabelle was indeed one of the very European writers who knew the Maghreb from the inside. According to Victor Barrucand, her Algerian editor and mentor, Isabelle was not only an extraordinary character, but a bold and courageous one who wrote about the humanity of the native and who espoused the Algerian's cause when it was not fashionable to do so: "There are," noted Barrucand in his 'Introduction' to *Pages d'Islam*, "many Algerias to be observed.[12] Where Louis Bertrand, for example, only met Latins and émigrés from Valencia, Isabelle wanted to see only natives" (12).

11. Stanislas Joyce, *My Brother's Keeper* (New York: 1958), 223.
12. Victor Barrucand, *Pages d'Islam*, "Introduction" (Paris: Fasquelle, 1920).

She was one of the very few Europeans who did not succumb to the romantic Oriental-Bedouin fever so endemic in her time.[13] Although as a child she fell under the spell of the Russian feminist, writer, journalist, and traveller, Lydia Pachkov, whose fabulous travel-accounts from the Middle East appeared regularly in the fashionable Parisian magazine, *Tour du Monde,* Isabelle's vision and experience of the Arab and Islamic world were at the antipodes of Pachkov's. For Isabelle the Maghreb was more than a theater of adventures, it was a permanent abode. Furthermore, even though she was a lifelong admirer of the sumptuous imagery of Pierre Loti, Isabelle's writing is, in a sense, the antithesis of Loti's. Isabelle's Orient is, in many respects, unromantic; she wrote almost exclusively about the degrading and dehumanizing effects of French colonial rule on the native population. In this regard alone, Isabelle's "écriture" is remarkably proto-postmodern and postcolonial: her treatment of Maghrebian reality is perceived by many readers in the Maghreb as an early attempt at what Meddeb calls "the rectification of the Orientalist consensus," something he too illustrates in his novel *Talismano.*[14]

That she was a *Heimatlose,* no doubt, sharpened her sense of humanity, and may explain the empathy she showed for the disinherited, whom a half-century later Frantz Fanon would call *The Wretched of the Earth.* The Maghreb depicted by Isabelle, at the height of the Algerianist school, represented by Louis Bertand and his "littérature de cartes postales," was neither exotic nor sentimental; it was steeped in people's lives, especially the ordinary among them.

Because she gave a voice to those who deliberately were left out of

13. Isabelle's collected work proves beyond the shadow of a doubt that she was indeed the first champion of decolonization, and belies the often unsubstantiated but typically reductive view, held for example by Rana Kabbani, that the "voyage East for Isabelle was primarily a gateway to sex . . . the East as a coffer of erotic delights and unlimited freedoms . . . and that Isabelle, like countless other Europeans, had come to the Orient on the flying-carpet of Orientalism." In "Introduction" to *The Passionate Nomad: The Diary of Isabelle Eberhardt,* op. cit., v–xii.

14. This is not to say that Isabelle was not sometimes "blind"—after all, she was a woman of her time and culture, and was, therefore, prey to a kind of Orientalizing romanticism, especially with respect to the nomads and the desert. Nor was she immune from racial and cultural stereotypes, namely about the Arab woman, her anti-type. Some of her attitudes about blacks, if taken out of context, are outright racist: "The disturbing and repulsive impression that Negroes produce on me comes almost singularly from the strange mobility of their faces with furtive eyes, with their features forever twitching with tics and grins. It is an invincible impression of nonanimal kinship that I feel childishly, at first sight, toward my brothers the blacks" *Ecrits sur le sable 1* op. cit., 247.

literature and history, Isabelle has been hailed posthumously as an advocate of decolonization.[15] Her sympathetic attitudes towards the natives rank her as one of the early critics of the colonial enterprise and its avowed civilizing mission. In this regard, Isabelle's work may have inaugurated the theme of decolonization in the Maghreb, for it expounded a sociology of colonialism and oppression whose critics and theorists would later include, among Francophone writers, the Martinican Frantz Fanon and the Tunisian Albert Memmi.

Her original social and psychological findings and observations articulate complex problematics that have continued to haunt Maghrebians for generations, namely the aftershocks of colonial rule on the native population: "In ten, twenty years' time," she wondered in her *Journaliers* "will today's young Algerians resemble their fathers and be as steeped as they are in the solemn serenity of their Islamic faith?" (22). In this regard, she was the first Francophone writer to delve into the complex problematic of the cultural alienation of the colonized, particularly of the tiny category of natives who benefited from the colonial system, known in French as the *évolués*. Isabelle spoke eloquently in her unfinished novel *Rakhil*, in the few pages salvaged from the flood, about the plight of North-African migrant workers in Marseilles, an important and current issue both in the Maghreb and France. Likewise, in *Trimardeur* she evokes problems pertaining to the living conditions, reception, and treatment of those migrant workers, problems which prefigure by over a half a century those raised by *Beur* writers, the children of second- and third-generation North-African immigrants in France.

THE FICTIONAL TYPE AS ISABELLE'S ALTER-EGO

Like the nomad who is doomed to repeat his migration and displacement, Isabelle repeats *ad infinitum* the same portrait of the *Heimatlose*, as if to convince herself of her own relevance and of the

15. For many Maghrebians, particularly Algerians, Isabelle looms in retrospect as an unswerving and staunch anticolonialist, and a defender of Arabic Islamic values and traditions at the height of the colonial undertaking. Today she is regarded by many as one of the precursors, if not the first, of Maghrebian Francophone writers. See particularly, Mohammed-Salah Dembri's "Isabelle Eberhardt est-elle Algérienne?" *Algérie Actualité*, 25 October 1970, and the more recent article by Djouher Mousseoui, "Signes et société," *El Moudjahid*, 10 July 1985.

worthiness of her quest. Her life is mirrored by the many facets of her fictional characters.

Isabelle's fiction is a world of extremes and excesses of all sorts. It revolves around a series of binary oppositions: Europe/Orient, exile/nomad, city/countryside, sacred (the Mosque)/profane (the whorehouse), etc. It is predominantly peopled with male characters and shows a special affection for nomads, Bedouins, legionnaires, Spahis, and other social outcasts—who are portrayed sympathetically, like herself, as innocent victims of Fate's misfortunes. If European women are notably absent in Isabelle's fiction, the only Arab women she writes about are *Bédouines*, and they are either prostitutes or *maraboutes*.[16]

A rebel, Isabelle was contemptuous of the submissiveness of women, and only befriended and wrote about those who refused the tutelage of males. In this regard, she saw in the Arab woman, not her alter-ego but her antitype: "Yes, indeed," she wrote to her Slimane, "I am your wife before God and Islam. But I am not a vulgar Fatma or an ordinary Aïcha. I am also your brother Mahmoud, the servant of God and Djilani first, rather than the servant of her husband that every Arab woman is, according to the *chera* (body of Islamic law)," (*Lettres intimes*, 336–37).

Her female characters, often portrayed as victims of frustrated love, and of social and moral constraints and misunderstandings, ultimately escape their unfulfilled life and seek oblivion in alcohol, drugs, prostitution or, in the case of *maraboutes*, mysticism. As viewed by the fiercely independent Isabelle, these forms of escape and rebellion are preferable to a life of mediocrity and enslavement: "Like all the women of her region, Achoura considered the sale of her body the only escape from want that was available to a woman. She had no desire to be cloistered again by marriage, nor was she ashamed to be what she was. To her, prostitution seemed legitimate, and did not interfere with her love for her favorite [Si Mohammed el Arbi]. Indeed, it never occurred to her to associate in her mind the indescribable bliss they knew

16. According to Cecily Mackworth, "Arab mythology contains a long tradition of female marabouts, several of whom had scoured the desert disguised as men. Lelle Aouda ben Sidi Mohammed was one of the most famous examples, and centuries later men spoke of the beauty and learning of the great chieftainess, her debauched early life, and her pious end as a cave-dwelling hermit" *The Destiny of Isabelle Eberhardt* (New York: The Ecco Press, 1975), 116. In some instances, Mackworth notes, especially among the Northern tribes such as the Ouled-Nail tribe, female maraboutism is the ultimate repentance for a life of prostitution (Mackworth, 61).

together with what she called, using the cynical *sabir* word, *"coum-merce,"* (*The Oblivion Seekers*, 33).

A typical protagonist is often a single man or woman confronting incredible social, political, and moral odds that occur as a result of an innate desire to be other than the original self. A typical itinerary of her characters is from North (Europe) to South (Africa), that of the city-dweller who leaves behind the comfort of Europe for the rugged life of the desert, who moves from materialism to spiritualism. Her female characters reverse this itinerary: they effect a passage from the desert to the city, from nomadism to a form of sedentary marginality, and from innocence to experience, to escape patriarchal hegemony. The men usually become vagabonds and beggars, and the women adopt the role of prostitute at the service of the garrison in the local "Village Nègre." For both men and women escape becomes a necessary condition for attaining the kingdom, although in Isabelle's case as with the nomad's and his/her various fictional avatars, always in *potentia*.

Her male characters, especially the Europeans, evolve through somewhat predictable stages. First, as with Isabelle herself, they un-dergo a profound transformation upon encountering the South. Often this transformation, which occurs gradually, like an initiation, starts with a revelation, the realization of a vocation, and the fulfillment of a destiny. Next, the protagonist is overwhelmed by the landscape, by a way of life; he is unburdened by social convention. Charmed by the land and the simplicity of the people and their customs, he slips into a solitary contemplation which distances him from his European col-leagues. Linguistic communion then allows him to bond with the people: "He (Jacques, the protagonist in "Le Major") studied conscien-tiously the raucous and melodious language, whose accent he liked immediately, and grasped its harmony with the fiery horizons and the petrified earth" (190–191). Love, the encounter with the other, is a matter of natural course. Invariably, as for Isabelle, her characters fall in love with a native: Isabelle/Slimane, Jacques/Yasmina (in *Yasmina*), Jacques/Embarka in *Le Major*, Andréï in *L'Anarchiste*, etc. The bond-ing is completed when the European character converts to Islam.

Isabelle's fictional project, as outlined in her pioneering story "Vi-sions du Moghreb," is to improve on and multiply, in innumerable versions and variations, the *taleb* prototype in order to people her landscape with kindred spirits. More than with any other character, Isabelle shows particular congeniality with the *M'tourni* (from the French *tourner*, the one who turns away from his religion and converts to a new one; a pejorative term used in the colonial period to refer to Muslims who convert to Christianity). Her most poignant fiction is titled only *M'tourni* [*The Convert*]; it is the quintessential Isabelle Eberhardt story, and in many respects reflects her own life. In *M' tourni*, Roberto Fraugi leaves his native Santa Reparata for Algiers and then the Sahara, where he settles permanently, converts to Islam, assumes a new identity, marries a native girl, and never looks back on his past or questions his destiny/Mektoub: "Roberto Fraugi was now Mohammed Kasdallah. . . . For it had been written that the cottage and the field he had dreamed of owning were to be granted him, only they were not to be in Santa Reparata. He would find them under another sky and on a different soil, in the Hodna country among Moslems, and surrounded by the vast sad horizon of the waste land" (*The Oblivion Seekers*, 42–43). For Roberto Fraugi/Mohammed Kasdallah and Isabelle Eberhardt/Mahmoud Essadi, "a feeling of ancient Islam, tranquil and mysterious," (*Journaliers*, 20), and the unbounded Sahara were the ultimate escape from North to South.

LIFE AS A PSEUDONYM

For escape, in Isabelle's sense, one might programmatically understand the body: her nomadism was the expression of her relentless effort to escape the limitations of her gender and the shame of her name. Her maternal name, Eberhardt, when her brothers and sisters went by the patronymic De Moerder, reminded her constantly of the absence of a father. Isabelle realized from early childhood that the "name of the mother" was a mere fig-leaf, a figment of the imagination, to cover the shame of her birth. This onomastic travesty bore the stigma of her "excommunication" from the De Moerder clan, and marked irrevocably her exile from the "name of the father" and from the ancestral fatherland.[17]

Having been deprived of a legitimate name, Isabelle sought to have all names—she would nomadize between an assortment of exotic

17. The preoccupation with onomastics is a fecund problematic in postcolonial Maghrebian literature in French that can be summarized by one of Khatibi's titles, *La Blessure du nom propre* (Paris: Denoël, 10/18, 1974). This topic was already discussed in his novel, *La Mémoire tatouée* (Paris: Denoël, 1971); to indicate his cultural alienation, Kateb Yacine uses his patronym (Kateb) as a first name (Yacine); Meddeb sees his name as a "stigma of colonial intervention," *Talismano* (Paris: Christian Bourgeois, 1979), 218.

names, male and female, Russian, French, and Arabic: Myriem, Mariem, Meriem, Nadia, Nicolas Podolinsky, Mahmoud, Si Mahmoud Saâdi, etc. In Algeria she passed for a Tunisian student, and in Tunisia for a Turk, in order to account for her accent. She would also nomadize between male and female identities to the anguished amazement of her relatives and friends: " . . . Remember," Isabelle urged her brother Augustin in one of her many letters, "that Edouard [Vivicorsi, Augustin's colegionnaire and Isabelle's correspondent] must never know that [Nicholas] Podolinsky and I *are one and the same person*" (Roux, 189–90).

For the young Isabelle, a male pseudonym was more than a prank or a sexual fantasy, it was a practical disguise, especially when she wrote about such "unfeminine" material as colonialism. One may wonder if the editors of *La Nouvelle Revue Moderne* would have published "Visions du Moghreb" if they had known it was penned by a female adolescent. For the aspiring artist, to use a pseudonym also meant identification with her literary idol: Pierre Loti. Like Pierre Loti, who was a great influence on her early hankering for the Orient, Isabelle had an irresistible attraction for masquerade and disguise. Julien Viaud had escaped into another self as Pierre Loti. And like Pierre Loti/Julien Viaud, Isabelle Eberhardt/Mahmoud Saâdi sought out literature as a space of onomastic, ethnic, sexual, and linguistic heterogeneity.[18] Significantly, her pseudonyms are either Arab or Russian, underscoring thus her claim to a double oriental heritage.

THE PRISONHOUSE OF GENDER

From her early Geneva days, Isabelle refused to be confined and condemned by her gender to the slavery of a domestic life. She found in disguise a means of escaping her "role," that is, domestic entrapment, the predicament of the overwhelming majority of women in her generation: "I have given up," she wrote in her *Journaliers*, "the hope of ever having a corner on earth to call my own, a home, a family, peace or prosperity. I have donned the cloak of the restless wanderer, one that

18. Jean Déjeux considers Isabelle one of the authentic Algerians who wholeheartedly opted for an Arab, Muslim Algeria along with the painter Etienne Dinet and the poet Jean Sénac (whose pseudoynm is Yahia el-Ouahrani), *Littérature algérienne contemporaine* (Paris: PUF "Que sais-je?" No. 1604, 107).

can be a burden too at times. I have written off the thought of ever coming home to a happy family for rest and safety" (4).

Isabelle, who felt that her body and gender were the primary forms of her exile, opted for a radical "deterritorialization" of herself by assuming a variety of male names and identities. In a letter to the Editor of *La Petite Gironde*, she traces back this cross-gender impulse to her childhood: "I was brought up as though I had been a boy. This explains the fact that for many years I have worn, and still wear, men's clothing" (*The Oblivion Seekers*, 85).[19] Later, in the Maghreb, she will opt for the cross-gender "burnous," a formless garment which resembles a woman's robe and a man's mantle.

Although rarely oblivious or unaware of her feminine identity, Isabelle, who was constantly in search of a surrogate father, identified completely with men, especially with her beloved brother Augustin. In order to "pass" as a man, she displayed strong will and motivation and took many risks. By the time she reached Algeria, she cross-dressed with baffling ease, unaffected by her ambiguous status in the public world, whether she were among nomads, women, or colonial officials.[20] By rejecting the symbolism of her female clothing, Isabelle transgressed and broke more than a dress code; she put into question not only gender roles and functions but also their political and ideological implications.

In socially and sexually segregated societies, such as the French colonial and Islamic ones, transvestism and the subsequent changes of name functioned for Isabelle as social and economic equalizers. Unable, for instance, to travel fourth-class as a woman, and with no money for a more expensive fare, Isabelle had to disguise herself as a deckhand and assume a masculine identity: "Once on the Berry [a ship plying between Bône and Marseilles] I sat up front," she recalled in her *Journaliers*, "disguised as Pierre Mouchet in my wretched sailor's outfit, and felt as sad as an emigrant being banished from his native soil"

19. Isabelle's letter to the Editor of *La Petite Gironde*, in *The Oblivion Seekers*, op. cit., 85.

20. In an appendix to *Dans l'ombre chaude de l'Islam*, her friend Victor Barrucand recalls a highly publicized instance of the natural quality of Isabelle's transvestism: "When Monsieur Loubet, President of France, came to Algiers, Isabelle Eberhardt was among those invited to the press banquet. As was her custom, she wore the attire of a Moslem man, being entirely covered in white wool, with no silk embroidery, no other spot of color save the brown camel's hair cords twisted tightly around her white Sahara-style turban" *The Oblivion Seekers*, op. cit., 84.

(48). The disguise reveals all the more poignantly Isabelle's psychic turmoil. In the metaphor of the "emigrant being banished from his native soil," we see at work Isabelle's compulsion to master her *heimatlose* trauma.

In order to break free from the role that society and convention imposed on her gender, Isabelle opted, as she confided in her *Journaliers*, for a "borrowed mask," that of the "cynical, the debauched and dissipated . . . the drunkard, the depraved and the brawler" (2). These are not only masculine but urban and aggressive roles that stand in counterdistinction to the peaceful life of the would-be nomad and the mystic, a life she referred to as her "beloved personality." This "mask" was merely a transitional, "borrowed" accoutrement to her "European" personality that she would readily forsake, in her adopted land, for her mystical personality. She longed, whenever she was in her European exile, "to don again, as early as possible, the beloved personality which is, in reality, the *true* life, to return there, in Africa, and to lead that life again" (2). On every flight to the Maghreb, she assumed her new identity ritualistically: "My hat bothered me, though, for it set me apart from Muslims," Isabelle wrote in her *Journaliers* upon her arrival to Algiers. "I went back to don my fez, and went out again with Ahmed . . . " (19).

Isabelle never missed an occasion, in her diaries and correspondence, to castigate the Dr. Grenier-type, "who seems to think that 'the habit makes the monk,' and that sporting a burnous or a woman's ferrachia makes one a Muslim?" ("Isabelle Eberhardt: Amazone ou paumée," 27). Isabelle may also have chosen to dress as an Arab man to subvert yet another form of cultural hegemony, namely the one that mandated that the natives "assimilate" and conform to the European dress code. Isabelle advocates, instead, reverse assimilation, namely that the Europeans, rather than the natives, adjust to the customs and traditions of the land. In her fiction, dressing up as the other becomes a matter of natural course. Her characters, like herself, "go native" out of sincere conviction, as a symbol of their new identity and life. To his fellow-villagers, Roberto Fraugi's adopting the local dress was a rite of passage in the process of his communal belonging: "His European clothing became ragged, and one day Seddik persuaded him to put on native dress. At first he felt as though he were in disguise. Then he found it practical, and grew used to it" (*The Oblivion Seekers*, 41).

Significantly, not only did Isabelle dress as a man, but as an Arab. In the context of French colonial North Africa, her cross-gender/racial transvestism was of special interest both to the Arabs and to the French. Although the indigenous people were aware of Isabelle's identity, they affected, out of a traditional sense of courtesy and honor, to believe the reality of Si Mahmoud, the travelling Tunisian student and seeker of Sufi knowledge. It is perhaps the Arabs' indifference to her disguise, as opposed to the declared hostility of the French colonial settlers, that endeared them to her. But dressing as an Arab, especially an Algerian Arab, was not without risk, especially when Isabelle ventured into Moroccan territory not yet "pacified" by the French. In a short passage significantly titled "Transformation," Isabelle underscores the political import of her clothing, especially in the charged context of Maghrebian internecine tribal rivalries: "Si Mahmoud, my child," she was told by the marabout of Kenadsa "if you want to leave the zaouia or holy shrine . . . you must change your costume. . . . The Algerian one you are wearing will surely cause trouble as you would be openly called *m'zani* [renegade]." For the Moroccans, especially the maraboutic people of Kenadsa, Algerian Muslims have sold out to the French and have thus become *m'zanat* or renegades. "And, thus, tonight, in order to go out, I transformed myself into a Moroccan man, shedding off the heavy costume of Algerian cavalrymen" (*Ecrits sur le sable*, 249).

Ironically, disguise is also entrapment, for sometimes the realities of Mahmoud and Isabelle are mutually exclusive. If for Isabelle, her assumed male identity and disguise served, in a man's world, as a natural protection, they were also an impediment which set her apart from the company of fellow women, on more than one occasion, especially that of Lella Zeyneb, the marabout's mother, whose authority and influence, although never seen, were felt everywhere in Kenadsa and beyond. In her "Notes de routes," we see Isabelle's longing to meet this mysterious and inaccessible woman impeded by the reality of Si Mahmoud, a male who is forbidden by strict codes of behavior to appear before a woman: "What is she like, this great Muslim lady whom I cannot approach since I am Sidi Mahmoud, and the people continue to treat me as such?" (*Ecrits sur le sable*, 255)

To the French, however, especially the settlers, Isabelle was a turncoat, a social pariah and "Arab lover." Her wandering in the Sahara was not to the liking of the Colonial Administration and she was under close surveillance: "Once again," she wrote in her *Journaliers*, "I had to establish that I was no English miss in Arab disguise, but a Russian writer" (59).[21]

In addition to her often noted eccentricity, Isabelle is also portrayed as a neurotic and unstable woman who, in the words of Capitaine Cauvet, one of the many intelligence officers charged with her surveillance, "professes fairly progressive ideas involved in the current feminist and socialist movement. I am more inclined to think," Cauvet added in his report to his superiors, "that she came to El Oued principally to satisfy, without inhibitions, in a country little visited by Europeans, her vicious penchants and her weakness for the natives" (*Ecrits intimes*, 262–63).

If gender-crossing, as discussed above, raises the psychologically crucial questions of male identity and authority, race-crossing, known in literature and psychology as the phenomenon of "going native," evokes issues of religion, race, nationality, and colonialism. Isabelle's seemingly contradictory aspiration to be both a man (the will to conquer) and an Arab (the conquered) was symbolic and emblematic of the sado-masochistic relationship that bound, in the colonial situation, colonizer (dominant) and colonized (dominated). As an Arab male, Isabelle was both victim and victimizer; she partook of the Arab's patriarchal arrogance and ascendency over women—her contempt for Arab women verges on homophobia—but also of his humiliation at the hands of the colonizers.

To be a female transvestite, a rare oddity at the time, was thus dismissed as a form of sexual deviance, but to be an Arab at that, in a racially, religiously, and culturally charged environment such as French Colonial North Africa, was more than enough to arouse concerns and suspicions: "We can understand your wearing men's clothes," Isabelle is often asked by the colonial officers, "but why wouldn't you dress up as a European man?" To those who question her transvestism, including Slimane her husband, she invariably and ambiguously answers: "It is impossible for me to do otherwise" (*Ecrits intimes*, 311).

One need only review her own statements and feelings about her disguise, a recurrent and obsessive question in her *Journaliers* and her "intimate" correspondence, to see that her disguise was chiefly a psy-

21. Many Arabs suspected she was in the employ of the French Colonial Administration; also, many French settlers regarded her as a spy in the employ of a rival colonial power. Neither allegation has, so far, been substantiated.

chological and symbolic ritual, rather than, as suggested by many of her detractors, a practical ruse.

A NICHE IN BABEL

One's ultimate exile is to feel a stranger within one's language. For Isabelle French was, to use Tahar Ben Jelloun's felicitous metaphor, "The House of the Others,"[22] a place where she never felt quite comfortable. This refuge was practical and temporary. In retrospect, Isabelle may have prefigured by at least half a century postcolonial Maghrebian literature in French, especially with regard to the status of the writer who uses a foreign medium. Isabelle would transform her alienation from the mother tongue into a literary vocation, yet another form of escape, another space of freedom that she yearned to conquer. For Isabelle the exile, language belonged, first and foremost, to its user and had therefore little to do with nationality or ethnicity. These sentiments would be echoed several generations later by a host of Maghrebian writers, namely Abdelwahab Meddeb, Abdellatif Laâbi, and Abdelkebir Khatibi, who conceive of language as a transnational phenomenon which plays only a secondary role as a criterion of literary belonging.[23]

Although she grew up speaking and reading Russian, a language which she knew intimately, French was the "public" language, which she used for communication outside the Villa Neuve, a *lingua franca*, the language of the world. The interplay between "private" and "public" usages of language and, later, when she became a Muslim and fluent in Arabic, the interplay between the sacred and the profane,[24] permeate Isabelle's writing, especially her letters to her Tunisian friend Ali Abdel Wahab:

Mais la vraie amitié, c'est vraiment (1) الأرواح ‎غنل une chose participant de la mystérieuse *essentia eterna* de nos âmes. Depuis quelque temps,

22. Tahar Ben Jelloun, "La Maison des autres," *Dérives*, nos. 31–32 (1982): 7–9.
23. See Abdellatif Laâbi, "Prologue," *Souffles*, no. 1 (1st semester, 1966), 4; for Abdelwahab Meddeb, "The state of a language depends on how it is used by its practitioners." In "Le Palimpseste du bilingue," in *Du Bilinguisme* (Paris: Denoël, 1985), 137.
24. In the context of French Algeria, the French language was considered by the average man, according to the Algerian poet Bachir Hadj-Ali, as a "langue d'ici-bas" [a language of this world], as opposed to Arabic, which became a "langue de mérite spitituel" [a language of spiritual merit]. Cited by Mostefa Lacheraf, *L'Algérie, nation et société* (Alger: S.N.E.D., 1978), 324.

dans la croissante mélancolie de ma vie, je commence à élaborer plusieurs pensées qui, (2) ان شاء الله تعالى m'accompagneront désormais (3) . الى نهار موتي

[But true friendship is really *the work of souls*, something partaking of the mysterious *essentia eterna* of our souls. For a while now, in the growing melancholy of my life, I have begun to entertain several ideas which, *God willing*, will henceforth be with me *till the day I die*] ("Isabelle Eberhardt: Amazone ou paumée?", 53).

In the above example, Isabelle uses Arabic concepts and script that are untranslatable into the other language. By refusing to translate, which is, in and of itself, an act of resistance that excludes the colonizer, she signifies all the more her belonging to this new culture and language, and her rootedness in her newfound land.

Like generations of Francophone writers, Isabelle wrote French from the outside, a practice that is not without its advantages. This external rapport with French gave her the freedom to engage in verbal inventions and audacious imagery, so as to make this *lingua franca* accommodate an Arab, Berber, and African ontology alien to it. Her writing teems with understatements, linguistic puns, and palimpsestic potentials. In her story "Yasmina," the courtship between Jacques and Yasmina is a perfect example of language and code mixing: "Il [Jacques] lui demanda à boire, par signes . . . *Ouch noua!* Qu'est-ce? . . . Jacques n'était plus un *Roumi*, un *Kéfer*. . . . Elle lui avait bien dit que l'on devait la marier à un *cahouadji* de la ville. . . .Tu t'appelleras *Mabrouk*, cela nous portera bonheur. . . . Il lui disait que sa vieille mère était bien malade, là-bas, *fil Fransa* . . . *Mektoub*, disait-elle . . . Ne pleure pas; *Ya Mabrouk*, c'est écrit . . . En ville, Jacques s'acharnait à l'étude de l'arabe algérien. Son ardeur faisait sourire ses camarades qui disaient, non sans ironie: 'Il doit y avoir une *bicotte* là-dessous' " (99–105). [He (Jacques) asked her for a drink (of water) in sign language . . . *Ouch-noua!* What is it? . . . Jacques was no longer a *Roumi* (foreigner, European) a *Kefer* (an infidel) . . . She told him that they would marry her to a *cahouadji* (a café owner) . . . Your name will be *Mabrouk* (the one who brings good fortune), this will bring us good luck . . . he told her that his old mother was sick *fil Fransa* (in France) . . . *Mektoub* (it's fate) . . . Don't cry; *ya Mabrouk* (you, Mabrouk), it is written . . . Once in town Jacques would immerse himself totally in the study of Algerian Arabic. His zeal did not go unnoticed by his colleagues who would say smilingly, and with a touch of irony: "there must be a *bicotte* (native gal) behind all this"].

This amorous discourse in the bilingual mode articulates at least three rhetorical devices: code-mixing, pidginization, and relexification.[25] Code-mixing occurs when two languages are used simultaneously, as in "Ouch-noua?/Qu'est-ce?" In this particular instance, the need for instantaneous translation is predicated by Jacques's initial ignorance of Arabic. As the story progresses and as Jacques's Arabic improves, we see fewer literal translations. Code-mixing is also used by Isabelle as a source of punning, as in "Mabrouk, cela nous portera bonheur," and "Mektoub . . . c'est écrit." With Isabelle, the European is always put at a linguistic disadvantage. It is Jacques who has to relexify his vocabulary in order to communicate with the native, as in "Fil Fransa." Both Jacques and Yasmina resort to *Sabir,* a form of pidginization known also as *Franco-arabe:* "Msiou" [monsieur], "coumerce" [commerce], "cahoua" [coffee], hence "cahouadji" [cafe owner]. Such terms as "bicot," "bicotte," refer to the colonial racist lexicon. "Il y a une bicotte là-dessous," is a pun on the familiar expression: "Il y a anguille sous roche" [There is more in it than meets the eye].

As clearly demonstrated in the above example, this seemingly linguistic sundering is more than textual nomadism among the various codes, it is also an enrichment of an otherwise ordinary prose. This desire to enhance her prose paralinguistically is expressed, especially in her *Journaliers,* through pictorial and calligraphic illustrations. The following example is a page from Isabelle's *Journaliers* reproduced by René-Louis Doyen in his "Introduction" to Isabelle's *Au Pays des sables.* The dynamic play of the French and Arabic handwriting is further enhanced by two sketches of *Zaouias,* or religious shrines. This jux-

25. Isabelle's own amorous discourse, especially in her letters to Slimane, is often articulated under the sign of bilingualism. The following is a fragment of a letter addressed to Slimane in which French and Arabic scripts are used symbiotically:

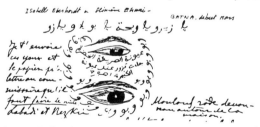

As we shall see further, Isabelle often enhances her bilingual scriptural practice with sketches.

taposition, on the same page, of word and image, makes Isabelle a precursor of aesthetic concretism, a practice that will become one of the trademarks of postmodern Maghrebian literature in French.[26]

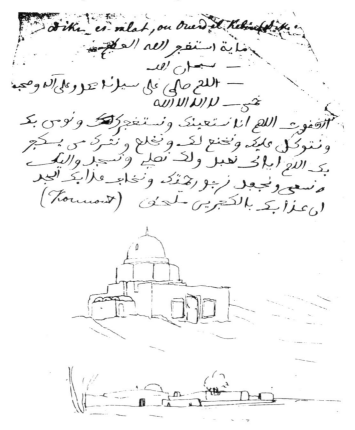

Isabelle used French as yet another disguise, a Harlequin costume, a trope through which she manipulated social, linguistic, and gender codes. As she subverted other forms of hegemony, Isabelle also sought to undermine the dominant French language by exiling it outside its ontology and traditions. Instead of its homogeneity, she set out to find and create an interlingual, international, and intercultural literary

26. Postindependence writers such as Khatibi, Meddeb, and Nabile Farès, to cite but a few, have exploited the artistic potential of the graph, and have, as Isabelle did first, resurrected a time-honored Islamic scriptural practice. The following example from Meddeb's *Phantasia* (Paris: Sindbad, 1986) highlights the importance of an originary graphic trace:

oeuvre. But how to break free from the monopoly of French, or for that matter from any "monolangue"? Again, Isabelle finds an answer in polyglotism, a form of linguistic nomadism, a trope through which she will attempt to express her polyphonic, plurivocal, and polysemic quest.

In this regard, Isabelle's writing, whether it be her letters, her diary, or fiction, is shaped by the tension, rhythm, and genius of more than one particular language: it is crisscrossed by currents of spoken and literate Arabic, Berber, Turkish, Greek, Latin, German, Russian, and Italian. Her letters, especially to her brother Augustin, are linguistic puzzles of schizophrenic proportions. In a typical letter to Augustin, she begins in French: "Souviens-toi aussi" [Remember also] "Quoi qu'il arrive après" [Whatever may happen after]; then Latin *"fac et spera . . . ;"* and Greek ["the old times and don't you ever sin"]; and on to Russian, "Da, pomni milyï, pomnie to i nadeïsa!" [Yes, remember this, my darling, remember and be patient!] (Roux, 191).

Isabelle could not have found a better polyglot space than in the Maghreb, her Babel. This concatenation of tongues and voices is one of the main constituents of her fictional universe. Like Jacques, the *Heimatlos,* one of her fictional alter egos, she sought to dwell in languages, her polylinguistic matrix: "He [Jacques, the Vagabond] listened vaguely to the chaotic Babel of conversation going on around him, deep voices joking in different languages, arguments inside the frail tents buffeted by the wind. His place was here now. He would curl up here, make a niche for himself among these companions, each of whom had his own secret past" (*Trimardeur,* 134). The Maghreb as a polylinguistic space, as posited and described by Isabelle, prefigures the discourse of multiplicity that Abdelkebir Khatibi calls "pensée en langues" in *Maghreb Pluriel.* Khatibi argues that the Maghreb has always

---

prennent forme toutes les croyances, كــن هيوني المعـتقــدات ; et que lui fût révélé في نفسك لصورجميع le troisième terme. analogie entre le *barzakh,* isthme, entre-deux, et le vide, qui lie/sépare le yin/ yang, ligne de partage, barre, trait d'union, inter- valle, intermédiaire, silence et pause, ٦ . Pour que brillât à la lumière du troisième œil l'om, اوم, اوم ou او, parole formatrice, inaugurant le texte, repérée dès l'an mil par Biruni équivalente à l'incipit isla- mique, *Au nom de Dieu, Très-Haut,* بسم الله الله, om, graphe à part, hors alphabet, forme

been a plurilinguistic space whose minimalist expression is bilinguism.[27]

By intertwining oral and written literary materials and incorporating indigenous ethnographical and anthropological elements into her fiction, Isabelle deterritorialized, in the sense made familiar by Deleuze and Guattari, the content of her writing completely and radically. She was the first to experiment and use polyglotism as a device to undermine the hegemony of "monolangue," one of the principal pillars of the colonial order. She was the first to present the Maghrebian ethos from the inside, using consistently the Arabic name "Maghreb" when the current and official term was North Africa, and first also to introduce indigenous words into the French language, beginning thus a long process of disenfranchisement of the dominant language. Words like *toub* [mud], *mleya* [woman's headress], *caîd* [local chief], *gourbi* [mud house], *diss* [herb], *roumi* [Roman, European], *guerba* [goat skin], etc., which express the Maghrebian reality, are not relegated to exotic indices; they are inserted unapologetically as constitutive elements of her writing.[28]

Isabelle was the first, as Edmonde Charles-Roux notes in her biography, to make literary use of the native's language, thus problematizing and relativizing the dominance of the conqueror's idiom: "Her treatment of Algerian reality did not acknowledge that there could be a dominant culture on Algerian soil, and that, for her part, she situated herself instinctively half-way between French culture and Arabic-Maghrebian culture. She was the only one to occupy this place. A Russian, she was the first Maghrebian writer of French expression" (Roux, 437).

Ironically, it is precisely to the extent that she is an untenable "entre deux," being neither French nor Arabic, both woman and man, aristocrat and vagabond, bacchante and mystic, that Isabelle is a veritable nomad. In her linguistic "corps à corps" with French to make it express a Maghrebian ontology, in her deterritorialization of her char-

---

27. Abdelkebir Khatibi, *Maghreb Pluriel* (Paris: Denoël, 1983).
28. One may regard this practice as Orientalist, but as we have argued above, Isabelle's Orientalism is anti-Orientalist, for it serves as a corrective to the French hegemonic discourse: although she was grounded in her European culture and ideology, Isabelle was, in her use of language, unique in her ability to go beyond them.

acters and subject-matter and in her use of the theme of wandering and nomadism, Isabelle was an ancestor to at least three generations of Maghrebian Francophone writers.[29] This literary genealogy may be construed, albeit posthumously, as the culmination of her search for identity and identification.

29. The practice of nomadic writing as a new creative space in literature, as advocated by such postindependence Maghrebian writers as Meddeb, Farès, and Khatibi, has been emblematic of the quest for identity and origin. It is also synonymous with the search for and recovery of a graphic trace as a new mode of aesthetic expression and a form of liberation from the language and culture of the Other. To proclaim oneself a nomadic writer today is to refuse to be confined to a fixed role or function. One need only review the lexicon by which Maghrebian writers refer to themselves to understand the extent of their nomadism: Kateb sees himself as *écrivain errant;* Meddeb as *sédentaire faussaire;* Boudjedra as *scribe;* Khatibi as *scripteur;* Ben Jelloun as *écrivain public;* Khair-Eddine as an *autodidacte.*

*II. Poetics of the Archipelago:
Transatlantic Passages*

MARYSE CONDÉ

Order, Disorder, Freedom, and the West Indian Writer

In a recent interview, the Martinican writer Edouard Glissant declared: "I don't believe that West Indian literature exists yet since literature supposes an action and a reaction between a public and an audience. I repeat that we West Indian writers, we are writing forewords to tomorrow's literature."[1] Last year when *Eloge de la Créolité* was published, two of his disciples, Raphaël Confiant and Patrick Chamoiseau, and a linguist Jean Bernabé repeated: "West Indian literature doesn't exist yet. We are in a state of pre-literature. Ours is a written production without an audience at home, deprived of the interaction between writers/readers which is necessary for any literature to exist."[2]

Although it seems difficult to state seriously that West Indian literature doesn't exist, we easily agree that there is a crisis, a malaise. But we don't blame it on the causes pointed out by Glissant, Confiant, and Chamoiseau. We attribute it to the very commands enumerated throughout the history of West Indian literature by the various generations of writers. For example, in *Eloge de la Créolité*, the authors state: "We must give a name to everything and true to *créolité* say that it is beautiful. Therefore we must see the human dignity of the "djobeurs," understand the life of the Morne Pichevin or of the vegetable markets of Fort-de-France, study how our storytellers operate . . . (*Eloge de la Créolité*, 40). Glissant, Chamoiseau, and Confiant are not the first ones to give commands to the future writers of our islands. West Indian

1. Interview given to Priska Degras and Bernard Magniez in *Notre Librarie* 74 (Caraïbes 2).
2. Jean Bernabé, Patrick Chamoiseau, Raphaël Confiant, *Eloge de la Créolité* (Paris: Gallimard, 1989), 14.

YFS 83, *Post/Colonial Conditions*, ed. Lionnet & Scharfman, © 1993 by Yale University.

121

literature born or not yet born has *always* been an object of deep concern.

We shall try to analyze the various commands decreed about West Indian literature, all of them contributing to the edification of an order very few writers have dared to transgress to introduce disorder. In conclusion, we shall try to see whether it is possible to hope for an era of freedom in West Indian writing.

ORDER

In 1927, in a journal called "La Trouée," a group of young Haitian intellectuals declared: "Literature is the cry of a people who want to say what boils within them." 1927: the American Marines had invaded Haiti twelve years earlier because of political upheavals. The Haitian people, who already knew political oppression, were discovering racism. History repeats itself.

A few years later, with the Marines still present in Haiti, the mulatto and upper bourgeois writer Jacques Roumain declared in "La Revue indigène": "Literature must be black and proletarian."[3]

In 1932, the manifesto called "Légitime Défense," signed by a group of Martinican and Guadeloupean intellectuals, was published in Paris. They had just discovered Marxism and in its name sentenced to death the bourgeois society to which they belonged. They also condemned its literature to death, stating "A foreigner would look in vain for any originality or depth, for the sensual and colorful imagination of the Black Man, or the echo of the aspirations of an oppressed people." On the eve of World War II, Suzanne Césaire, in the journal "Tropiques," uttered her famous command: "Martinican poetry shall be cannibalistic or shall not be."[4] As for Césaire himself, in *Cahier d'un retour au pays natal [Return to my Native Land]* speaking of the role of the poet, he summed up all these ideas saying "My mouth will be the mouth of those who have no mouth, my voice the voice of those who despair."[5] From that time on the foundations of order were laid. Even those who are not very familiar with West Indian literature know some

---

3. Jacques Roumain in "La Revue indigène."
4. Suzanne Césaire, *Misère d'une Poésie, Tropiques* (repr. Paris: Jean-Michel Place, 1978).
5. Aimé Césaire, *Return to my Native Land*, trans. Emile Snyder (Paris: Présence Africaine, 1968), 61. *The Collected Poetry*, translation with introduction and notes by Clayton Eshelman and Annette Smith (Berkeley: University of California Press, 1982).

of the basic rules, and we don't intend to repeat them again. One may simply say that they were inspired by the theory of social realism which was favored in some quarters, since the victorious Soviet Revolution had heralded what seemed to be the dawn of a new era for the oppressed all over the world. They were also influenced by Sartre who, in 1948, wrote the foreword to the first anthology of French-speaking black poetry.

> 1. Individualism was chastised. Only the collectivity had the right to express itself.
> 2. The masses were the sole producers of Beauty, and the poet had to take inspiration from them.
> 3. The main, if not the sole, purpose of writing was to denounce one's political and social conditions, and in so doing, to bring about one's liberation.
> 4. Poetic and political ambition were one and the same.

Therefore, pictures of individual love and psychological turmoil were banished. Any description of nature was forbidden. Lyrical outbursts about the mountains or the sea and the sky were left to the so-called "exotic poets" writing at the beginning of the century, who had been ridiculed and sentenced to literary death. The hills were the refuge where the Maroons had escaped the sufferings of the plantation, the trees the silent witnesses of an eternal exploitation. In the celebrated opening lines of *Return to my Native Land*, Césaire gives an example of this ideological description of nature. Looking at the magnificent bay of Fort-de-France, he exclaims: "At the end of the dawn, flowered with frail creeks, the hungry West Indies, pitted with smallpox, dynamited with alcohol, stranded in the mud of this bay, in the dirt of this city sinisterly stranded" (Césaire, *Return to my Native Land*, 40). Is it not time to somehow rehabilitate the so-called exotic poets?

Victor Segalen has shown that exoticism can be considered the first perception of difference: "The knowledge that something is not yourself."[6] In the case of the exotic poets of the West Indies, one could say that to celebrate their land was the first, timid appropriation of their own world. They were celebrating their land *before* celebrating their peoples. Not *instead* of doing so. Their poetic abilities were ridiculed. "Not art," said Césaire contemptuously, "not poetry. Only the ugly

---

6. Victor Segalen, *Essai sur l'exotisme: une esthétique du divers* (Montpellier: Fata Morgana, 1978).

leprosy of imitation."[7] He was forgetting that in those days, to imitate to perfection was already a transgression. The black man was not entitled to have any talent, and during slavery to be caught reading a book meant death.

The new order didn't affect only poetry. It also affected history, sociology, and philosophy. West Indian society was not studied *per se*, as an autonomous object. It was always seen as a result of the slave-trade, slavery, and colonial oppression. This past was the cause of every social and cultural feature and thus explained everything: the relationships between men and women, the family system, as well as oral traditions or popular music. It is impossible to deny that the West Indian past weighs heavily on the present. Nevertheless, the plantation system in which this society evolved, the promiscuity of the white master, the arrival of new ethnic groups such as the Indians, are factors responsible for its characteristics as well. Not everything can be explained through slavery. West Indian society came to be considered as a Paradise perverted by Europe. Everything prior to colonization was idealized. Consequently, from the image of Africa, the motherland, were carefully eradicated any blemishes such as domestic slavery, or tribal warfare, and the subjugation of women.

In *The Wretched of the Earth*, Frantz Fanon was the first to realize the dangers of such idealization. But in turn, he blames it on Europe, stating: "Colonialism . . . never ceased to assert that the Negro was a savage and by Negro was meant not the Angolan or the Nigerian, but the Negro. . . . Therefore the efforts of the colonized to rehabilitate himself and escape the attacks of colonialism are to be logically understood on the same level."[8]

At the end of the Second World War, communications were resumed. The intellectuals from the West Indies and Africa were able to meet again and plan for the future. The *Société Africaine de Culture* was created in Paris, a few years after *Présence Africaine*. What was the purpose of this *Société?* Once again, let's consult Frantz Fanon: "This society . . . will limit its activity to a few exhibitions: it will try to prove to Europe that African culture does exist" (*The Wretched of the Earth*, 148).

---

7. Aimé Césaire, "Présentation" du no. 1 de la revue *Tropiques* (repr. Fort-de-France, 1941).

8. Frantz Fanon, *Les Damnés de la terre*, préface de Jean-Paul Sartre (Paris: Maspéro, 1961 [1967]), 145; *The Wretched of the Earth*, preface by Jean-Paul Sartre, trans. Constance Farrington (New York: Grove Press, 1963 [1977]).

Among these exhibitions:
In 1956 in Paris, the First Congress of Writers and Artists of the Black World.
In 1959 in Rome, the Second Congress.

It was during this Second Congress that Sekou Touré, the late president of Guinea, delivered his speech on "The political leader as the representative of a Culture" and declared: "There is no place for the artist or for the intellectual who is not totally mobilized with the people in the great struggle of Africa and suffering mankind."[9] Such sentences become very ironical when one knows of Touré's ulterior active imposition of suffering on the Guinean people. However, despite these reservations there was a wonderful, generous dream in those days. The dream of a black world which would not be broken up into distinct nations by the colonial languages, and the various colonial systems of governments. A black world which would speak through one voice, through the univocal voice of its poets and writers. A black world which would recover its dignity and pride.

All that was soon to disappear. The end of World War II marked the beginnings of decolonization in Africa. Year after year, through a series of reforms and conflicts, the African countries arrived at political independence. The African poets and writers who had been close to the *Société Africaine de Culture* and to *Présence Africaine* became heads of state, prime ministers, ministers, thus completing the collusion between politics and literature. The islands of the West Indies, however, became and remained "French Overseas Departments." The black Americans went to fight racism at home. Thus the dream of a united black world was shattered.

Just before the end of the war the posthumous novel of the Haitian writer Jacques Roumain, *Gouverneurs de la rosée [Masters of the Dew]*, was published.[10] If one compares this novel to *Return to my Native Land* by Césaire, one cannot help being struck by the structural similarities. In both cases, we have two messianic male heroes (Manuel and the Poet) whose ambition is to change their societies and thus rehabilitate the exploited Black Man. On the literary scene, these two

9. Sekou Touré, *The Political Leader as the Representative of a Culture*, 2d Congress of Black Writers and Artists (Rome: 1959); *The Political Leader Considered* (Newark, N.J.: Jihad Productions, 1975).

10. Jacques Roumain, *Gouverneurs de la rosée* (Paris: Editeurs français réunis, 1946); *Masters of the Dew*, trans. Langston Hughes and Mercer Cook (London: Heinemann, 1982).

works were to have the same effect: obliterate for years to come any literary production prior to themselves. Like *Return to my Native Land*, *Masters of the Dew* became a sacred text, a fundamental text. According to a Guadeloupean critic, every West Indian novel is nothing but the rewriting of *Masters of the Dew* and *Return to my Native Land*. The reason for the critical acclaim of *Masters of the Dew* cannot be purely aesthetic. As Alain Robbe-Grillet puts it: "There are no masterpieces for eternity; merely works marked by their time."[11]

With less obscurity and incandescence than Césaire, with a lesser concern for the black world, now limited to the islands, *Masters of the Dew* provides the West Indians with a perfect image of themselves and their islands. Freud said that the finality of art is to reconcile the people with a reality which they don't like. If this is true, in this extraordinary poetic novel the West Indians have everything they can dream of. *Master of the Dew* established a model which is still largely undisputed to this day.

1. The framework should be the native land.
2. The hero should be male, of peasant origin.
3. The brave and hardworking woman should be the auxiliary in his struggle for his community.
4. Although they produce children, no reference should be made to sex. If any, it will be to male sexuality.

I cannot resist the pleasure of quoting the passage in *Masters of the Dew* where Annaïse and Manuel make love for the first time:

> "Yes," she says, "I shall be the mistress of your house. I shall serve you at table and I shall stay standing while you eat and you will tell me 'I thank you, my woman' and I shall tell you 'As you like it, my master.' At night, I shall lie by your side. You will not say anything, but to your silence, to the touch of your hand, I shall reply 'Yes, my man,' because I shall be the servant of your desire." [131]

5. Of course, heterosexuality is the absolute rule.
6. Society should be pitied but never criticized. All its errors should be redeemed by the male hero. In *Masters of the Dew*, Manuel has been compared to a black Christ giving his life for the small community of "Fonds Rouges."

It is the privilege of Edouard Glissant to have united all these tendencies: the end of the Pan-African dream and the desire for a national

11. Alain Robbe-Grillet, *Pour un nouveau roman* (Paris: Gallimard, 1946), 131.

literature to build a theory which slightly improved upon the existing order. It seems to me that the differences between Césaire and Glissant have been exaggerated. It is a fact that Glissant never really adopted the Pan-African ideal. However, his close connections with *Présence Africaine* and the Société Africaine de Culture illustrate a definite concern for the future of the black world. He shares with Césaire the confusion between political and poetic ambitions and the belief in the importance of the community. (In *Le Discours antillais* he says: "The question any Martinican should ask himself is not: 'Who am I?' which is meaningless; but 'Who are we?' ").[12]

Glissant's most important contribution to West Indian literature is the introduction of a new dimension, the one of language. Language is the cord which links the West Indian to his land, to his past, to his history. The cord which links the West Indian to the West Indian. "The Theory of *Antillanité*," he explains in *Le Discours antillais*, "aims at exploring all aspects of the African element, which is modified but always present in our societies, and the root of language, which is reinforced through multiplication. Derek Walcott perverts the English language in the same way that Nicolás Guillén perverts Spanish, in the same way that V. S. Naipaul asserts his origin while denying it. Maybe we don't all speak Creole. However, we speak variants of the same language" (Glissant, 182).

Glissant was certainly the first West Indian intellectual to stress the linguistic dimension of colonialism and the problem of diglossia in the islands. But more important than this analytical contribution is his stress on the relationship between the writer, his people, and language. The reproach of obscurity and abstruseness which is constantly hurled at him is but the consequence of his essential belief: language for the West Indian writer is the only way of shaping the future. Glissant is also responsible for the reintroduction of nature and the environment in the West Indian novel. But not nature *per se*. The description of nature remains symbolic if not ideological, symbolic. In his own words, he associates the hills with the habitation where the white master used to live, and the plain with the daily life of the black man. Political consciousness is thus a symbolic journey through the island. That is the reason why rivers play such a major role in Glissant's works. They flow across flat lands and highlands. Like language, they unite men to men, then ultimately merge with the sea which is the

---

12. Edouard Glissant, *Le Discours antillais* (Paris: Seuil, 1981).

symbol of freedom, reconciliation with oneself, and political consciousness.

As I said earlier, Glissant tries to provide future writers with what
he thinks will be a more elaborate model for fiction:

> 1. Characters should not be individuals, but the collective expression
> of the West Indian soul. In a recent discussion in an undergraduate class
> at Berkeley, he explained why in *Malemort* the characters are grouped
> by three (Dlan-Médellus-Silacier) and speak collectively.
> 2. Nature should be part of the story just like another character. This is
> particularly obvious in *Le Quatrième siècle*.
> 3. However, it is language itself which can be regarded as the main
> object of the novel. The cohabitation of Creole and French creates a
> new language, the adventures of which are the real subject of the novel.
> For Glissant, the question is not Creole *or* French, but Creole *and*
> French.

However elaborate and attractive this model may be, it has not been
adopted by the majority of West Indian writers, who remain attached to
such things as characters, plots, realistic descriptions of people and
places, and who, above all, reject the very complexity of Glissant's
language. Therefore, for many years, although "antillanité" has been
accepted as a theory perfectly suited to the realities of the islands, the
literary model it implies has not been able to impose itself.

Then came Raphaël Confiant and Patrick Chamoiseau, the two
writers who, together with the linguist Jean Bernabé, call themselves
"Le Groupe de la Créolité." Like their elders in "Légitime Défense,"
they signaled their entrance into the literary world with the publication of a manifesto called *Eloge de la Créolité*. Like Césaire in *Return
to my Native Land*, the opening lines possess the violence of a declaration of war: "Neither Europeans, nor Africans, nor Asians, we proclaim
ourselves to be Creoles. This will be a mental attitude. More, a watch-
fulness, a sort of mental envelope which will sustain our own world in
the confrontation with other worlds" (*Eloge de la Créolité*, 13). In these
first pages too, although they state what they regard to be the limitations of "antillanité," they pay homage to Glissant, whom they consider to be their inspiration, their model and master. They inherit from
Glissant the desire to make the inventory of their West Indian society,
perceived as autonomous and complex, and, above all, a concern for
language. However, whereas Glissant paid respect to Creole *and*
French as the two languages the West Indian possesses, the new writers
lay a heavy emphasis on *Créole*, considered to be the sole mother

tongue. "Whenever a mother did everything she could to get her child to learn French and in doing so repressed his Creole tongue, what she did was to strike a mortal blow to his imagination and to exile his creativity forever" (ibid., 14).

However, it would be simplistic to believe that "créolité" is the mere rehabilitation of the Creole language. It is the reappropriation of oneself, of that "formidable migan" which created the West Indian personality. It is an aesthetic. Moreover, it is the future of the world. "The world is moving towards a state of *créolité*" (ibid., 52). In their novels, Raphaël Confiant and Patrick Chamoiseau give an illustration of their theory. There is no doubt that both writers produce very good fiction. But apart from the sumptuous invention of a language (especially in the case of Chamoiseau), we see only minor changes in the prevailing West Indian model, minor changes in the order. Here are the most striking innovations:

1. The characters are not confined to the usual trilogy: *béké*, (white planter)/black man/mulatto. (For instance, Raphaël Confiant introduces an East Indian, up to now the forgotten soul of Guadeloupean and Martinican literature.)
2. Sexuality (especially in Confiant's novel)[13] is no longer absent, but is exclusively male sexuality.
3. The male characters (women remain confined to stereotypical or negative roles) don't have the messianic ambition to modify their world, like Manuel for instance. On the contrary, in *Chronique des sept misères*, Patrick Chamoiseau presents a deliberate satire of the "revolutionary behavior" of a *female* student:

It is around this time that a revolutionary student arrived who goaded us with her ideal as if it were a whip. Her voice covered the cries of the market women calling to customers and worrying about their breadfruits ripening or their "caimites" opening up in the heat. . . . She used to shout also: "You must organize yourselves, rationalize your production, gather your energies into a cooperative . . .' "[14]

Maybe it is too early to ask these writers to illustrate their theory fully. As a rule, theory comes before practice. Therefore, we have to refer ourselves to their manifesto *Eloge de la Créolité* in order to imagine fully the themes of the literature to come. In this respect, *Eloge de la*

13. Raphaël Confiant, *Le Nègre et l'amiral* (Paris: Grasset, 1988).
14. Patrick Chamoiseau, *Chronique des sept misères* (Paris: Gallimard, 1986), 118.

Créolité gives an impression of *déjà vu* or *déjà entendu*. Moreover, reading it, one seems to witness the emergence of a new order, even more restrictive than the existing one.

The tedious enumeration of the elements of popular culture which is made in the first pages of the manifesto leaves very little freedom for creativity. Are we condemned *ad vitam aeternam* to speak of vegetable markets, story tellers, "dorlis," "koutem" . . . ? Are we condemned to explore to saturation the resources of our narrow islands? We live in a world where, already, frontiers have ceased to exist. Guadeloupe and Martinique, for better or for worse, have entered the European Common Market and welcome on their soil thousands of men and women from all sorts of countries. Half of the population of each island lives abroad. Part of it no longer speaks the Creole language, although they remain Creoles, since a damaging simplification, albeit made by a school of sociologists, equates identity with language. In new environments one faces new experiences which reshape the West Indian personality. For those who stay on the islands, changes occur also. As Glissant himself puts it, the Caribbean Sea, which he opposes to the Mediterranean, is not a closed area. On the contrary, it opens onto the world and its varied energetic influences.

West Indians should be as changing and evolving as the islands themselves. Above all, creativity is a complex process which obeys no rules. A writer confined to a small and isolated village of the West Indies is free to dream of "Another Land" and make of it the subject of his/her fiction. Creative imagination goes beyond the limits of reality and soars to areas of its own choice. In fact, dream is a factor which has always been neglected in West Indian literature. It constitutes the object of some of the most magnificent writings of the world.

Does its power frighten the West Indian writer?

DISORDER

In a Bambara myth of origin, after the creation of the earth, and the organization of everything on its surface, disorder was introduced by a woman. Disorder meant the power to create new objects and to modify the existing ones. In a word, disorder meant creativity.

Apart from one or two names, the female writers of the West Indies are little known. Their works are forgotten, out of print, misunderstood. The best example of incomprehension remains the criticism of Mayotte Capécia's *Je suis martiniquaise*[15] by Frantz Fanon. In *Black Skin, White Masks*,[16] he singled her out to illustrate what he calls "le complexe de la lactification," the desire to be white and thereby to go down in history. First of all, Frantz Fanon takes a very dangerous stand. He deliberately confuses the *author* and the *object of her fiction*. Although Mayotte says *Je*, nothing proves that she was writing about herself. And even if she were! Let us recall that this novel was written in 1948. At that time, all the societies which had suffered from the wrongs of slavery and colonial exploitation were alienated in the same way. In *Masters and Slaves*, Gilberto Freyre explains the desire to "wash one's blood" which affected the blacks as well as the mulattoes in multiracial Brazil.[17] Mayotte Capécia was simply no exception to the rule. This unjust criticism has forever cast a slur on the book and overshadowed its other interesting aspects. For instance, it contains a deep and penetrating picture of Mayotte's father, whose irresponsibility and mistreatment of her mother might well be partially responsible for Mayotte's hatred of the black man. Contrary to what Frantz Fanon thinks and says, *Je suis martiniquaise* is a precious written testimony, the only one that we possess, of the mentality of a West Indian girl in those days, of the impossibility for her to build up an aesthetics which would enable her to come to terms with the color of her skin.

At the beginning of the century, long before Césaire desperately tried to redeem the black man's image, Suzanne Lacascade in her only novel, *Claire-Solange, âme africaine,* constructed a theory of the climates in order to prove the superiority of the colored woman over the white one.[18] It is obvious that neither Suzanne Lacascade nor Mayotte Capécia had a particular gift for writing, but the oblivion in which they have unfortunately been relegated is not due to their lack of literary skills.

Whenever women speak out, they displease, shock, or disturb. Their writings imply that before thinking of a political revolution, West Indian society needs a psychological one. What they hope for and

15. Mayotte Capécia, *Je suis martiniquaise* (Paris: Cornéa, 1948).

16. Frantz Fanon, *Black Skin, White Masks*, trans. Charles Lam Harkmann (New York: Grove Press, 1982 [1967]).

17. Gilberto Freyre, *Masters and Slaves* (Berkeley: University of California Press, 1986).

18. Suzanne Lacascade, *Claire-Solange, âme africaine* (Paris: E. Figuière, 1924).

desire conflicts with men's ambitions and dreams. Why, they ask, fight against racism in the world when it exists at home, among ourselves? There is nothing West Indian society hates more than facing the reality of color prejudice which reminds it of the days of slavery, of the time when to be black was a curse and to possess a fair skin was regarded as a blessing. Color prejudice is precisely the exclusive theme of Michèle Lacrosil's novels. Her first novel, *Sapotille et le serin d'argile*, portrays a girl's internalization of the inferiority complex during her childhood. Her second one, *Cajou*,[19] reads like the diary of a mental patient who cannot come to terms with life and takes refuge in death. It would be too easy to dismiss Michèle Lacrosil, as it is often done, by saying that she portrays a time gone by. West Indian society is not sure it is cured from the alienation Michèle Lacrosil portrays so vividly. Therefore it is forced to question itself. Is today really different from yesterday? Have we really changed? Aren't we at heart still the same people?

At the conclusion of *La Vie scélérate*,[20] the young narrator Coco expresses the literary viewpoint of the author when she states:

> Maybe I shall have to write this story? Maybe I shall have to pay my debt and so doing displease and shock everybody? Mine will be the story of very ordinary people who in their very ordinary ways had nevertheless shed the blood of others. I must write my own story and this will be my own personal homage to those who are no more. My book will be very different from the ambitious ones that my mother had dreamt of: 'Essay on the Revolutionary Movements of the Black World' and the like. . . . It will be a book without either great torturers or dignified martyrs. But it will, however, be loaded with flesh and blood. The story of my people. [*La Vie scélérate*, 340]

Mental breakdown, madness, and eventually suicide, are common themes among women writers. As I indicated earlier, Cajou commits suicide. Because of the difficulties of their sentimental lives, Télumée in *Pluie et vent sur Télumée Miracle* by Simone Schwarz-Bart,[21] as well as Thécla in *La Vie scélérate*, temporarily lose their minds. The heroines of *Le Quimboiseur l'avait dit* and *Juletane* by Myriam Warner-Vieyra are both mentally disturbed.[22]

19. Michèle Lacrosil, *Sapotille et le serin d'argile* (Paris: Gallimard, 1960); *Cajou* (Paris: Gallimard, 1961).

20. Maryse Condé, *La Vie scélérate*, (Paris: Le Livre de Poche, 1987).

21. Simone Schwarz-Bart, *Pluie et vent sur Télumée Miracle* (Paris: Editions du Seuil, 1972).

22. Myriam Warner-Vieyra, *Le Quimboiseur l'avait dit* (Paris: Présence africaine, 1980); *Juletane* (Paris: Présence africaine, 1982).

Sexuality is another taboo in West Indian literature, and when reference is made to sexuality, it is to male sexuality. We have already discussed the portrayal of Annaïse, the servant of Manuel's desire in *Masters of the Dew*. The uproar about my novel *Heremakhonon*[23] was largely caused by Veronica, the heroine, expressing her own sexuality. For the first time a woman had the right to enjoy sex and to say it. But the most striking transgressions of the order imposed by the male writers are related to the image of men and to the image of Africa.

The family system of the West Indies has been the object of intensive studies. In 1928, the Jamaican researcher Edith Clarke wrote an unsurpassed classic, *My Mother who Fathered Me*,[24] echoed a few years ago by *Sé kouto sèl*, an essay based upon over seventy interviews of Guadeloupean women conducted by France Alibar and Perrette Lambèye-Boye.[25] Although widely set apart in time, both books registered the same complaints. Due to the absenteeism and irresponsibility of the fathers, the victimized mothers are forced to be the breadwinners and to assume the education of the children. However, in spite of this sociological reality, we have been fed upon triumphant portrayals of messianic heroes coming back home to revolutionize their societies. . . .

In *Pluie et vent sur Télumée Miracle*, Simone Schwarz-Bart was the first to dare to shatter this myth and place West Indian women where they belong—at the forefront of the daily battle for survival. This novel is too well known and the Lougandor dynasty of women too famous to be presented again. We must, however, say that few critics have done justice to the disturbing quality of *Pluie et vent sur Télumée Miracle*. Apart from a rejection of motherhood in the novel, we find the portrayal of a "bad mother," Victoire, and of a "bad woman," "a witch," personified by Laetitia. While Télumée is compared to a heliconia of the mountains, Laetitia is compared to a water lily. Thus, Schwarz-Bart associates her with the great goddesses of the West Indian pantheon who derive their powers from water: *Maman dlo, Yemanya.* . . . Télumée, creature of the air, "négresse planeuse," "flèche de canne à sucre" fights in vain against her. Before being hailed by the critics

---

23. Maryse Condé, *Heremakhonon: a Novel*, trans. Richard Philcox (Washington, D.C.: Three Continents Press, 1982).

24. Edith Clarke, *My Mother Who Fathered Me*, preface by Sir Hugh Foot, introduction by M. G. Smith (London: Allen & Unwin, 1979 [1966]).

25. *Sé kouto sèl* (Paris: Editions Caribéennes: Agence de Coopération Culturelle et Technique, c. 1981).

abroad, *Pluie et vent sur Télumée Miracle* received a great many adverse comments at home. It was thought to be pessimistic, negative, and fatalistic since it contained no elements of the conventional revolutionary bric à brac. The only allusion to social turmoil ends abruptly with Amboise's death. Eventually *Pluie et vent sur Télumée Miracle* was recuperated by some West Indian university critics who turned it into a female version of *Gouverneurs de la rosée.* By so doing, they deprived it of all its irreverence and could therefore celebrate it as a feminine masterpiece.

However, transgressing the image of the male is nothing compared with transgressing the traditional image of Africa. We shall not recall the quarrel over *Heremakhonon, Ségou,* and other novels about Africa written by myself and Myriam Warner-Vieyra. Those who want to veil their faces before the harsh realities of Africa cannot accept *our* truth. Let us quote Julio Cortazar, a Third World novelist who has fought all his life for the freedom of creativity: "It is the destiny of literature to provide for beauty. It is its duty to provide for truth in this beauty."[26]

FREEDOM

As we can see, we are far from this permanent questioning of text and context which characterizes literature today. In *Le Livre à venir,* Maurice Blanchot declared:

> The essence of literature is to escape any fundamental determination, any assertion which could stabilize it or even fix it. It is never already there, it is always to be found or invented again.[27]

On the contrary, in the West Indies, literature seems to exist to provide the reader with a few reassuring images of himself and his land. Although West Indian literature proclaims to be revolutionary and to be able to change the world, on the contrary, writer and reader implicitly agree about respecting a stereotypical portrayal of themselves and their society. In reality, does the writer wish to protect the reader and himself against the ugliness of the past, the hardships of the present, and the uncertainty of the future? Can we expect the liberation of the West Indian writer in the years to come?

Eloge de la Créolité gives a negative answer. However, other forces

26. Julio Cortazar, Lecture given at the University of California, Berkeley (1977).
27. Maurice Blanchot, *Le Livre à venir* (Paris: Gallimard, Idées, 1971 [1959]), 293.

are at work, such as the new mentality of our youth and our increased contacts with the rest of the world, especially the Americas. Among the writers themselves, a few dissenting voices, not just female voices, although still covered by those of the majority, make themselves heard and give cause for hope.

JOAN DAYAN

France Reads Haiti:
An Interview with René Depestre

In July 1990 I traveled from Paris to the Midi, to the site of Cathars and Troubadours to visit René Depestre, the Haitian poet, novelist and essayist, who had recently moved to Lézignan-Corbières, amid vineyards and mountains. I was not prepared for the glorious old house, surrounded by trees of all kinds, gardens, and birds singing—a feeling of the tropics in Languedoc-Roussillon. I recalled my only other visit with Depestre in 1980, two years after he had left Cuba. He was bitter. He sat in his office at UNESCO, in front of a window looking out onto the Eiffel Tower. He spoke of politics and his dismissal of all he had once fervently held dear: "I don't give a damn about politics; turn the page."

Depestre had come to terms with the end of his dreams of "eros and revolution." "Joie à Lézignan." So reads one of the rave articles about Depestre when *Hadriana dans tous mes rêves* won the Prix Renaudot in 1989. Depestre is now a Gallimard author. In these interviews I sought to explore the complexities of Depestre's treatment of women and to ask what it means to write about a place so often imaged as excess, dismissed as savage. How does one write about Haiti when, in the words of one Haitian critic, "you're Frenchified to the heart"? Who tells you what to remember, or how to feel? How coercive finally is it when your editors are well-known French writers (e.g., Claude Roy) you've long respected, no matter their politics?

There are obvious dangers in my asking such questions. An outsider, how can I presume to know or to judge a literary representation as licit or illicit? Can there be an incorrect usage of an image? Perhaps

YFS 83, *Post/Colonial Conditions,* ed. Lionnet & Scharfman, © 1993 by Yale University.

the question is who has the *right* to represent whom? Vague claims of "authenticity," as Depestre would no doubt argue, are as dubious as those terms he now distrusts: "identity," "nationalism," or "revolution." I did not finally ask many of the questions that haunt me. Instead, I tried to let Depestre tell his story: a story that moves uneasily between lyricism, love, and his recognition of that particularly "elegant" racism he has confronted in France, which he feels is as much his country as his "native land," Haiti.

*   *   *   *

INTERVIEW, 16 JULY 1990

Joan Dayan Which book of poetry do you feel is your best?

René Depestre The book I wrote with the most innocence, the most generosity is *Un Arc-en-ciel pour l'occident chrétien*. Because then I had a certain inner security, a certain rhythm of belief in Cuba, much confidence in what the Cubans had done. They had found an original way in the revolution that I believed could be reconciled with my harsh experiences in Czechoslovakia. So, I wrote a profoundly Haitian book, where I could recuperate the gods of my childhood and integrate them into my adult preoccupations. The beliefs of my youth, especially vodoun, coincided with my experiences as a revolutionary in Cuba. I tried again to find the meaning of vodoun, which was revolutionary in its origins. Not only at the beginning of the revolution in Saint Domingue, but throughout slavery vodoun remained a continued protest against Catholicism, against colonization, against enslavement. If the black gods could be the vehicles of the revolutionary message then, I thought they could sustain that voice even now. Also, there is more maturity in the formal plan of this book. I manipulated all kinds of fantasies and integrated them into my reading. It is historical chronical, poetry, drama, and ritual. If someone asked me which book I would hold on to of all that I have written, it's *Un Arc-en-ciel*. It's the least indulgent or individualist. It's always good when an author can finally integrate his personal concerns into a collective mythology.

J. D. How was *Un Arc-en-ciel* received in Paris?

R. D. Very poorly. It is a book of great violence. The gods descend to the South of the United States in the blood of the poet there to do vengeance for oppression. In France critics saw it as an antiwestern book, yet at the end, there is a reconciliation with "Our Lady of Ashes" and her joining of a western icon of beauty and love with a Haitian: Helen, the Virgin Mary, and Erzulie. This final synthesis resulted in criticism by blacks who thought I had compromised, that I had not gone far enough.

J. D. Tell me a bit about your own knowledge of the gods. In *Fonds des nègres* Marie Chauvet claims in a footnote to her preface that her vodoun ceremonies have their source in Louis Maximilien's *Le Vodou haïtien,* a rather cunning wrong lead, since her descriptions seem to come from first-hand observation, and in their details and specificities bear little relation to Maximilien's more abstract and European-style meditations. How would you talk about the base for your use of vodoun?

R. D. The gods, and the songs of the vodoun gods, all that has origins in my memory, in things that I saw and lived in Jacmel and Port-au-Prince. My adolescence was filled with the gods and services to them. My mother would take us to ceremonies on Saturday nights, but of course, any Haitian—whether they admit it or not—would know the ceremonies. The poem is a synthesis of my experiences: Catholicism and vodoun lead to an evangelical vision of the world, my sign of the cross. A final message in the name of tenderness and love. I keep the door open.

J. D. You have bitter memories of the collection you wrote a few years later, *Poète à Cuba,* which we discussed when you left Cuba for Paris in 1979.

R. D. Yes. This book was the sum of my experiences in Cuba. It never appeared there; though accepted by an editor and a union of writers, the bureaucrats blocked the book. Censored by the Central Committee, they called me in and read it poem by poem, selecting the lines in each poem that must be eliminated. If I had agreed to accept this mutilation the book would have been published. I would not accept the automutilation imposed by these police of dreams. The book appeared in France with a preface by Claude Roy, and even then I tried to signal my good will. I tried to respond to his preface which was very severe in his condemnation of communism. He went much further in his fine prose than I had in my poetry. Yet I believed then that I might remain in Cuba, that they would leave me in peace with my writing. Today, I find my response, "Lettre de Cuba à Claude Roy," a very weak text. Claude Roy was right. He asked the question, "Could one be a poet in Cuba?" And circumstances have shown me that I could not. Imagine. I write a book called *Poète à Cuba*, and they keep my manuscript in a drawer for two years before giving it to an officer of the Central Committee of the Communist Party in Cuba. It was inadmissible. In my poem "Légende de la Deuxième Vie de Vladimir Ilitch Lénine" I imagine that Lenin returns to his homeland and comments on the faults of the Soviet Union. He sees all the statues of Lenin, idols, empty icons of revolution, and wonders where he is amid the relics of a country that has transgressed his thought.

J. D. You have turned to prose instead of poetry, writing novels and stories. After *Un État de poésie*, begun in your last years in Cuba and completed in Paris, you wrote *Alléluia pour une femme jardin*, *Hadriana dans tous mes rêves*, and the soon-to-be-published *Eros dans un train chinois*. Does this turn have anything to do with your departure from Cuba?

R. D. I think it's a false problem: my writing in prose or writing in poetry. I had always wanted to write in prose. When I was seventeen or eighteen years old, I saw myself as a prose writer, but when I arrived in France and saw the French literary corpus, the works of Stendhal, Balzac, Zola, Mérimée, Maupassant, and the others, I knew I had to be very humble, even if my poetry was carried away by the life and rhythms of Haiti. For prose I had to have a new talent. I had to wait. Of course, in Haiti everyone talks, everyone needs to tell a story. Those memories of tales told helped me to write my first novel, *Le Mât de Cocagne*. And now, I discover that for me prose is very important.

J. D. Do you think prose helps you to get at the right representation of vodoun? I am very interested in your uses of vodoun as motive for characterization and plot, especially in *Hadriana*.

R. D. In *Hadriana* I refer to the vodoun of my childhood, of my youth. It is not perhaps the actual vodoun today, where the gods are adrift and derailed in sometimes horrible ways. For a long time I looked back to the tutelary gods of my early years, those gods of my mother who lived in the countryside where I lived. The rather happy gods of another time. Vodoun had not yet entered into the decline into which Duvalier had plunged it. For Duvalier aggravated the Haitian crisis. He provoked the explosion of every traditional structure of the peasantry. And since vodoun is preeminently an agrarian religion, it was fatal. Duvalier disarticulated the Haitian imaginary, which is essentially constituted by vodoun. Vodoun is the kernel of the Haitian imaginary. And Duvalier knew it: if he could get to that, then he could distort and pervert the minds of a country.

J. D. We've started talking about the gods, and I'd like to go further. Tell me more about how you think vodoun has changed? Which gods get to be bought. I've heard about the *loa acheté*.

R. D. Many, because the process of the gods' formation is open-ended. Today still gods are born, die, and disappear. There are the great beneficent tutelary gods like Legba, Damballah, Erzulie, the Ogoun, Papa Loko. The gods who are the fathers of the religion. They still live. They are present. But there are all kinds of other gods: gods of politics, occasional gods. One always fabricates gods. And you can buy and sell gods. Odd, given the fact of slavery. Gods going off to the highest bidder in a land of ex-slaves! But gods are in the image of men and women, and they're always present, even in the deepest, most secret of life's rituals.

Some gods are more poetic than others in their histories. For each god has a history. I heard people tell stories about the gods, a true history of the gods, their biography. People recounted their adventures: how they lived, what their childhood was like, their fights over women. They have the same passions and experience, the same trials as those who invented them. Now, Dessalines is the only Black Jacobin who has been divinized. De Gaulle might also be turned into a loa, any one very well known in the world scene. It's a real phenomenon, the creation of the gods. Marilyn Monroe might one day appear a model for Simbi, or Erzulie. For the peasants are not necessarily attached to the black race. It has been said that the American marines struck the Haitian imagination for their beauty, authority, and violence. So affected, one ends up integrating these qualities into the vodoun pantheon. Of course, it is necessary to have a big ceremony, to celebrate the new god, who must be accepted by the houngan [priest], who will then hold the necessary service. They say that Erzulie-gé-rouge was born out of the blood of the revolution, a whole *romancero*.

Today the gods know the same vicissitudes as other Haitians. They take the boats like the "boat people," men, women, children, and gods. They were in Cuba during the American Occupation of Haiti, when Haitian migrants worked in the fields of sugarcane owned by American companies. The loa themselves are victims of the general *zombifica-*

tion of Haitians. It's quite significant, because it is one of those rare societies where the gods feel themselves implicated—politically, erotically—in the destiny of men today. The gods are a constituent part of Haitian sensibility and determine their conduct in daily life.

J. D. The individual as conceived in vodoun is more complicated than a simple soul-body dichotomy, right?

R. D. The problem of identity in Creole, the self or the I, is something quite different than in French. The articulation of what it means to think in vodoun has never been studied. No one has done an analysis of a Creole ontology. Yet I believe that the concept of the person is tied to the problem of the zombi and to the other metaphysical problems one confronts in vodoun. For example, each human being is composed of a *gros bon ange* and a *petit bon ange*. The body is *le cadavre corps*, opposed to *l'esprit*, but no simple dichotomy is allowed here, since to understand the distinction between the gros bon ange and the petit bon ange, we would have to think about something like mind and like soul, but the division is not hard and fast. We need a Haitian metaphysics, a kind of anthology of the notion of being in vodoun. But there are no philosophers of vodoun. Haitians are not very philosophical.

J. D. Do you think one day you'll write a book in depth on vodoun?

R. D. If I write a historical novel, vodoun will be at its core, its essence, a return to that moment when it was an ideology of liberation, an ideology of revolt in all its force. There are still many things that remain to be done on vodoun, while it is still living, rather than in fifty years when it will perhaps be a dead religion. Doubtless, something will remain, like sorcery. If you modernize a country, however, sorcery will disappear very quickly, since it is quite fragile, tied to the material and spiritual insecurity of Haitians.

J. D. Let's get back to the question of exile. You've said that you don't like the word.

R. D. For me it's critical that I wrote of my experiences as a Haitian, but a Haitian who has lived everywhere and who feels at home everywhere. I have never accepted the division between being a Haitian or being an outsider. I have never left Haiti. I am not a writer of exile nor a writer of the diaspora. As for myself, I have never known the diaspora. I was Milanese in Italy, Brazilian in Rio, and now in Lézignan, I am Lézignanian. But *au fond* I always remain a man of Jacmel.

J. D. As you know, I have questions about your treatment of women in *Alleluia* and *Hadriana*. For now, let me ask why did you choose a French woman to be the ideal of beauty and incarnation of Jacmel in *Hadriana*?

R. D. That's a good question, since I began by choosing a Haitian woman. In the beginning Hadriana was a true Jacmelian. But I had a lot of difficulty going forward with my story. For a couple of weeks I wondered what had caused this difficulty. I changed her name from Adriana to Hadriana, which pleased me. Then, I began to wonder what if Hadriana was a French woman? If I had made her Haitian, it would have been a traditional novel. Now, by introducing one of the most contradictory elements in the history of Haiti—France and the French—it became something else. Imagine. A zombi seizing the bon ange of a white. I broke with a tradition that made all zombis Haitian. For the first time I presented the experience of a person of the white race, which introduced into the system of fear and belief an unusual element. I ruptured the myth and interrogated it. Of course, Haitians are obsessed by the French, who made them slaves, who made them suffer. And now, it is a French woman who suffers, yet who loved Haiti, and who loved Haitians. Hector, Patrick, all Haitians. The French were masters, but we should not oversimplify things. They were other things as well. I wanted to inject an element of doubt into the myth— especially in the myth of nationalism, so blatantly exploited by Duvalier. So, it worked. I could write. The block disappeared. Also, remember that the categories of color are not rigid in vodoun. Erzulie who's white loves a black, Ogoun. The claims of color were invented by politicians in Port-au-Prince, building on the rhetoric of the American Occupation.

J. D. It wasn't that the French woman was more beautiful, could symbolize better what you called "la beauté de Jacmel"?

R. D. (Laughter) Oh, no, the négresse Elize in *Le Mât de Cocagne* is much more beautiful than Hadriana.

J. D. You've said that your next book *Eros dans un train chinois* is a kind of divertissement, playful and funny.

R. D. Ah, yes. Eros is a vodoun god, and here I wrote my little bit of scandal. A journey with sex in China, Japan, Brazil, and the United States. Gallimard wanted to call it *Eros vagabonde*, but I wanted to keep my original title. I see the book as the conclusion to my erotic phase, my celebration of women.

INTERVIEW, 18 JULY 1990

J. D. In many reviews of your work, you are described as a writer-in exile: "un homme qui cherche son identité en exil," as Jean Jonassaint puts it. Do you see yourself as an exile?

R. D. Now I would respond differently than in the past, but I think that for all men who leave their country, their identity is threatened, but today I think that the notion of identity itself is in crisis. I don't see things as I once did. The word is like a drawer into which everyone puts whatever they want. If I must make use of the concept today, I refer to it with caution, not as before when something called identity corresponded to a real need of those peoples who fought for their independence and against decolonization. All these concepts were forged among the oppressed, and were then recuperated by others, and today we confront an absolutely confused usage of identity. There are so many outmoded terms that remain: negritude, revolution, or identity.

J. D. What puzzles me in your disavowal of what we might call a political terminology is that the "oppressed" remain.

R. D. Yes, but one has removed the concept from a context forged in the concrete and precise struggles of decolonization. This concept has been recuperated for all kinds of reasons, no matter by whom. So, the words make no sense, but more seriously, this recuperation was made in two directions: on one hand, by those who have indigenized colonial violence. For example, I'm thinking of the theory of authenticity that was advanced by Mobutu, and then recuperated by those of the Third World who used the concept of identity in order to justify a return to a national past, to a cultural heritage that would lead to liberation. Today we see that the most retrograde regimes defend their point of view by harping on identity. When a concept dies, when a concept goes mad, you must mistrust it and look for other kinds of explication.

J. D. Which terms, then, in order to replace identity, or more precisely, identity in exile?

R. D. As I have always told you, *I am not an exile*. I am far from Haiti. Besides, I live in a country with which I have much in common, a country that has marked Haiti in many ways. I bear the French part of my history, as I do the Haitian, but I do not set up a dichotomy between them, between these two components, because I have finally been able to synthesize my personal and my professional life. France has formed my sensibility. Most importantly, because France informs the composition of vodoun through Catholicism. Vodoun is not a phenomenon that was brought over from Africa into America without being changed by the effect of transplantation. It marks a phenomenon of *créolité.* Vodoun could be said to have suffered from the shock of the collision of African and Catholic beliefs. Vodoun is a Creole product—what the slaves had to put forth as a defense and most of all, as a means of their identity through history.

Then, there is the French language. After all, Creole is itself a product of certain linguistic customs inherited from Africa and France. Thus, whatever aspect of life one might envisage, one finds this syncretism, this synthesis of many elements of multiple cultures. We are the products of a historic *métissage* that continues even now. Thus, when you say that I have found my identity in exile, that means that I have never lost it. I left Haiti with the elements of my identity intact, and they have not been lost.

J. D. And what about the question of nationalism?

R. D. Our identity has been inflected into nationalism. Identity has been recuperated for the benefit of nationalism. I am a patriot, but I am not a nationalist. The nationalists are at the heart of all the misfortunes of the twentieth century. And in Haiti, it is nationalism adrift, a nationalism *sans foi ni loi,* the worst of nationalisms, that has destroyed freedom. I am horrified by nationalism.

J. D. You said yesterday that the Third World is no longer useful as a concept, that it is "worn out." Can you explain what you mean?

R. D. That the concept no longer applies to reality, because like other words, it is an invention. They called us *blacks,* they called us *negroes.* They did not consult us. We were never asked. I call this process a disguise, and we were always forced to wear masks. We have entered into life, into modern life under cover of masks, under a false identity. The role of the intellectual in his critical function is to unmask. For that reason notions like "cultural identity" or "Third World" that have been operative for many years need to be reevaluated. We are now at a crossroads. For that reason, I am extremely prudent and vigilant about those instrumental concepts. Now, in those countries called "Third World" are most of the "loco" tyrants who have indigenized the methods of colonization.

J. D. You mean that all the colonialist strategies. . . .

R. D. . . . . have been interiorized, deformed, presented under cover of identity. For that reason I believe one must mistrust abstract *tiers-mondisme*. Note that there are no longer theoreticians of such a thing. Now, the tyrants themselves manipulate all of the theory of times past. But it's enough that one put all the cards on the table and begin again to think and reflect.

J. D. But what about the people of Africa and the Caribbean? Because truly it is a completely different situation for them.

R. D. It's up to them to reflect. It's up to the intellectuals who have the force of criticism in the society to have the courage to abandon the well-tried paths to begin a new life.

J. D. Well, let's speak a little about *Hadriana*, because *Hadriana*, the title interests me a great deal. Quite different from your other titles. Is the name a symbol?

R. D. I never think about symbols while writing. Only afterwards, after reading the critics.

J. D. And Hadriana as woman, she represents. . . .

R. D. No, I did not want to represent. No. In putting pen to page, a writer does not attend to pedagogical things like that: I am going to choose a name, this name as bearer of symbols. When I took the name Hadriana, it was by chance. The name pleased me. For me, the name had a certain sensual connotation. It's lovely, Hadriana. I had written it first as Adriana, as one usually writes the name. And then, somehow I felt a sort of malaise. I had difficulties manipulating this word. And then, I put an "h" before it, and I saw that graphically, it was already better. If someone had told me afterwards that perhaps it is the "h" of Haiti—a way of introducing in the very first letter of the name Haiti into the text—I certainly had not thought of that. For me, it was a love story that I wanted to write.

J. D. A love of Jacmel, right?

R. D. No, a love of women. I wanted to write a story of love for a beautiful, young woman. I situated my love in Jacmel, because that was the place of my own adolescence.

J. D. But this love story would have been totally different if the events of the novel had taken place in another country. . . .

R. D. Today I would put my love story in Paris. Perhaps in recounting the story of Hadriana, I have tracked down my own history.

J. D. But, without insisting too much on this point, I would ask you if the novel is not a kind of return to Jacmel?

R. D. No. That was not my objective. I did not want to make a return to Jacmel. If you want to read it like that, that's fine. So, I'm tied to my origins. Yet I can still make an aesthetic usage of my memories of a young man. I resist the idea that I wanted to render homage to Haiti. That is not my main objective as a writer. But if it seems to be that for my readers, fine.

J. D. Now, what about "zombification"? In your opinion, doesn't *Hadriana* stress a deep link between love and zombification?

R. D. No, there is no connection. In the popular imagination of the people, there has been this problematic of zombis, and it has marked the experience of lovers. But I do not want my readers to turn my book into a history of zombification.

J. D. But this "essai sans lendemain" poses a number of propositions about zombification, an elaborate theoretical exercise, right in the middle of *Hadriana*.

R. D. That's because I'm not only addressing Haitians, and so, I must give information that will help other readers. The phenomenon of zombification is not only a fact of *mentalité*, but it is a phenomenon of the social life of the country, of Haiti's history, as it was elaborated as a concept in the realities of the colonial plantation. So, since I live outside of Haiti, I wanted to give my readers, who are not Haitian, a certain sense of a reality they would not otherwise know. I know that I run the risk of introducing a didactic element in the center of my narrative. But the business of zombis has always mattered to me. In my opinion, the notion of zombification replaces the theory of alienation. It is the concrete form of the alienation of a people. In Haiti, zombification tells the same story that one finds in other societies, but it is the colonial form of the impoverishment of being.

In the Haitian context, a myth has been invented that tells of alienation, the last ditch effort of those who are truly oppressed, from whom everything has been taken, even *self-awareness*, even the awareness of your body, or the feel or value of your body. Such a mutilation of being, that terrible zombification began with slavery.

J. D. In writing *Hadriana* did you think of Jacques-Stephen Alexis's *Chronique d'un faux amour*, another story of a virgin zombified on what would have been her wedding night?

R. D. No, I didn't think of anything. No. But the zombi myth permeates all the paths of Haitian sensibility. It is a menace that has always existed in Haiti. It is obviously a powerful legend in the Haitian imaginary, those zombis who hover around and threaten virgins. And in writing *Hadriana*, I have not closed this cycle of belief. One can see how the same story has been treated in Alexis, in my work and that of other writers. A myth can have infinite forms of expression among those writers of a country who grew up knowing a legend. Now that you've mentioned Alexis, I recall that perhaps I made something of a bow to Alexis when I made an allusion to a young woman who had gone to a convent in France, at Saint Gervais. My mother told me about a woman who had been sent to France. One always talked of women who had been victims of an attempted zombification and having escaped were sent to live in France. And one night in 1956, before he wrote *Chronique d'un faux amour*, Alexis and I, sitting around with Ponge and Richard Wright, spoke about those virgin victims.

J. D. And in Alexis's *L'Espace d'un cillement*, La Nina is described simultaneously as virgin, as zombi, and as prostitute.

R. D. Yes, because this obsession with the zombi is perhaps the most interesting fact of cultural life in Haiti. And further, it corresponds to a reality which is the state of the Haitian people. An explication that presents itself immediately to mind: Haiti is a zombified country, a country that has lost its soul. Political and colonial history has plunged Haiti into an unrelenting state of total alienation.

J. D. Do you think that the French can understand this story of Hadriana as you would like?

R. D. Yes. One of the pleasures I've experienced since this book came out is to see how very intelligent readers, most of all Belgian critics, have seized all the most complex turns of this book, things that I might not have thought of myself. I need time in order to understand what I have expressed, because I have a too rational side, a need to explain everything, which is the need of the essayist, or perhaps it's my demonic side compelled to know everything. It is better to work out of the surrealism of one's own personality when you write fiction or poetry. But I am a battlefield. There are so many tendencies that I try to unify, and my work is an attempt at unification, perhaps a continuing effort to unify the self.

J. D. I have another question, perhaps too facile, but I'll ask it anyway. Do you think that contemporary Haitians reading your novel will respond differently from the French? And what do you make of this different receptivity?

R. D. Yes, of course. For Haitians, there is no need to explain about zombis, so it is redundant in their opinion to spend so much time in the novel in such a discourse. They can contribute so much to my tale, for they have memories that might put them in touch with zombi adventures that I do not know, since one speaks only of death and zombis in Haiti. The death that one saw every day in the colony of Saint-Domingue: gratuitous death, unavoidable death.

J. D. The gods (loa) of death, the Guédés, have always intrigued me. They are also images or spirits of eroticism. So, I'm moving back to my earlier question about the connection between love and death, or zombification.

R. D. Perhaps there is some key to how one knows death through eroticism, through dance, through lovemaking. One dances death in Haiti. And often in the countryside when there is a burial, the moment one removes the body from the house, the dance begins. I have described this dance in the moment when they leave the church with Hadriana, when they remove her shroud, when the gods themselves take the shroud in their hands and they dance with Hadriana. She felt that. She said in her story that they made her corpse dance. It was the last time that someone invited my superb Hadriana to dance.

J. D. You mentioned yesterday that vodoun is adrift, *à la dérive*. Perhaps now only Cap'tain Zombi remains as a loa, an effective spirit. . . .

R. D. Yes, because he remains identified with the actual condition of the Haitian people. He is the last of the loas, like the last of the Mohicans. Cap'tain Zombi will perhaps be recalled as "the last of the Mohicans" of vodoun.

J. D. In *Un Arc-en-ciel pour l'occident chrétien,* you described Cap'tain Zombi as a character who had attained a synesthesia of all the senses. That is not part of your vodoun "mythology" is it?

R. D. No, it's my personal surrealism. I fashioned a man-god who could provoke a *dérèglement général de tous les sens,* because Cap'tain Zombi is a human temple of strange and unwonted mutations. But I formed him through a surrealism that was collective as well as individual: a method that would contain French literary history as well as my other spontaneous surrealism that corresponds to Haitian sensibility, that forces you to see things from all sides, and at the same time—this crazy kind of excess and immoderation.

J. D. I would like you to explain this sentence in *Hadriana:*
Laisse tomber la mise en forme de ces propositions faussement férues de mythologie et de sociologie de la décolonisation. . . .

R. D. After writing that, I often wondered why I put such a sentence in my novel, but it was a way to take my distance from theories of decolonization, forseeing the actual demise of the concept. For the writer, it was a transition, a way to return to the flesh, to the beauty of Hadriana. I now feel that my own life marks out such a return: the end of a theory like marxism that accounted for thirty years of my work.

J. D. You said that one could read *Hadriana* like a work of mourning, the death of your illusions.

R. D. Yes, as if I had lived in my flesh the debacle of the ideology of a century. I am thinking of marxism as thought, as a theory of revolution and the reformation of the world, as a theory of the disalienation of man. Perhaps in this section of *Hadriana* I delved into myself in order to exorcize my demons, known and unknown.

J. D. Would you agree that in all your work, especially recently, there are two extremes in conflict, in a kind of oscillation? I am very interested in this suspension or tension between oppositions: one cannot eliminate one or the other, neither dogma nor invention, mind nor body.

R. D. Yes, for me, there are two assumptions that are always there, determining my every idiosyncracy, my personality, my individual history: a terrible need for passion, an extreme sensuality that I see in myself. When one speaks of my relations with women, for example, notions like "make love," or even "fuck," words that are usually employed to speak about possession, always seemed so insufficient that I have tried to see the male and the female point of view. I think that you can live as woman and as man: there is always a sort of reciprocity in the act of love. Thus, there is this thought, this sharp awareness of the ontology of fucking, as well as an extreme need for rigor and analysis. For me, that is my contradiction, but in writing, I think I have made these contradictions fruitful.

J. D. You always speak so absolutely about your "Adieu" to politics, but as I read *Hadriana* it seems to me that you have not been able to put aside entirely the question of politics.

R. D. There is no doubt that I have longed to say goodbye to politics. When I wrote *Bonjour et adieu à la négritude,* one could perhaps read that as "Hello and Goodbye to Politics." If the notion of revolution itself has failed, it would be illusory for me to continue to sleep with a phantom: the great zombi of modernity, it is revolution, alas. The great zombi.

J. D. Let's return to the eroticism of your books. You mentioned that your eroticism was not that of Bataille. And yet you cite Bataille as primary epigraph to *Alléluia pour une femme jardin,* which could be read as a kind of diary of conquest. Why?

R. D. I pay a casual homage to him, since I have found there are always affinities between various cultures, what I used to call "a universal humanism." I pay homage to all kinds of conditions. Libertinage, for example, as I called it, "géolibertinage." The problem of libertinage is not my own, but I am paying homage to libertines who have lived this kind of sensuality.

J. D. But this kind of tribute has caused many to think of your work as sexist. . . .

R. D. Yes, as macho, also. Machismo exists in our culture, in the Caribbean, and it is quite possible that I have not disengaged myself from these trappings, and that they manifest themselves to readers. I have always read about the great libertines with interest: I read Sade especially. Such things have always been part of human experience.

When I pay homage to Bataille in my epigraph I greet a brother from another culture whom I understand. I have read Henry Miller carefully, who has written of sexuality with tremendous force, as if it were an epic of the senses, even if I do not share his direction. He has turned women into objects, treating them often with brutality, as if he exhibited a kind of wounded tenderness, for he seems to be scared by women. The brutality is thus a mask for his fear of women. And that I do not understand, that fear and terror. Maybe that is why, in the case of Bataille, death must always be present, the dark lurking at the limits of eros. Such a fear, fear of sex, fear of women both attractive and repellent I have never felt. For me, the knowledge of the body and its pleasures are very far from death.

J. D. Yet, even in Haiti, there are contradictions in the confrontation with "love." For example, Erzulie, perhaps the most enigmatic of the loa. She is a goddess of love, but she is also very harsh. I have described her as a loa of love who forbids love. Is such a contradiction imposed upon the god by "western" ethnographers or does it reflect the practices of many peasants in Haiti?

R. D. That's a difficult question, but a good theme: how can one begin to study the eroticism of the Haitian loa, to get at their relations between each other and their servants. I am thinking about Legba, the phallic side of Legba, the "god of the crossroads."

J. D. But that phallic side is not very pronounced in contemporary Haiti, is it? Instead, Legba is aged and limping, with a gnarled crutch or cane between his legs.

R. D. Yes, the phallic strength has disappeared. Many of the traits of earlier days have now disappeared, because vodoun is in decline. The beginning of vodoun's decline goes back to the beginning of the last century, during the great agrarian crises, for vodoun has always been a religion of the land. The most violent crises in Haitian life have been over land. The business of land explains every conflict of the nineteenth century, all the battles between peasants and large landowners, since Dessalines.

J. D. René, I've noticed that often when you speak of your favorite writers, you do not mention women. . . .

R. D. Ah, no? Well, let me begin then. Yourcenar, Simone de Beauvoir and George Sand, I like them all very much. I also like Colette, perhaps most of all, for she is a sensual writer, not too preoccupied with philosophy, but so natural, and that's marvelous. She writes in such an extraordinary way, with a grace that gives her words a savor that is unique to the French language. In my library there are many women. They do not occupy a second place in my imagination. I've not read just their bodies (laughter). In Haitian literature, there is Marie Chauvet. Besides her, there aren't many women writers who matter in Haiti. Among Americans, I like Carson McCullers most. I really like those women who write in such a way that they transcend any division like masculine or feminine. There is no "feminine literature," only literature.

J. D. Now to return to the subject of your proposed book, *Mes années cubaines. . . .*

R. D. It will be my farewell to the Revolution. In order to remain faithful to my intellectual being, to my artistic integrity, I had to leave Cuba. But right now, I don't want to talk much about it.

J. D. We keep returning to the question of politics, or revolution. But I want to be more precise and narrow the question to that of racism, the ongoing problems of blacks in the twentieth century. We've not gone beyond that, have we?

R. D. No, that has not been overcome. It is the study of this question that must be done. But with a new method, since the old categories don't apply.

J. D. In my opinion, the question of color, what Césaire writing about the Haitian Revolution called "the terrible negro question," has not changed.

R. D. Because the misfortunes of perception continue. I see the evil still. I wrote *Bonjour et adieu à la négritude* in order to try to explain the semantic traps of racism: the way a biological trait could be used to justify a metaphysical truth. I was not understood, very few readers understood me, or perhaps most did not want to be bothered with these difficult questions. They did not understand me, because they are prisoners still of the old schemas of colonization. Finally, people are still locked into the traditional explications of black, of white, and the images these often spurious oppositions engender. What I was dealing with was the question of constructing *the other*. I guess I put more passion, more of myself into this book than any other. But silence followed its publication. It tore me apart. I had expected another kind of reception to this collection of essays.

J. D. Yes, here you responded to Fanon and to Césaire, in the attempt to explode those ongoing myths of inferiority. . . .

R. D. *They did not read me. They did not see me.* Finally, this part of my work, what you once called the theoretical part, was ignored. The French, especially. They prefer *Hadriana,* or the fiction of a poet, but the essayist in me has been obscured, blocked, because I said things that were too disturbing, that unsettled the normative assumptions of the intelligentsia here. What, after all, is the last refuge of the colonialist? The continued perception of a self at the cost of someone else's identity. Consciously or unconsciously: since no one told me, no, beware, but silence is so much more elegant, isn't it? There was an article in *Le Nouvel Observateur,* and a very perceptive article by a young Belgian novelist now dead, Conrad de Trieze. *Le Monde* published a very superficial article, and then in *L'Humanité,* the Communist journal, there was a serious article that caught my message.

Politics wounded me so much. Yet now I know that I must help the French to understand, and I will do it through my books. I must write. I have not yet written the book that can justify my spending my life so far from Haiti. To gain authority, to be heard, to be sure that one will read the troubling things that I still have to say, means that I must have patience. For a historic guilt still weighs down European culture. But this terrible complicity is disappearing. We are confronting a new period. And the French public will return to those texts they avoided. That is part of the struggle. But you should not say they will *never* read those things that disturb the status quo. I have confidence in their intelligence, and in France, because it is a country of culture. At least, I have found a way to begin the dialogue.

JOAN DAYAN

France Reads Haiti: René Depestre's *Hadriana dans tous mes rêves*

> I'm about to eat the blue flower
> The lotus which changes my native land
> Into a mere checkroom at the airport.
> —Depestre, "The Last Degree of Exile"

THE PLEASURES OF EXILE?

In *Peau noire, masques blancs*, Frantz Fanon analyzes what it means to be colonial, what happens to the black man of the Antilles when he finds himself in a white world. For Fanon language is crucial. To speak is to exist absolutely for the other. What does it mean to acquire the language of *la nation civilisatrice?* "To speak means to be in a position to use a certain syntax, to grasp the morphology of this or that language, but it means above all to assume a culture, to support the weight of a civilization."[1] Adapting Hegel's idea of the mutual adaptability of slave and master to the relation between two kinds of speakers (those who speak French and those who do not), Fanon knows that the coordinate rituals of language separate the "colonized" from the majority of people in his "native land." To acquire a "civilizing" language, then, is to be an exile in your own land: a boon of utterance that makes you complicit with a history of directives and redefinition that can cost you your identity.[2]

The Afro-Caribbean writer risks being "choked on foreign" as the

1. Frantz Fanon, *Peau noire, masques blancs*, trans. Charles Lane Markmann (New York: Grove Press, Inc., 1967), 17–18.
2. Edward Kamau Brathwaite, throughout his essays and poetry, has attempted to combat what he sees as an ongoing domination by the discourse of literate whites— "the European 'great tradition' "—in the West Indies. Linking postemancipation and colonial periods with the slave period, he argues in *Folk Culture of the Slaves in Jamaica* (London and Port of Spain: New Beacon Books, 1974), 31: "It was in language that the slave was perhaps most successfully imprisoned by his master, and it was in his (mis-)use of it that he perhaps most effectively rebelled."

YFS 83, *Post/Colonial Conditions*, ed. Lionnet & Scharfman, © 1993 by Yale University.

Jamaican novelist Erna Brodber puts it in *Myal*, her novel about the many kinds of "spirit thievery."[3] When considering a writer like René Depestre, in exile from Haiti for forty-five years, except for a nine-month visit in 1958, we need to remember and complicate our reading of Fanon. Celebrated in France as "the sensual writer of the islands" or as "the voice of Haiti," Depestre does not like the word "exile," for he says it does not apply to him. "Exile is an external phenomenon, something like a mask. You can wear it if you like, but it is never a psychological problem or truth."[4] In a fascinating interview with Jean Jonassaint, Depestre, when prodded to talk about writing in French for a French audience, answered:

> To return to the question of "the French tool," if you don't use it, you're condemned to silence, you would have to fall silent, in exile. For me, it's not a debate, it's a false problem. *One can make a maternal usage of no matter which language when one is sufficiently impregnated with his country.*[5]

Is the concept of deracination rendered spurious when Depestre places himself as a Haitian *au fond* who has found his home or "abri" in France? In Haiti, Depestre was possessed by France, and now that he is "anchored" in France, only now, does he feel he can fully inhabit Haiti, which he describes as "a once fabulous but now extenuated Eden." How is Depestre's position as "un nomade enraciné" [a rooted nomad] different from Césaire's ever-elusive and delayed "return to the native land"? Finally, what is exile a metaphor for: what does it mean to call a writer an "exile" or "nomad"?

Writing about his mother in 1988, Depestre recalls: "She made us speak French at the house . . . She repeated unceasingly that our future was in French. . . . I was obsessed by France, thanks to my mother, who made me read Jules Verne, Alexandre Dumas, and Emile Zola, in order instinctively to develop my culture."[6] To become cultured, as so many Afro-Caribbean writers have recognized, is to learn to live through the

3. Erna Brodber, *Myal* (London and Port of Spain: New Beacon Books, 1988).

4. Depestre, conversation with author, 14 July 1990. Unless otherwise indicated, translations from French are my own. See pp. 136–53 in this volume.

5. Jean Jonassaint, *Le Pouvoir des mots, les maux du pouvoir: des romanciers haïtiens de l'exil* (Paris: Editions de l'Arcantère and Montréal: Les Presses de l'Université de Montréal, 1986), 192.

6. Depestre, *A ma mère: 60 écrivains parlent de leur mère*, ed. Marcel Bisiaux and Catherine Jagolet (Paris: Presse Mercury, 1988), 140, 143.

books that make inheritance an act of will: a desire to know, to learn, and to perpetuate a literature. As Derek Walcott put it in his controversial "The Muse of History":

> Forget the snow and the daffodils. They were real, more real than the heat and the oleander, perhaps because they lived on the page, in imagination and therefore in memory. There is a memory of imagination in literature which has nothing to do with actual experience, which is, in fact, another life.[7]

Exile, defined most broadly as "enforced removal from one's native land," begins at home. The power of idealized language or privileged text to disengage a writer from something called "real life" puts some writers in a difficult bind. But for a writer like Depestre, who has now articulated his personal romanticism while celebrating what he calls a "veritable bulimia of reading," there is only one truth, the "aesthetic" (Jonassaint, 188).

> Exile is usually considered as mourning, a lack; the search for one's native land, the return are obsessional. Personally, I have a joyous idea of exile. Poetry and literature have now allowed me to synthesize the contradictions of my life.[8]

In Paris at the Café Flore in November 1988 two writers celebrated. Erick Orsenna had just won the Prix Goncourt for his novel *L'Exposition coloniale* and René Depestre the Prix Renaudot for *Hadriana dans tous mes rêves.*[9] Before turning to the ruptures, representations, and silences in the French press as it reviewed *Hadriana*—what one headline described as a story about "La Vierge chez les païens paillards"—I want to introduce Depestre to those readers who might not have followed his career as poet and political man.

Born in Jacmel, Haiti in 1926, during the American occupation (1915–1934), Depestre is one of the most significant Afro-Caribbean writers, whose work must be considered if we are to understand the complex histories of Haiti, the impact of vodoun on artistic expression,

---

7. Walcott is responding no doubt to Brathwaite's complaint that West Indian writers have been educated into something that means nothing to them in "real life." See "The Muse of History," *Carifesta Forum: An Anthology of Twenty Caribbean Voices* (1976): 126.

8. Depestre, "René Depestre: Citoyen de l'exil," *Millésime* (1990): 119.

9. Thirty years before Depestre's award, Edouard Glissant received the Renaudot for *La Lézarde.*

and the high costs of being a celebrated writer in France. Besides the Prix Renaudot, *Hadriana dans tous mes rêves* won "Le Grand Prix du roman de la société des gens des lettres," "Le Grand Prix du roman de la ville de Montpellier," "Le Prix du roman de l'Académie royale en Belgique." Since 1988, the novel has sold nearly 200,000 copies. Gallimard has published his most recent works and an edition of his selected poems. The "Poètes d'aujourd'hui" series of Pierre Seghers has introduced French readers to Depestre's life and work.[10] The documentary film maker Jean Rouch had wanted to turn *Hadriana*, this tale of "l'amour fou" and "la Walpurgis caraïbe" into film, but Gallimard and Depestre feared Rouch would emphasize the details of vodoun practice, thus making central what was supposed to serve as mere backdrop to the main subject, the love story.

When I first read Depestre's poetry in 1970, he was a relatively unknown poet living in Cuba.[11] He had wandered through a series of locales and ideologies, enduring those exiles and returns that constitute what he calls his "successive selves" or his "system of multiple identities." While Depestre now synthesizes his disparate experiences by saying, "I have many loa [spirits] in me,"[12] some of his critics are suspicious of his turns in disposition or style, his cult of *le revirement*. They argue that like a chameleon Depestre has changed himself into whatever the situation required, taking on disguises, putting on the garb of revolutionary when fashionable, but quick to shed that skin in the apolitical pressures of the eighties.[13]

Determined by varying uses of exile, Depestre's writings can be read as a formidable tension between an unattainable past and an unsatisfactory present. His desire to make art out of a remembered

---

10. Claude Couffon, *René Depestre* (Paris: Seghers, 1986).

11. See my introduction to Depestre's work and translation of *Un Arc-en-ciel pour l'occident chrétien, A Rainbow for the Christian West* (Amherst: University of Massachusetts Press, 1977). The second major translation of Depestre's work is Carrol F. Coates's *The Festival of the Greasy Pole*, which includes an excellent introduction to Depestre's novel *Le Mât de cocagne*—Depestre's romance of one man's fight against the brutal reality of the Haiti of Papa Doc Duvalier—called "Zoocrates Zacharias," the "great electrifier of souls."

12. Depestre, conversation with author, 15 July 1990.

13. Depestre's fellow Haitian writer Pierre Clitandre is so aware of this tendency, especially among Haitians, to question and denigrate the "'revirement de René Depestre'," that he wrote a moving "Open letter" to Depestre in *Le Figaro* (15 November 1988) 20–26: "The ambiguity of your 'revirement' (reversal, change or conversion) is caused by the rather simplistic fact that some continue to believe that you must still be a political activist in your sixties."

Haiti, though sometimes imprisoned by memory, marks all of his works with a consistency that can only be called obsessive: a quest that keeps turning in on itself. As "navigator of forbidden seas"—with the slaves' sea journey from Africa to the New World ever in mind—Depestre journeys through a series of landscapes, increasingly solitary, from Dahomey to the United States, to South Africa, to Cuba, to Brazil, to France, all "far from Jacmel."

Let us fix a point of departure in a life that has continuously reinvented origins, lamented ends, and defied constancy. Depestre's writings and recollections take us back to the Haiti of Breton, Wifredo Lam, surrealism and the "bloodless revolution" of 1946 (which resulted— due to the efforts of Depestre and other young intellectuals—in the overthrow of President Elie Lescot and earned for Depestre the title "l'enfant terrible"); to the Paris of Fanon, Césaire, Senghor, and Damas, and the transformations of *négritude*; to Haiti in 1958 during Duvalier's first years of power, before he had consolidated his totalitarian regime in the name of black nationalism; to a Cuba in full revolution in 1959; and finally, back to Paris in 1979.

From his first book of poems, *Etincelles*, published in Haiti in 1945, to *Hadriana dans tous mes rêves*, published in Paris in 1988, readers have reacted strongly to Depestre. Condemned as Marxist polemicist, lyrical opportunist, or bourgeois eroticist, his career has been fraught with ideological struggle. Depestre's major exiles (from Haiti in 1946, from France in 1951, and from Cuba in 1979) resulted from his refusal to falsify or screen the competing claims of poetry and politics, and his insistence on the reciprocity between a private and public voice. What Depestre finally decides to do with history—what had been his belief in a collective context for personal expression—in *Hadriana* turns out to be a critical factor in his reception by the French reading public: proving that the aesthetic is never not political.

In a letter to the French writer Claude Roy (now his editor at Gallimard), later published as a preface to *Poète à Cuba*, Depestre explained his version of "marvelous realism," which joined the "poet" and "the man of political fire": "the revolutionary poet, a man burning with reality, truth and imagination . . . must explore the real and imaginary, proceeding both from social necessity and individual desire."[14] Returning to France in 1979, Depestre carried with him *Poète à Cuba*, proclaiming his return to "lyricism" and his farewell to the

14. Depestre, *Poète à Cuba* (Paris: P. J. Oswald, 1976), 20.

revolution. Speaking in terms that reminded me of Walcott's "I have no friends / but the oldest, words" (*Another Life*), Depestre explained that he had failed in politics and would dedicate what remained of his life to his writing.[15]

Though written in and about Cuba, Cuban officials had forbidden publication of *Poète à Cuba*. According to Depestre, they never forgave him for not censoring himself, for daring to speak against state dogma. That the collection of poems was published in Paris in 1976 is ironic, since the work grew out of Depestre's confident answer to an article in "Le Nouvel Observateur," which announced that one could not live in Cuba and remain a poet. In response to the article's negative answer to the question, "Can one be a poet in Cuba?," Depestre attempted to redefine the concept of revolution by eroticizing it: "Comrade Eros said to the world: / I will not be a cuckold of socialism / The State, it's me, I fuck therefore I am." Thinking back no doubt to his 1955 debate with Césaire, known as "The Debate Over National Poetry," and Césaire's warning not to ponder too much on "the relation between poetry and revolution," Depestre wrote the more serious "Poète à Cuba":

> Back in Paris, at a cafe table,
> People who have never yoked a poem
> To the beauty of a revolutionary ox
> Wonder: "Can one be a poet in Cuba?"
>
> My latest poem has muddied clothes . . .
> It answers doubts about the rapport
> Between poetry and Revolution
> It has the audacity of a rocket soaring
> To the moon and is a rebel against all liturgy
> *And every dogma out of the Stalinist kiln.*

After this collection, which proclaimed his "daring Haitian magic" as antidote to the sterile dictates of Stalinist polemic, Depestre began to write himself out of the class struggle. Lest this phrase seem too reductive, I recall Depestre's words of about twenty years ago, "The Revolution has generated my poetry; without it my senses would be adrift."

Something happened to Depestre's sense of vodoun and treatment of the gods once he left Cuba. Without a certain kind of struggle, a specific history, it seems that the gods lost a context that could resist their conversion into decor or exotica. In Haiti the appearance of the

15. Interview with Depestre at UNESCO in Paris, 17 July 1980.

gods depends upon their involvement in a social world: the spirits respond to the demands of quite specific sociopolitical situations.[16] Depestre's *Un Arc-en-ciel pour l'occident chrétien* (1967) remains his most hybrid and successful work. Like Césaire's *Cahier*, Depestre's *Un Arc-en-ciel* tries to make a new language out of the givens of French and the remnants of African culture perpetuated and transformed in the islands. Written in Cuba, this ambitious long poem records Depestre's attempt to come to grips with poetic usages of Creole, the voice of the Haitian people, as well as with vodoun, their collective historical and religious experience.

Writing a social history of the Caribbean in the diaspora, Depestre makes his history janus-faced, looking both to truth and fable. In the blood of a poet, "a tempest-nigger," the vodoun gods make an epic journey from Haiti to a judge's parlor in Alabama, "the violent Dixie pit." Staying close to the form of vodoun ceremony, Depestre begins his "Epiphanies of the Vodoun Gods" with Atibon Legba, the god of the crossroads, the old and limping spirit of the crossroads. All that remains of his great phallic power in Dahomey is the gnarled crutch-cane that he carries.

> I am Atibon-Legba
> My hat comes from Guinea
> So does my bamboo cane
> So does my old suffering
> So do my old bones
> *A Rainbow for the Christian West*, 123]

In this poem of tradition and revolt, Depestre incarnates Legba's past revivified and made new on Southern soil. It is striking to note that when Depestre returns to Paris and "lyricism" in 1979 publishing, what is to date his last volume of poems, *En Etat de poésie*, he turns himself into an unwelcome, ruined Legba without hope of renewal: "At the door of the foyer, there's no one / to wish welcome to my old bones / Armed men who live in the mountains / have furiously spit on the good news / that my poet's feet brought to their soul" ("Words on a Night in June").[17] The solitary nature of the poet of *En Etat de poésie*, the diminution and mourning that fill these pages, bearing titles like

16. See Dayan, "Vodoun, or the Voice of the Gods," *Raritan* (Winter 1991): 32–57.
17. Depestre, *En Etat de poésie* (Paris: Les Editeurs Français Réunis, 1980), 37.

"Epitaph," "Goodbye to Tobacco, to Smoke," "Autumn Blues," or "The Last Degree of Exile," suggest that exile, at least that final exile from Cuba, is not always a pleasure. Further, these poems of loss and nostalgia for things past set the stage for *Hadriana dans tous mes rêves*, a novel about necromantic virility, zombis, and a white virgin revenant.[18]

READING LIKE A TOURIST

> because life is not a spectacle
> —Césaire, *Cahier d'un retour au pays natal*

In Erna Brodber's *Myal*, Ella O'Grady Langley, a mulatto (half-Irish and half-Jamaican) marries Selwyn Langley from Philadelphia. Brodber tells a New World Pygmalion story: the whitening of an already "alabaster baby" comes with "the powdering and the plucking of eyebrows, the straightening of the hair, all of which a loving husband did." But the reason the "creator loved his creature" lies in Ella's "life story," which Selwyn urges her to keep telling. He listens to her stories of Grove Town, Jamaica, rewrites her and steals her spirit by putting her, and her people into his own text of a de-naturalized, deformed, but exotic island, the play *Caribbean Nights and Days*, which he senses will be "the biggest coon show ever" (Brodber, *Myal*, 43, 80–81). He converts Ella's home into a tourist's paradise, replete with breadfruit, star-apples, rose-apples and mangoes, with black characters "polished, wet, polished again and burnished," with white chalk around their mouths. "The major character was a white-skinned girl . . . chased by outstretched black hands grabbing at her and sliding, and being forced into somersaults as they missed their target throughout *Caribbean Nights and Days* (*Myal*, 83–84).

When certain tourists visit the Caribbean, they know what they want. Paradise is fixed in their minds as a place of gorgeous colors, secret or forbidden rites, a nature gone wild but corrected for the paying consumer. The vacation-package works as a "get-away," a "place in the

---

18. *Hadriana* is the first in a trilogy of erotic stories, what Depestre calls his "divertissement." *Eros dans un train chinois*, which Gallimard wanted to title *Eros vagabond* was published in 1990, and *Les Aveugles font l'amour à midi*, stories which take place in Cuba, is in progress.

sun," and "carefree living" *because* the visitor does not have to get involved with the people or the place. The most popular vacation spots are those set far away or sealed off from the daily grind of local lives, a world where you can forget your troubles, turn your lounge chair to the sea, accept a kind of cultural amnesia and dream about beauty, sex, and magic.

What do some readers of the Caribbean novel want? I ask this question because it helps us to think about which fictions become popular, indeed celebrated, while others do not get reviewed and remain unrecognized. It is much easier to be an observer of a spectacle and not be implicated in it, especially if the subject pertains to the colonial situation or the race question. *Hadriana dans tous mes rêves* demonstrates the way a series of representations can be disconnected from historical contexts many readers would prefer to forget. After all, *Hadriana* is a love story, and Depestre confirms the emotive ethics of his fable when he ends the tale by asserting "the joys and sorrows of love have no history."[19] More important, the response of French critics to the story, their terms of praise, help us to understand how pervasive is the desire for a certain kind of Caribbean, how urgent the demand for a package of themes and images, how predictable the call for scandal and *divertissement.*

Before turning to certain critics and their praise of the flowers, voodoo, zombies, perfumes, fairies, magic, nostalgia, phantoms, orgies, drumbeats, and sex, the French promotion of "Haitian Nights and Days," I offer a brief summary of *Hadriana dans tous mes rêves.* Hadriana, "l'éternel de la beauté française" incarnates Depestre's native land, Jacmel. But she dies, or seems to have died, at the moment that she is to be married, when she pronounces the ritual "yes" at the altar. Her loss marks the end of a once paradisiac Jacmel, causing "ruin, fire, hurricanes, drought, the presidency-for-life, malaria, the State, erosion, the homo papadocus, all blending into each other in a kind of perpetual osmosis" (111).[20] But Hadriana is not dead, the virgin has been turned into a zombi by wicker sorcerers and is sought by the great

---

19. Depestre, *Hadriana dans tous mes rêves* (Paris: Gallimard, 1988), 191. All subsequent page references noted in text.

20. For a sharp deconstruction of Depestre's fictions of eros, carnival, and zombification, see Lizabeth Paravasini, "Writers Playin' Mas': Carnival and the Grotesque in the Contemporary Caribbean Novel," *History of the Literature of the Caribbean,* vol. 3, ed. A. James Arnold (Charlottesville: University Press of Virginia, forthcoming).

and feared phallic butterfly, Balthazar Grandchiré. After her "zombification," the black inhabitants of Jacmel make a cult of the "dead" white lady, "whom they loved and admired like a fairy," dancing around her in what Depestre calls a "collective embolism," or "general thrombosis." Depestre's theater of the marvelous makes the unthinkable or the unknown accede to scenic accommodation. Vodoun practice, once merged with carnival and black magic, becomes the sensational background for another adventure, a more sentimental game: the narrator's own quest for his beloved and virginal object of desire.

Described by one critic as "an amiable and talented bird of the islands as we like them," Depestre has undergone a somewhat strange regeneration and reconstruction in France. In those heady days following the award of the Prix Renaudot, reviews of *Hadriana* appeared in countless papers throughout France.[21] In publications as diverse as *Le Monde, France-soir, Le Figaro, L'Humanité, Libération, L'Indépendant, Dépêche, Le Quotidien, Le Magazine littéraire, Le Soleil, Le Devoir, La Presse, Midi Libre, La Quinzaine littéraire,* Depestre's novel inspired an orgy of naming. He was called the "Haitian nomad," the "Lézignanais," "the tropical man," "the lover," "the garden-man," "the rooted nomad," "the poet of the future," "A Creole Blaise Cendrars," "Haitian and Citizen of the World."

Critics note a rupture between the Depestre of 1967, the "tempest-nigger" moving through the "grass" of his negritude—as well as the theorist of *Bonjour et adieu à la négritude* who wrote what remains the most critical recent analysis of the fetish of color in neocolonial culture—and the nomad in Lézignan-Corbière, standing before his "écritoire," what he calls his "pulpit," composing his books, "like Victor Hugo, with his oval face and chalky beard." He lives in the town called Albert Camus in Lézignan in the Midi, the "country of wine and writers," and is quoted as liking Flaubert, Aragon, Zola, and Balzac (*L'Indépendant,* 11/22/88). Depestre's past life as militant communist is taken up in fragments and then reconstituted to conjure the glorified symbol of "the writer," who has finally chosen art over politics. This conversion story is no doubt helped by Depestre's own self-portrait: "Today I am a peaceable man who cultivates his garden in the style of Voltaire" ("Citoyen de l'exil," *Millésime*).[22]

21. I thank Depestre for generously making available to me the numerous reviews of *Hadriana*. These reviews appeared following the Renaudot, 1988–89.

22. Note that even while Depestre theorized about the reduction of blacks into

Like Brodber's seasonal fruits all lumped together out of season in *Caribbean Nights and Days,* Depestre's complex series of pasts, his separable identities, are collapsed into a caricature of the prodigal son who has returned to France, the land of letters. He is both orientalized as "the Haitian man" and reclaimed as the "spirit" of Lézignan, the nomad who has chosen the south of France, Languedoc-Roussillon, as "his adopted country." Further, the doubly displaced or happily re-placed Depestre writes a story of "tropical sweet scents" for the reader willing to surrender to "Caribbean eroticism," to "the luxuriance, the excess, the paroxysm, the trance of the writing":

> The joy and the very astonishing health that impregnate these stories make one forget the grave problems that trouble the Third World and restore those qualities that the tourist sometimes discovers.[23]

Abandon to the magic of "wild," rhythmic, and poetic writing" is the key to reading *Hadriana.* Critics warn that Europeans must "let themselves go," forget Descartes, and read themselves into the magic of Haiti, "the land of zombis." Jacques Folch-Ribas writes: "The story is fiery, it reads well, you're seized from the first lines by the beauty, the suffocating heat, the music, the odors—like the tourist descending from the plane right into the Caribbean."[24] Seething with "deflower-ings, aphrodisiac emanations, sexual exploits, forbidden extasies," the text exerts an irresistible sorcery on its readers" (*Est. Eclair,* 1/17/89). "Nothing seems to rattle the gaiety of the tropical man, even in those moments where Depestre sets forth grave deeds and theories" (*Public,* Lebanon, 11/88). "What better escape from the woes of postmodernity than a return to the myth of the happy savage, those "who have noth-ing to lose or to gain," who "live in a nearly perfect accord with the heavens and the earth" (*La Quinzaine littéraire*). If Depestre's French Hadriana is creolized in the eyes of the beholder, *Hadriana dans tous mes rêves* becomes proof of one writer's ability to convert dross into

---

commodities, he was often caught up in his own aesthetic conversions of women into "a social fetish," so many lovely bodies served up to recuperative male fantasy. See Dayan, " 'Hallelujah for a Garden-Woman': The Caribbean Adam and His Pretext," *The French Review* (March 1986): 581–95.

23. Anne-Fabre Luce, "Les Noces du désir et de l'amour," *La Quinzaine littéraire,* writing about *Alléluia pour une femme jardin.*

24. Newspaper not identified on copy of review.

gold: to make something beautiful out of the chaos, excess, and brutality of a "savage" and macabre Haiti.

"A RENAUDOT IN THE COUNTRY OF VOODOO"

> You don't have to believe in zombis or vodoun
> in order to be carried away by this story,
> metaphor of all dispossessions.
> —Tahar Ben Jelloun, Le Monde (6/17/88)

On 10 October 1991, after the coup that ousted President Jean-Bertrand Aristide from Haiti, while soldiers (not shooting "indiscriminately" as the news reported) killed over a thousand civilians, most often in their homes, the "Morning Edition" of National Public Radio offered its listeners five minutes of discussion about Haiti. Lee Hochkstader, the Washington Post correspondent in Port-au-Prince, declared, "No one is in charge of Haiti. Haiti is in a state of nature." And when asked if things had returned to normal yet, he answered: "To the extent that anything is normal in a country where there is voodoo."[25] Since the departure of "Baby Doc" Duvalier in 1986, writers have blamed Haiti's troubles on vodoun, most often a vodoun misrepresented as criminal secret societies or sorcery. As I noted in 1988 when I recalled "Haiti after Duvalier," misery, poverty, and the facts of a society riddled with greed, where the unlettered majority always "pay through their teeth," something called "voodoo theocracy," serves to derail our attention from economic and political facts.[26]

Making zombis and vodoun a trope for "barbaric" Haiti was a favorite strategy of the "civilized" world once the former French colony of Saint Domingue became the first Black Republic in 1804. As Michel-Rolph Trouillot has argued: "The more Haiti appears weird, the easier it is to forget that it represents the longest neocolonial experiment in the history of the West."[27] In placing Hadriana in this rather gothic

25. I retain the common American spelling of "voodoo" when quoting from those reviews that use the term as analogous to black magic, orgies, zombies, and the sensational trappings so attractive to foreign audiences.

26. Dayan, "The Crisis of the Gods: Haiti After Duvalier," The Yale Review (Spring 1988): 299–332.

27. What Michel-Rolph Trouillot calls "the myth of Haitian exceptionalism" has "practical consequences": "When we are being told over and over again that Haiti is unique, bizarre, unnatural, odd, queer, freakish, or grotesque, we are also being told, in varying degrees, that it is unnatural, erratic, and therefore unexplainable." See Trouillot, "The Odd and the Ordinary: Haiti, the Caribbean, and the World," Cimarron (Winter 1990): 3–13.

context of regression and fanaticism, I am making certain demands on "fiction." For Depestre's "romance," which seems to put its readers right in "voodoo country," is part of a tradition, a phantasm of barbarism, most extremely displayed in the nineteenth century in Europe and the United States.

"The barbarian is at the gates!" The former slaves of Hugo's "black" revolution in *Bug-Jargal*, "a mob, a masquerade, a sabbath, a carnival, a hell, a something terrible and farcical," like Gustave d'Alaux's *L'Empereur Soulouque et son empire* (1856)—an account of the terrors of Soulouque's reign in Haiti—alludes to the fascination in "the barbaric element" ever present in the masses of Haiti, who were irredeemably African. Categories like fiction, history, or anthropology become interchangeable in this discursive move between the constructed extremes of "civilization" and "savagery."

Now, unlike his nineteenth-century Haitian predecessors, who sought to disassociate Haiti from vodoun, who fought French tales of cannibalism and magic with claims that in Haiti "all is French: in everything here we model ourselves on France,"[28] Depestre seems to join with other black writers of the diaspora who return to the gods, to the call of a past denigrated by the "standard" histories. But Depestre's recollection is more deeply shaped by a very French surrealism than by vodoun practices, with its fragments of rituals, and recollected or reexperienced gods that make belief a reliving of history. I distinguish between the strident movement of induced trance, the "dérèglement de tous les sens," or Breton's "crazy love," and the continued practice of memory that marks the relation between humans and gods in the New World. Toni Morrison in *Beloved* called that unsettling dialogue "rememory": the return or rehabitation that makes the spirit, or spirits survive. No easy accommodation or spectacular frenzy, for the image or god possesses and pushes the past into the present, even when "disremembered or unaccounted for."

In *Hadriana dans tous mes rêves* the French reader is served up what one reviewer called "a fully Caribbean verve," and in a sense, this idealization contributes as much to false generalizations about Haiti as any denigration by Spenser St.-John or those other accounts of the "Magic Island" or "Black Baghdad." Such a celebratory description falsifies, because it never begins to think about what that "verve"

---

28. L.-J. Janvier, *Les Détracteurs de la race noire et de la République d'Haïti* (Paris: Marpon et Flammarion, 1882), 27.

might be, how that "gaiety" might work, in terms of other more ordinary, but pressing truths about some daily lives. There is, as some Haitian novelists, particularly Marie Chauvet, have demonstrated, an abject underside to the more poetic and monumental representations of Haiti: starvation, fear of the powers connected to the government in Port-au-Prince, and the endless laws, constitutions, and injunctions that the rural and urban masses cannot read, as well as the illnesses that cripple and rot the flesh.

Does Depestre, because he is Haitian though Frenchified to the bones, have a responsibility to present Haiti in a way that resists mythologizing? And why should he have to bear the burden of facts other writers ignore when writing the fantastic? These are crucial questions, for Depestre himself would probably argue that they do not apply to him. He is writing "marvelous realism," and has proclaimed: "Les idéologies sont grises, l'amour non!" (La Presse, Montréal, 2/25/89). Unfortunately, everything can become an ideology. When do we not live in ideology? What matters is what materials contribute to the illusions of cultural work.

When the metamorphoses of Hadriana can be perceived as "mixing the horrors of death with the laughter of carnival," "blasphemous rites" and "saturnalia" coincident with "the vengeful magic of vodoo," then what kind of attitude or belief is formed about that land named Jacmel, Haiti? How can readers hearing news of another coup, another massacre, expect anything else from such a bizarre people? Some reviewers have stressed that the unbridled love-death scenes of this "crazy story" in the "hot tropics" are not to be found in "our pale, reasoning, christian latitudes" (24 Heures, Lausanne, 11/15/88). "Too much, it's too much, will judge indomitable cartesians! We are here in voodoo land" (Libre-Belgique, 11/15/88).[29] With such inevitable difference established, we need go no further. The phallic butterfly Balthazar can pierce sleeping virgins throughout Jacmel, Erzulie can lasciviously lift her dress, the black gods can copulate around Hadriana's coffin, but readers do not have to worry about the human context out of which these images are wrenched. For where are the humans in this "island of dreams"? One reviewer makes the link between the improbable and the actual. Talking of the strange life-in-

29. Recall another cold Cartesian judgment of a place called Granbois in Rhys's reinvention of Rochester in Wide Sargasso Sea: "Everything is too much. . . . Too much blue, too much purple, too much green. The flowers are too red, the mountains too high, the hills too near." Jean Rhys, Wide Sargasso Sea (N.Y. and London, 1966, 1982), 70.

death of Hadriana, whom Depestre describes as "the Creole fairy," "the white little angel," he writes: "Pseudodeath or pseudolife? Why look for an answer when the incredible belongs as naturally to the destiny of Haitians as the fatality of dictators."[30]

WHO IS HADRIANA?

> "I want to adorn you like a divine betrothed, an ineffable bride, a celestial being."
>
> —Villiers de l'Isle-Adam, *Axel*

A Haitian remembers Jacmel. Homage to a beautiful woman inspires him to retell old tales about the lusty, seven-breasted Germaine Villaret-Joyeuse. Love of a virgin-zombie inspires the memorialist to describe scenes of "bewitched testicles" and "dazzled penises and vaginas." What meaning does the virginal whiteness of Hadriana lend to Patrick's fantasies? Critics were nearly unanimous in celebrating *Hadriana* as "a song of love" or "a novel of pure love." What kind of love?

The engagement of Hadriana with Hector Danoze and the life-time longing of Patrick, the narrator, for Hadriana operate against a background of phallic transgressions and lascivious stories. Reviewers have described Hadriana, who happens to be the daughter of a French industrialist in Haiti, as an "angel of grace and perfection," an "incomparable fairy," a "blond fairy," "a beautiful, a young and ravishing bride, of the white race," "this dazzling phantom of savage beauty." Unlike Antoinette, the creole heroine of Jean Rhys's *Wide Sargasso Sea*, who finds herself torn between two extremes, or two illusions—the black Caribbean and white England—Hadriana experiences a gradual creolization that comes to fruition with her apparent death. Her zombification does not lead to madness, but is a kind of conversion ritual, a recuperative fantasy. For as Depestre presents it, she opens up to the magic of eros only when she has fallen victim to the zombi potion.

As Depestre's heroine, Hadriana had felt love for everyone, a "lust for life." After her "death," she is quoted as having said: "If I die young, I would like my death to be lived by all those who would have loved me,

---

30. Newspaper not identified on copy of review.

with drums and masques during the days of carnival" (65). Yet Depestre finds the ultimate romance in the "false death" of his heroine. She is zombified not to be put to work by malevolent sorcerers, but to be put out of commission, unhinged, and passive. Full sexuality is experienced as subjection.

"The narrative of Hadriana" ends the novel. She begins her story by saying, "I died on the most beautiful day of my life." Dying before she can experience sexual consummation, "my own thunderbolt of marriage," her recollection of zombification—which began as she entered the church—unfolds as an intensification and synesthesia of her senses. It is as if her sex must move irresistibly toward the climax so rudely thwarted. Tremulous, she watches herself enter an odorous, viscous, and effervescent scene of pure sensual experience, a kind of great cosmic fuck. At the altar, her fiancé Hector Danoze turns into the "Yes" she is to utter. The sacrament of marriage, the ceremonial affirmation becomes a "formless and phosphorescent flesh," described as a "sound-light-body-empyreanmatic," which puts itself into her sex:

> And my sex, identified with a last breath, hallucinatory, affirmative, began slowly to climb through me like a column of mercury in a barometer. I felt its mounting movement in my innards, then in my digestive apparatus. It left a strange emptiness in its wake. It made a stop in my heart which was hardly beating. . . . I felt it again climb toward my throat. It would have strangled me before balancing its burning weight on my tongue. With my whole mouth in four lips I screamed out the final Yes of life to my Hector and to the world! [148]

At that moment, she dies. This orgasmic yes, coming after this excruciating description of utter penetration, acts as a kind of prolepsis to the yes she might have uttered on her wedding night.

Further, this weird description of love-death recalls the antics of the butterfly "Balthazar Granchiré" (in Creole chiré means "gash" or "tear"; and used idiomatically for "fuck" or "fucked," his last name could be translated both as "Bigfuck" or "Biggash"). The grotesque winged phallus, a "satan of a phallus" that violates unsuspecting virgins, causes enchanting orgasms that "wreak havoc in . . . beautiful lives": "Balthazar puts his penis into the vagina of young virgins, penetrates them to the heart where he stops, then resuscitates them by innoculating them with a counterpoison that makes them submissive to his desire" (26). We cannot read Hadriana's erotic delirium without recalling the savage deflowerings of Balthazar, whose force pulsed through the bodies of his victims like a "devastating hurricane." The sleeping and penetrated "superb adolescents" awaken "in terror, savagely deflowered, with blood everywhere."[31]

It is somewhat surprising, after reading Hadriana's libidinal, self-inflected requiem, that French critics have persisted in calling *Hadriana* a "story of pure love" or "song of love." Apparently, in a land of excess, fable, erotic miracles and unbridled invention, one presence—the virgin zombi—haunts readers as an unattainable ideal. As icon of sexualized religiosity, Hadriana, her whiteness, purity, and love, even if creolized, engenders a cult of Beauty. The critical conversion of Depestre's fantasia into praise of innocence, perfection, and chastity demonstrates how easily *Hadriana* can be inscribed into prior texts, or more precisely European pretexts. Heathens, pagans, and natives become backdrop to an ever-reclaimed image of ideal woman. By playing on strategies of idealization in the French reading public, Depestre has demonstrated how a romantic idea of woman—white, virginal and dead—plays into racial fantasy: black wantonness in quest of a dream of whiteness.

Through Hadriana's narrative, Depestre proves that the contamination so feared by the "civilizers" has already happened. The polluting stain of desire has already become part of the body and soul of Hadriana. Thus, while objectifying the object of *his* desire, Depestre succeeds in crossing boundaries that some critics manage to ignore. Hadriana, in her tale of zombification, though never *actually* possessed by Balthazar, reenacts the experience of her friends, their "fabulous flight," their "uninterrupted orgasm" and their "season of dream." The only difference is that unlike Hadriana, these girls are described as seduced by pleasure: Depestre's unfortunate reprise of the "every girl wants to be raped" syndrome.

How are we to read Hadriana's oneiric adventure? Passive, responsive to a thrillingly mystical intercourse, she suggests that her initiation into vodoun was made possible by sorcery: "vodoun mythology had entered my life. Its gods, its dances, its drums held no fascination

31. Depestre explained to me that Balthazar Granchiré was a legendary figure in numerous stories he heard throughout his adolescence (conversation, 16 July 1990). Although I have never heard or read of this oversexed butterfly in Haiti, Balthazar is identifiable with something called "le dorliss," a supernatural being found in Martinique: "Unknown in Guadeloupe, the dorliss is this phallus that . . . dispenses pleasure in the bed of sleeping virgins, regardless of their age." See Hélène Migerel, *La Migration des Zombis: Survivances de la magie antillaise en France* (Paris: Editions Caribéennes, 1987), 65.

for me until the moment when one of its lewd butterflies, manipulated by secret societies, had poured zombi poison into my iced lemonade" (178). Her narrative reads as revelation, a strange turning inside out to discover the blackness in herself. Whether or not we appreciate Depestre's use of transgressive sex, his blur of sorcery and vodoun in Hadriana's erotic (or Haitian) awakening, we should recognize how Depestre attempts to subvert the myth of "true womanhood."

Hadriana, whose desire seems to have no limits, is implicitly identified with Erzulie-Fréda, the nearly white loa of love, the embodiment of gorgeous femininity in Haiti. There is always another side to every extreme incarnation, and the elite Erzulie has her dark counterpart in the popular Erzulie Dantor. This cursory division into dark and light lady is far more reductive than Erzulie's numerous and varied manifestations in Haiti, than her insistent ambiguity and pressing anomaly.[32] But Depestre chooses to adopt the less threatening trope of the double lady. A "dazzling" Erzulie of "astounding sensuality" dances before the catafalque of Hadriana and then she and the mambo Madame Losange—possessed by Saint Jacques le Majeur—together mime "a fabulous fuck" (78).

Though critics recognize the "reconciliation between black and white" represented in the final coupling of Patrick and Hadriana, they have ignored another more daring scene where black meets white. White Hadriana has her black equivalent or double in this "young girl in bridal veil" who, possessed by Erzulie, dances before her "false corpse":

> I saw the unknown, a Black of extreme beauty, remove her veils and move naked toward my coffin. She leaned forward. Her two breasts were hanging above me. I had the longing to bite into their high upstanding feast: big tits swollen with life and lyricism, round, firm, suspended over my famished abyss, I recognized my own nipples disguised as the breasts of the negress in this carnival of my marriage. [163]

This celebration before Hadriana's catafalque typifies Depestre's obsession with describing women's anatomical parts as signs of plenitude and cause for rejoicing. Yet while reading descriptions of nuns falling to the ground in shock at the sight of the profane rites of vodoun and the setting for Hadriana's death—candles, the aroma of incense,

32. See Dayan, "Caribbean Cannibals and Whores," *Raritan* (Fall 1989), 45–68, and "Erzulie: A Women's History of Haiti?" in *Beyond the Hexagon* (forthcoming).

the altar, canticles and ornaments of the Church—I could not help thinking of another woman's response to her wedding. It is difficult to forget Sara, the "shadowy orphan" of Villiers de l'Isle-Adam's *Axel,* that extraordinary hymn to the Absolute. Dressed in funereal garb, Sara prepares for her sacred nuptials with Christ. When the priest asks, "Answer! do you accept the Light, the Hope, and the Life?" Sara, the "sacred virgin" answers "No." As punishment, she is imprisoned in a burial vault, with the threat: "You will be the bitter bride of this nuptial night." Buried, Sara escapes, and reawakened by Axel, is initiated into the mysteries of love, passion, and occult knowledge.

In Depestre's romance, priests fight with vodoun practitioners for the body of Hadriana, Latin phrases intermingle with drums and the "musical fury" of a "pagan homage" (77). The words "Christ the Redeemer" are drowned by the sounds of carnival. Sara utters the "no" that leads to her initiation into the "Occult World" and the "Passional World." The climax of the story is "the supreme choice" of Axel and Sara to renounce the earth, the soil of illusion, and to choose the "perfect" and "absolute" ideal, the ultimate moment of the spirit. Hadriana falls dead at the altar after pronouncing the "yes" that marks her entry into the "secrets of vodoun." For Depestre, arcane knowledge is present, physical, and public. Yet while claiming that he denies the morbid sex-in-death that is so much a part of the European mentality, he still writes a fable of sexual awakening that makes the most of a woman's dissolution. Sara escapes only to find Axel and join him in renouncing the pleasures of the flesh, while Hadriana, "burning with virginity," escapes to Jamaica and meets Patrick in order to do the sex she had only envisioned (191).

A happy ending? A virgin zombified awakens into Patrick's possession. Hadriana has endured a fake death, and a counterfeit deflowering only to be possessed by him. Sexual thralldom? The entire carnival celebration around her body could be seen as what Freud in "Contributions to the Psychology of Love: The Taboo of Virginity," describes as the "ceremonial mock-coitus," the crucial phase of the "marriage ceremonies of primitives." Horror of blood, the breaking of the hymen, necessitates a two-part scenario of marriage: the public performance of penetration and then the husband's unique entry.

Hadriana dans tous mes rêves is prize-winning for it serves up the most cherished, masculine mystifications, even as it seems to subvert them. What is a woman's sole function in life? To please her man.

Recall the stunning description of a young girl's preparation for "the consummation of love" in Zora Neale Hurston's *Tell My Horse: Voodoo and Life in Haiti and Jamaica*.[33] In Part I of *Tell My Horse,* Hurston thinks and thinks again about the plight of "Caribbean Women," forced into a servitude called marriage, betrayed by their husbands, who own them body and soul. Think about the following as a gloss on Hadriana's zombification, her life-in-death, which seems like a prolonged titillation of her senses prior to her consummation with Patrick. An old woman specialist prepares the girl for her life as bride. On the day of the wedding, she massages her body with oil. She concentrates on the breasts, moves finally toward the nipples, stimulating them with a "warm feather." The massage continues. The girl swoons, is revived with rum spiced with marijuana, swoons again, as she is touched to frenzy. "She is in a twilight state of awareness, cushioned on a cloud of love thoughts." In this condition she is instructed: "You have the happiest duty of any creature on earth and you must perform it well. The whole duty of a woman is love and comfort. You were never intended for anything else. . . . That is all that men ever want women for . . . ." All this talk and touching arouses the girl who begs to be taken to her husband. She can't wait.

WHITE ZOMBI

> The zombi . . . those figures of Antillian legends tinged with exoticism. Believe nothing of it? They are there, on the soil of France, even in dead winter.
> —Jacket blurb for *La Migration des zombis*

Hadriana's tomb is empty. Jacmel is desolate. In sublime apotheosis she reappears in Jamaica thirty-nine years after her disappearance in 1938. Patrick, who describes himself as "zombified by Cuba," is revitalized in Kingston, Jamaica, where he teaches "aesthetics" to nubile, moist-lipped young women, whose shapely legs seem "ready for more savory labors" (135). Like Hadriana, Patrick (or Depestre) has undergone years of exile, culminating in what he describes as his "false

33. Zora Neale Hurston, *Tell My Horse: Voodoo and Life in Haiti and Jamaica* [1938], reprinted in 1990 (New York: Harper & Row Publishers), 17–20.

death" in Cuba, where his "body and soul" were bled to death by socialism (135).

Critics have celebrated the union of Hadriana and Patrick as a joyous synthesis, a "fabulous métissage" (*Magazine litéraire*, 6/88). In *La Quinzaine Littéraire* (5/16–31/88), Agnès Vaquin writes: "The end of the idyll of the black Patrick and the white Hadriana is that of a fairy tale. It's up to readers to read into this what they want, even the happy marriage of the two races and the successful integration of the white woman, by the grace of Caribbean *amour fou.*" This interpretation is crucial. For while Jacmel remains ruined, zombified, a waste land, Patrick and Hadriana alone can transform a world of servile limits into a future of liberated ecstasy. In *Le Monde* (6/17/88), Tahar Ben Jelloun writes that "Depestre's native land, Jacmel, is now devastated. It survives miserably with its myths and its phantoms. Everything there is desolate."

But what myths and phantoms does Depestre conjure for his readers in France? Hadriana's story is preceded by what has by now become Depestre's most pervasive concern, his theory of zombis (125–33). "My native land what is it but a collective zombi?" The saving graces of Hadriana and the fiery writing of Depestre have no effect on godforsaken Jacmel. Depestre abandons the inhabitants of Haiti to their fate, apparently forgetting their continued struggles against dictatorship, repression, and poverty. All that remains of his Haiti is a portrait of black, poor, apathetic husks of humanity, who can never awaken into freedom.

The zombi has always mattered for Depestre. From his early *Minerai noir*, which retells the conversions of humans into slaves, identities crushed in brutal commodification, to the wild promise of the "human future" captured in "Cap'tain Zombi" in *Un Arc-en-ciel pour l'occident chrétien*, to his perceptive theoretical writings, Depestre evokes the zombi as the most powerful emblem of anonymity, loss, and neocolonialism. The business of capital made possible what Depestre had described in *Bonjour et adieu à la négritude* as this "fantastic process of reification and assimilation" that "means the total loss of my identity, the psychological annihilation of my being, my zombification."

Now Depestre excludes himself from the general horror of a specific system. His private love story is superimposed on a ground of Jacmelian malaise. Even a past politics cannot help, for Cuba has become part of the rhetoric of "zombification." Who loses their soul, their spirit, their will in *Hadriana?* Not Hadriana, not Patrick, but the

Haitian people, whose "memory"—their creative operations of re-
trieval, preservation, and endurance—have very little to do with Depestre's dirge. Again, for some French critics *Hadriana* is "a beautiful
story of love between two beings, but also between two civilizations,
two cultures . . . in a mutual spirit of fraternity" (*Public*, Lebanon,
11/88). In the midst of what Depestre calls "the Haitian disaster," he
says that he searches for "new ties with France . . . a sort of brotherhood, a sort of French Commonwealth" (*La Presse*, Montréal,
11/15/88).

The hour of reconciliation sounds. Hadriana, saved from the
clutches of a regressive and static destiny, becomes "a metaphor for all
dispossessions": "She is the symbol of an entire people that a merciless
dictatorship has for decades tried to zombify" (*La Liberté Dimanche*,
19–20/11/88). What kind of "homage to Antillean culture" is
Hadriana dans tous mes rêves? A story that promotes the comfortable
illusion that a *white* can take on the burden of *blacks*, symbolically
redeeming those who are finally irredeemable.

Remember that the most common meaning of zombi in Guadeloupe and Martinique, for example, is a stolen or evil spirit. In Haiti
originated the belief in a zombi "in flesh and bones," a human poisoned
in order to appear dead and then resurrected by a sorcerer to work as a
slave, usually in some foreign land. Has Depestre been zombified by
French fame? Has he been turned into nothing more than the "spirit"
of Haiti who labors on the soil of France? I conclude with one reviewer's rather ambivalent celebration of Depestre's life and work: "I
wonder if René Depestre might not himself be a zombi converted and
reincarnated as a writer . . . transmuting all the occult forces of the
homo papadocus into great luminous flashes, metamorphosing himself into a butterfly of writing" (*Spectrum*, 1/89).

MIREILLE ROSELLO

"One More Sea to Cross:" Exile and Intertextuality in Aimé Césaire's *Cahier d'un retour au pays natal*

l'exil s'en va ainsi dans la mangeoire des astres portant de malhabiles
grains aux oiseaux nés du temps
—"Birds" in *Ferrements*

The people of Martinique and Guadeloupe will perhaps never recover from their exile, will perhaps never even succeed in defining it.[1] Exile will thus be, for a long time to come, the raw material of the texts of Aimé Césaire, Edouard Glissant, Maryse Condé, and of many others. Like their books, these writers, born in the Antilles and educated in metropolitan France, fall outside the traditional classifications in anthologies of literature, eluding the canon which does not know what place to assign them. Although retrieved by the hegemony and placed among marginal categories (Caribbean texts, Francophone texts, Black literature), the works of Martinican and Guadeloupean writers will

1. It is arbitrary and useless here to try to put into operation a clear-cut difference between "exiles," "émigrés," "expatriates," etc. . . . What the French Antillean leaves is neither a country nor a homeland that the islands are French territories. Nonetheless, writings resulting from this displacement betray the same anguish that Edward Said describes when he analyzes individuals deported by the will of a totalitarian state in his essay entitled "Reflections on Exile," *Granta* 13 (Autumn 1984): 157–72. While the exiles' hope of return, although generally illusory and forever deferred, remains the longed-for solution to their distress, Martinicans and Guadeloupeans who leave for metropolitan France are not yet in a position, at first, to idealize the "native land" they voluntarily abandoned. In addition, exile is not necessarily geographic and the Martinicans and Guadeloupeans who remain in their "native" land may very well suffer from the syndrome of exile. The diglossic situation that always forces the speaking subject to situate him/herself in relation to a language and culture can serve as a symbol of this perpetual gap in relation to an inaccessible home. For a discussion of the terms that attempt to classify rigorously the misery of different forms of exile, see the text by Robert Nixon, "London Calling: V. S. Naipaul and the License of Exile," *The South Atlantic Quarterly* 87.1 (Winter 1988): 1–38, in which he analyzes "the medley of terms—exile, emigrant, émigré, expatriate, refugee, and homeless individual" that may be used.

YFS 83, *Post/Colonial Conditions*, ed. Lionnet & Scharfman, © 1993 by Yale University.

always be elsewhere, but an elsewhere that one will choose at times to appropriate and assimilate: Martinique and Guadeloupe, departments of France, Aimé Césaire, "great Black poet."[2] Whatever the label imposed upon these texts, it is clear that the canon violates them when they are reduced to the "Oneness" of "French," "Francophone," "Black," or even "Antillean" culture, when it minimizes the differences that separate them from the traditions within which they are classified. The dubious privileges accompanying literary fame and recognition cannot offset the loss of a vital part of their multiple identity.

The study of the "theme" of exile will relieve none of this pain. Exile here does not yet have a satisfactory definition, it is not resolved by a "return" to the "land." Texts which "come from" the islands and which "return" there are stricken not by Exile but by a *series* of exiles; they suffer from an impossible departure and return, they are marked by the ambiguity of an eternal movement of "detours."[3] For Edouard Glissant, "retour" and "détour" thus become inseparable, and the quasi-homonymy of these two words invites us to look towards language to find what might be a possible definition of a "native land" for writers in the Antilles.

When Glissant writes that the Martinican who decides to leave his island "n'emporte pas sa patrie à la semelle de ses souliers" [does not take along the homeland on the soles of his shoes] (*Discours Antillais*, 74), he suggests in effect that exile has a link, often obscured, with the language one uses, in this case with French, whose clichés and proverbs are incompatible with the lived experience of Antilleans. We will see how with Césaire, the French language becomes the object of appropriation and is transformed into a strategic instrument of resistance. We do well, however, to remember that for Antillean writers of French language and culture, every unexplored intertextuality risks being an unfortunate missed opportunity: the monolithic French Language is not necessarily equipped to talk about a "land" that is not one, about a "native land" that is not an origin, about a "return" that would

2. The title that André Breton gives to the preface of the 1947 edition of *Notebook of a Return to the Native Land*, "Un grand poète noir" in *Cahier d'un retour au pays natal* (Paris: Présence Africaine, 1983), 77–87, reduces Aimé Césaire's identity to a racial composite. It is true that in 1947 it was crucial not to obscure the element that was used as a pretext for the oppression of various groups tossed together under the heading "Black," but Breton's formulation makes of Césaire a cultural "man without a home."

3. On this subject see the chapter of the first book of Edouard Glissant's *Discours antillais* (Paris: Seuil, 1981), 28–37, entitled "Retour et Détour" ["Return and Detour"].

only be another departure and a new detour, about joyous departures that are transformed into unhappy exiles and become little by little the acceptance of "wandering," [4] about an infinite and irremediable exile. I will use two texts as examples, because from them was born the intuition that, among certain Antillean writers, the notion of exile is the result of a long process of recognition, and that often it is only a posteriori that a voluntary and wished-for departure is reinterpreted as a disaster—an agonizing separation, but one that is overshadowed by an Antillean culture imagined as nothing-ness, a void.

I. A "NOTEBOOK" AND "NOTES"

In 1939, Césaire, who from then on would consider himself an "exile" in Paris, finished *Notebook of a Return to the Native Land.*[5] Forty years later, Maryse Condé, having returned to Guadeloupe after a "detour" through Europe and Africa, borrowed from Césaire the essence of his title and spoke of her exiles in an essay entitled "Notes on a Return to the Native Land." The two titles resemble each other, recall each other, echo each other. An example of a problematic intertextual dialogue, is Maryse Condé's title a reference-homage to the father of Négritude, to the Master of Antillean literature whom the novelist recognizes henceforth as her own? Does this title signal the end of a literary exile and the adoption of a cultural homeland? It appears that both elements coexist, and that the title may also be a pastiche, a disabused wink at a pathetic (literary) history that does not allow writers to change problematics, that condemns them to an unending repetition; it is paradoxical, at the exact moment when Condé alludes to a Césairian "native land" which might constitute a possible origin, to choose as a theme the absence of origin, and thus the difficulty of "return."

From generation to generation, Antillean writers who have gone to study and work in France have had in common the perception that their initial departure was *not* an exile—indeed, the opposite seems true. Maryse Condé describes her adolescence as long years of

---

4. Maryse Condé, "Notes sur un retour au pays natal" in *Conjonction: revue franco-haïtienne.* Supplément to 176 (1987), 23. All translations are mine when no published translations are indicated in the notes.

5. I will use Clayton Eshleman and Annette Smith's translation from the bilingual edition *Aimé Césaire: The Collected Poetry* (Berkeley: University of California Press, 1983).

boredom, and speaks of her island-*"prison"* and of the "mer qu'on ne regardait que pour avoir le désir de *s'échapper des Antilles"* [the sea one looked at only to have the desire to *escape* from the Antilles] (Condé, 9, my emphasis). "Le pays natal se réduisait pour nous à un décor, le décor d'un constant ennui" [The native land was reduced for us to a setting, the setting of constant boredom] (Condé, 10). "Donc, quand j'ai quitté la Guadeloupe, . . . j'avais l'impression que j'allais enfin commencer à vivre" [Thus, when I left Guadeloupe, . . . I had the impression that I was finally going to begin to live] (Condé, 10). This first voluntary departure is euphorically described as the end of a confinement, as a liberation. One may be surprised that Maryse Condé's remembrances echo Césaire's own declarations, when he asserts to Lilyan Kesteloot: "J'ai quitté la Martinique avec volupté" [I left Martinique with exquisite delight][6]. At this stage, as if the Césairian experience had not entered into the Condé's History, there is no origin. The concept itself of exile seems impossible to forge. The place from which exile could possibly be defined has been completely annihilated by the colonial situation. Literally, the native land has been erased:

> Si on m'avait demandé à ce moment-là "Qu'est-ce que ton pays natal?" Je n'aurais *rien eu à dire*; j'aurais dit que c'était peut-être deux ou trois palmiers à côté de la mer qui *encadraient* le *vide le néant*. [Condé, 10, my emphasis]

> If someone had asked me at that time "What is your native land?" I would have had *nothing* to say; I would have said that it was maybe two or three palm trees next to the sea framing *nothingness*, the void.

The native land is a "nothingness," a "void," and therefore in leaving, Martinicans and Guadeloupeans leave nothing towards which they could eventually return. It is only later, *retrospectively*, that Antillean intellectuals can rediscover a "homeland" by representing the people of the Antilles as already exiled—uprooted from Africa and from themselves. It is thus striking to discover that the two texts of Maryse Condé and Aimé Césaire, although separated by a literary generation, take up the same problematic in almost exactly the same terms. In 1987, Condé speaks of her adolescence as a period during which the Antilles are not *representable*. Condé confesses that in 1954, the date of her first departure, "[elle n'avait] jamais entendu

6. Lilyan Kesteloot, *Aimé Césaire* (Paris: Seghers, collection poètes d'aujourd'hui, 1962), 18.

prononcer le nom d'Aimé Césaire" [She had never heard the name of
Aimé Césaire] (Condé, 10). For her, everything happens as though the
Négritude movement and the publication of *Tropiques* had gone unnoticed.[7] What is remarkable in Condé's narrative is the persistent
impression that she has no literary past from her native soil. Even
Césaire, to whom she owes her title, is discovered after her departure,
in metropolitan France. The "native land" is a silence, it is peopled by
words which could be hers: it has "nothing to say." No precursor existed for her, and oddly, her text resembles Césaire's own in which he
admits that Antillean literature did not exist for him as he prepared to
leave Paris ("Quand je suis rentré à la Martinique, qu'est-ce que je
connaissais? La littérature française: Rimbaud, Claudel, Baudelaire"
[When I returned to Martinique, what did I know? French literature:
Rimbaud, Claudel, Baudelaire].[8] The recognition of exile will thus be
paradoxical since the "land" is not the idealized homeland towards
which nostalgia turns. Césaire and Condé will undergo in Paris the
experience of their foreignness, of their alienation, of a negative exile
in relation to a metropolitan community which excludes them but
they will not know where to place their loyalty, their sense of belonging, their return. Maryse Condé says: "La première découverte que je
fais, c'est que je ne suis pas française" [The first discovery I made, is
that I am not French] (Condé, 10). It is only after having arrived in Paris
that Condé joins the itinerary of the authors of the preceding generation and begins to suspect that the island was in fact already exiled
from its African origin. Nonetheless, even this origin is henceforth
mythic and illusory; tempted by the "great Black womb," she realizes
that it does not want her[9] and that the return to the Black continent is,
as Glissant says, "un espoir raturé," [a deleted hope] (Glissant, 105).
Under these conditions, "return" emerges as the only possible choice,
but by elimination, by violence. The political and literary awakening
which results from contact with France also renders return the only

7. Retrospectively, here again she refers the reader back to Frantz Fanon's analysis
in *Peau noire, masques blancs* (Paris: Seuil, Collection Points, 1952) concerning the
difficulty Antillean writers encounter in gaining access to noncanonical works. See
especially the chapter "L'Expérience vécue du Noir" (88–114).
8. Jacqueline Leiner, "Entretien avec Aimé Césaire" in *Tropiques* I, 1–5 (April
1941–April 1942), 8.
9. See the novel *Hérémakhonon* (Paris: Editions 10/18, 1976), which recounts this
"detour" through Africa, and Françoise Lionnet's analysis of this novel: "Happiness
Deferred: Maryse Condé's *Hérémakhonon* and the failure of Enunciation" in *Autobiographical Voices* (Ithaca: Cornell University Press, 1989).

possible strategy for an author determined to participate in the birth of an Antillean nation and writing. Condé insists that it required "bravery" on her part to accept to return to this prison she had left, to what Césaire had described as "ces quelques milliers de mortiférés qui tournent en rond dans la calebasse d'une île . . . l'archipel arqué comme le désir inquiet de se nier" [these few thousand deathbearers who mill in that calabash of an island . . . the archipelago arched with an anguished desire to negate itself] (*Collected Poetry, Notebook*, 46).

The result is that one has the impression that the return to the land resolves nothing, that the departure for Martinique and Guadeloupe are logical political decisions, but that strangely, for Antillean writers, the "return to the native land" is yet another form of exile. Exile here is perceived as a permanent gap, no longer between the speaking subject and a clearly identified cultural or national identity, but between the "I" and the community within which that "I" temporarily finds itself (speaking). Every displacement, every attempt to return, every new departure renders the "I" more and more aware of the gap, of his or her difference. The revealing element of this incessant exile, of this return constantly deferred, is thus the meeting of the "I" and a community by which he or she tries to become adopted, which he or she tries to recognize as a homeland; this repeated endeavor could be compared to what Glissant calls "mise en Relation" [putting into Relation].

II. CÉSAIRE/BAUDELAIRE: "WINGED TRAVELLERS"

With Césaire, this "mise en Relation" is accomplished by the poetic word. The *Notebook of a Return to the Native Land* is not, like the "Notes" of Maryse Condé, an autobiographical narrative in prose which retraces after the fact the steps leading to an awareness of exile. A prophetic vision of what will be the return, this long poem allows the "I" to anticipate the same discoveries as those of the narrator of "Notes on a Return to the Native Land." In the *Notebook*, the "mise en Relation" is achieved by the confrontation of the poetic language of the "I" and the language of the community within which he finds himself. The passage I will examine here, which critics customarily call the streetcar scene, seems to me an extraordinary moment of textual putting into relation, a moment of awareness in which the narrator becomes hyperconscious of manipulating a language and a culture which also manipulate him. The "I," at first tempted by the recourse to assimilate (here an individual solution), is two steps away from enclosing himself in his unconscious exile, and risks becoming irrevocably "other." But this episode also coincides with the discovery of a solution, a moment of illumination for the narrator who remembers and tells the story.

I would like to show that in this passage, a reference to "L'Albatros" by Baudelaire which at first seems to slip its way into the poem as though by accident, is immediately picked up, unmasked, and systematically explored by the "I" who refuses to obscure the work of language, which is capable in turn of serving and harming him, of enriching and impoverishing him, of including and excluding him, of liberating and oppressing him. I cite one following the other the poem by Baudelaire and the meeting between the narrator and a "grouchy nigger" in a Parisan streetcar:

> Souvent, pour s'amuser, les hommes d'équipage
> Prennent des albatros, vastes oiseaux des mers,
> Qui suivent, indolents compagnons de voyage,
> Le navire glissant sur les gouffres amers.
>
> A peine les ont-ils déposés sur les planches,
> Que ces rois de l'azur, maladroits et honteux
> Laissent piteusement leurs grandes ailes blanches
> Comme des avirons traîner à côté d'eux
>
> Ce voyageur ailé, comme il est gauche et veule
> *Lui, naguère si beau, qu'il est comique et laid!*
> L'un agace son bec avec un brûle-gueule
> L'autre mime, en boîtant, l'infirme qui volait!
>
> Le Poète est semblable au prince des nuées
> Qui hante la tempête et se rit de l'archer;
> Exilé sur le sol aux milieux des huées
> Ses ailes de géant l'empêchent de marcher.[10]
>
> Often, to pass the time on board, the crew
> will catch an albatross, one of those big birds
> which nonchalantly chaperone a ship
> across the bitter fathoms of the sea.
>
> Tied to the deck, this sovereign of space,
> as if embarrassed by its clumsiness,

---

10. Charles Baudelaire, *Les Fleurs du Mal*. With translations by Richard Howard (Boston: David R. Godine, Publisher, 1982), 11–12, my emphasis.

pitiably lets its great white wings
drag at its sides like a pair of unshipped oars.

How weak and awkward, even comical[11]
this traveller but lately so adroit—
one deckhand sticks a pipestem in its beak,
another mocks the cripple that once flew!

The Poet is like this monarch of the clouds
riding the storm above the marksman's range;
exiled on the ground, hooted and jeered, he cannot walk because of his
great wings.

[Baudelaire, 13–14]

Et moi, et moi, moi qui chantais le poing dur.
Il faut savoir jusqu'où je poussai la lâcheté. Un soir dans un tramway en
     face de moi, un nègre . . .
La misère on ne pouvait pas dire, s'était donné un mal fou pour
     l'achever. . . .
Et l'ensemble faisait parfaitement un nègre hideux, un nègre grognon,
     un nègre mélancolique, un nègre affalé, ses mains réunies en prière
     sur un bâton noueux.
Un nègre enseveli dans une vieille veste élimée. Un nègre comique et
     laid et des femmes derrière moi ricanaient en le regardant
Il était COMIQUE ET LAID,
COMIQUE ET LAID pour sûr.
J'arborai un grand sourire complice . . .
Ma lâcheté retrouvée!

[Césaire, *Collected Poetry*, 62]

And I, and I,
I was singing the hard fist
You must know the extent of my cowardice.
One evening on the streetcar facing me, a nigger . . .
Poverty, without any question, had knocked itself out
to finish him off. . . .
And the whole thing added up perfectly to a hideous nigger, a grouchy
nigger, a melancholy nigger, a slouched nigger, his hands joined in

---

11. The translation of this sentence does not allow the reader to fully appreciate
the complexities of Césaire's work of appropriation: for the sake of more accurate
comparison, I suggest: "This winged traveller, how awkward and weak he is! Formerly
so splendid, how he is comical and ugly"

prayer on a knobby stick. A nigger shrouded in an old threadbare coat.
A comical and ugly nigger, with some women behind me sneering at
him.
He was COMICAL AND UGLY,
COMICAL AND UGLY for sure.
I displayed a big complicitous smile . . .
My cowardice rediscovered!

[*Collected Poetry*, 63]

For M. a M. Ngal, "this scene takes root in the daily colorfulness of
the Latin Quarter. It was really lived."[12] Although Ngal devotes an
entire chapter of his study on Césaire to the "school of foreign matu-
rities," concentrating especially on an inventory of philosophical and
literary influences, he does not read the streetcar scene as an example
of intertextuality.[13] Classified under the rubric "other sources" (Ngal,
202), this passage is considered one of the scenes that depict "the
collective experience of the 'nigger' in time and space" (Ngal, 202). I
would like to suggest that the "comical and ugly nigger" underlines
what is problematic in the rewriting of a space-time "nigger" when one
writes in French. This scene which Ngal considers "banal" (202) does
not escape the problems of literary influences. To the contrary, it
shows how these influences are problematic: this passage from the
Notebook is the meeting of the "grouchy nigger" and the narrator, but

12. In regard to this, Ngal cites the interview he had with Aimé Césaire in 1967:
"Some of it is lived . . . . He was a guy who used to hang around the Latin Quarter. His
name was Hannah Charley. A very strange man, half crazy . . . but who was also half
philosopher, half bum, who often visited the Latin Quarter and questioned every black
student. He had moments of prosperity and moments of poverty. He was originally
from Guadeloupe. The scene doesn't only refer to him, I had to mix in other people,"
quoted in Mbwil a Mpaang Ngal, *Aimé Césaire: un homme à la recherche d'une patrie*
(Dakar: Les Nouvelles éditions africaines, 1975), 203.
13. Ngal has researched the echoes that are produced for a "French student" between Césaire's texts and canonical texts. A system of correspondences is established
between Césaire, Rimbaud, Claudel, Saint-John Perse, Péguy, the surrealists, etc. . . .
Other essays, notably Jean Bernabé's "La Négritude césairienne et l'occident" in
Négritude africaine, négritude caraïbe: les littératures d'expression française, Acts of
the colloquium that took place at Paris-Nord University (Paris 13), 26 27 January 1973,
Centre d'études francophones (Paris: Editions de la Francité, 1973) seek to propose
"intertextual dialogues" between the works of Césaire, Corneille, and Giraudoux, for
example, as described in Bernadette Cailler's *Proposition poétique: une lecture de
l'oeuvre d'Aimé Césaire* (Paris, Québec: Naaman, 1976), 32. And in her chapter entitled
"Le Mot ou une écriture en situation," Cailler seeks in addition to define the *nature* of
the tie that links related texts. For her, the language of "Négritude poets" is proof of "an
intertextuality of particularly dense writing in which knowledge and refusal, abandon
and revolt are intimately intertwined" (ibid).

also the meeting between the writing of Césaire and that of Baudelaire. The episode puts into relation two black men but also two poets, two discourses. It also puts into relation the space-time of individuals and the space-time of writing. It enables us to witness the creation of the production of communities in formation, of the resulting conflicts, and of the manifold choices occasioned by these manifold meetings.

The streetcar scene is written around a Baudelairian reminiscence that abruptly becomes aware of being a quotation: not only is a "textual dialogue" established (Cailler, 32), but also the text catches itself in a blatant (and dangerous) use of "sources," "origins." This awareness is closely tied to the referential context of the scene and makes the Baudelairian reference coincide with a moment in which the poet confesses an (auto)betrayal. The progressive modification of this connection with the other's poetry becomes a political act; the poem masterfully demonstrates that intertextuality is not limited to a problem of literary form, but touches in addition a community much larger than the restricted circle of critics. The putting into relation of two complicitous or rival texts serves at the same time to create boundaries between communities of readers and to put these boundaries into question, to underscore the differences and similarities between the readers and characters of the *Notebook*, to create networks of belonging and exclusion in relation to which the poet (and the reading "I") must define their place, their nostalgia, their exile.

The work of putting into relation follows three stages that correspond to three successive references to the same poem by Baudelaire: "A comical and ugly nigger, with some women behind me sneering at him. / He was COMICAL AND UGLY, / COMICAL AND UGLY for sure." The repetition of the same adjectival phrase avoids obscuring the process of putting into relation, which would otherwise risk transforming the poem into a passive intertextual assimilation on the part of the black poet (recognizing the distinction Léopold Senghor established between "to assimilate" and "to be assimilated").

The first appearance of the phrase "comical and ugly" creates a simple and binary world in which the "grouchy nigger," grotesque and scorned, is contrasted with the sneering women with whom the poet identifies. At this point in the narrative, the narrator presents us with the "nigger" isolated from everyone else, and who no longer has anything in common with the assimilated poet, both supportive and an accomplice of the women, unaware of any tie he may have with the wretched character he curiously eyes. The tie between the poet and his race has been cut by the language he uses. The adjectives "comical and ugly," to which no punctuation marks draw our attention, at first infiltrate the poem without the narrator noticing that they are a "ready-made," part of the language and culture; the Baudelairian reference at first appears without any signs of quotation, without distance, irrevocably absorbed by the word that the poet thinks he is speaking, but that in fact speaks him. Part and parcel of the language called French, the reference could quite easily at this stage remain obscure, without requiring the poet here to claim that he has drawn his inspiration from the restricted community of "étudiants français plus ou moins cultivés" [more or less cultured French students][14] among whom he could feel at home. Readers will not suffer from a feeling of incompetence if they do not identify "comical and ugly" as a quotation. Some will probably have the intuition of an intertextual moment without the sense of the passage becoming irremediably obscure for all that if the vague memory does not become clearer. Every Francophone can be satisfied with understanding the expression which is, like the narrator's language, perfectly assimilated.

This reference, which is not necessarily one, demonstrates the theoretical possibility of cultural "assimilation" that certain researchers consider impossible,[15] but of course renders it extremely problematic; for how can one delight in this form of assimilation since the expression "comical and ugly" is used to oppress him whom I have just constructed as "other": the Black, the poor Black, he who from now on has nothing more in common with the poet, and who is treated as an object of curiosity and derision. By choosing these two adjectives, the "I" excludes himself from a whole group of wretched and grouchy "niggers" to which he absolutely refuses to belong. He has mastered the language of the colonizer sufficiently well to be able to consider his words an origin without quotation, a free message without ties. In contrast, for example, to the tradition of African-American slave narratives, whose authors often use the authority of a well-known or powerful white to support the truthfulness of their account, Césaire

14. Césaire himself describes himself at that time: "I was subjected to the same influences that all more or less cultured French students were subjected to at that time," quoted in Leiner, 8.

15. Albert Memmi, in *Portrait du colonisé* (Paris: Petite bibliothèque Payot, 1973), maintains on the contrary that assimilation is not only undesirable for obvious ideological reasons, but is also quite simply impossible because in reality, the colonizer does not want it at all. See the chapter entitled "Impossibilité de l'assimilation" (153–55).

does not need to cite Baudelaire to talk about a "comical and ugly nigger." But at the very moment at which he has the impression of possessing language, language possesses him since it forces him to convey the ideology of which it is the carrier. The more the poet appropriates this language, the more he makes it his own, the more quotation marks, that is, an awareness of distance, are absent, and the more he exiles himself from this people of grouchy niggers with whom he no longer recognizes the slightest affinity, the slightest resemblance. The first appearance of the reminiscence is probably accompanied by the same "exquisite delight" as the first departure for Paris—the poet undergoes an exile of which he is not conscious, his foreignness has become alienation. The sign of this alienation is a moment of the "verbal delirium" which Mudimbe discusses,[16] of the gap between ideology and the speaking subject which Glissant, Fanon[17] and Sartre denounce in their theoretical works. In "Black Orpheus," Sartre notes that school teaches the "Negro" not just the words "black" and "white," but rather the existence of a hierarchic coupling: "en le livrant au nègre, l'instituteur lui livre par surcroît cent habitudes de langage qui consacrent la priorité du blanc sur le noir" [in passing it to the Negro, the instructor gives him [her] in addition a hundred habits of language which consecrate the priority of white over black.][18] If a certain social stratum manages to achieve assimilation, it must have adopted "l'idéologie donnée avec l'enseignement. Elle deviendra vite le véhicule de la pensée officielle" [the ideology given with schooling. It will quickly become the vehicle of official thought] (Glissant, 70). Exile consists then in being from nowhere, in being only the "vehicle," the point of passage of a language, in losing oneself as Edouard Glissant claims:

> Comment ne pas voir qu'une communauté ainsi accoutumée à l'emploi des mots qui pour elle et si visiblement ne correspondent à aucune

16. See especially, *L'Odeur du père. Essai sur les limites de la science et de la vie en Afrique noire* (Paris: Présence africaine, 1982). In this essay, Mudimbe masterfully describes the delirium from which the discourse of the Occidental who attempts to describe the Other suffers, but also the delirium of the discourse of the African who talks about his/her own continent. The idea of a "separating distance" which would serve as a sign of the cultural gap within a discourse is to be related to Césaire's poem and to the poetic representation of the awareness of a textual putting into Relation.

17. The very first chapter of *Peau noire, masques blancs* is devoted to the relationship between the "Black and language." "To speak," writes Fanon, "is essentially to assume a culture, to bear the weight of a civilization" (13). The metaphor of the burden is remarkably significant in the context of Césaire's poem in which the Albatross tries in vain to take flight.

18. Jean-Paul Sartre, *Black Orpheus*, trans. S. W. Allen (Paris: Gallimard, 1969), 27.

réalité sinon projetée en phantasmes, peu à peu *se perd* dans un usage irréel, et par conséquent irresponsable des mots.

How can one not see that a community thus accustomed to using words which for it, only so obviously, correspond to no reality, if not one projected in fantasy, little by little loses itself in an unreal, and consequently irresponsible, usage of words. [Glissant, 123, My translation]

If the first appearance of the reminiscence is an integral part of the language of the poet and ideologically influences the rest of his text, the second stage of the work of "mise en Relation" is a *revelation* in the sense that photographers use the term: an image appears suddenly there where before nothing was visible. "COMICAL AND UGLY" stand out from here on in capital letters which do not explicitly acknowledge the status of quotation but graphically represent a moment of awareness; for us, the two adjectives are henceforth unavoidable, hypervisible, we can no longer ignore them. The two words demand our attention as though their enlargement corresponded to the moment at which they suddenly became audible for the poet as elements foreign to his own language.

The capital letters establish a distance, a difference between the one who blames the "grouchy nigger" and the speaking subject. From now on, the "I" will be forever distanced from the group with which he had been trying to identify. Not that the poet is seeking to refute responsibility for his judgment, but a foreign presence appears around which alliances will establish themselves.

By accentuating the reference invisible up till then, by graphically admitting that these two adjectives are out of the ordinary, the poet accomplishes a doubly subversive act; he voluntarily exiles himself from words which he had thought were his own and from the reassuring ideology which made of him an assimilated member of society. In representing, through his poetic language, a moment of awareness, in putting us in presence with the moment at which he realizes that he is quoting, he admits first that he was taken in by what he thought was his own language, he sets himself apart, on the outside, he makes Baudelaire, this canonized white poet, the origin of his discourse. The narrator discovers that he is alienated, that another speaks in his place. The textual "mise en Relation" "separates the poet from a universe that he erroneously thought was his."[19] And suddenly, the meaning of

19. Aliko Songolo, *Aimé Césaire, une poétique de la découverte* (Paris: L'Harmattan, 1985), 45.

the whole passage is altered, as if by magic: all at once, the meaning of the two adjectives is enriched and transformed, because the context has changed, and because the reference to "the Albatross" has modified the forces present. This passage of the poem seems to me to offer a remarkably economical representation of a moment of awareness, which, for Césaire, had perhaps lasted for years. The conclusions of the Négritude movement, notably the decision no longer to permit colonialist ideology to contaminate poetic language, the search for an authentic Black voice, are distilled here into a moment of revelation which can act as a founding myth. The Baudelairian intertext, even if it is perceived as a text testifying to colonial power, thus becomes liberating.

The nigger suddenly becomes a positive image, that of a free and majestic bird, misunderstood by the crewmen who "to pass the time" have exiled it far from the natural habitat to which it was marvelously adapted. The streetcar becomes similar to the "deck" of the ship, and suddenly appears as a last resort compared to the aerial space the albatross masters. A first connection becomes clear between the grouchy nigger and the poet: like him, the poet is an exiled "winged traveller" who has crossed the seas on the decks of boats of men. Without bringing in racial solidarity, which the colonial situation has perhaps irremediably destroyed or rendered impossible to define, the text forces the poet to perceive resemblance where before he had only wanted to see the incongruous presence of the comical and ugly Other. Departure, voyage, and winged traveller take on an entirely new meaning, painting a portrait in which the "I" is forced to recognize himself. In an interview with Daniel Maximin, Césaire described the *Notebook* as the "departure," "le grand coup d'aile, il y a Icare qui se met des ailes et qui part" [the great flapping of wings, Icarus is there putting on his wings and leaving.][20] Two identical images refer henceforth to the wretched Black and to the poet, the textual putting into relation that at first oppressed the unassimilated Black now turns ironically against the poet who sought to exile himself voluntarily. In spite of all the efforts of the assimilated narrator to distinguish himself, it becomes clear that he cannot ignore the fate that the "crewmen" thrust upon the albatross because he himself is part of the race of winged travellers. At present, two groups face each other, and it is impossible to ignore

20. Daniel Maximin, "Aimé Césaire: la poésie, parole essentielle" in *Présence Africaine* 126 (1983), 11.

that their relationship is marked by a violence before which the poet cannot remain neutral. It is clear that the two groups confront one another in a tragic struggle that cannot leave the poet (literally) in/different: he must resign himself to choosing his homeland, he must see himself as "albatross" or "member of the crew" and the choice is no longer so easy as when it was a question of allying himself with the "women" who made fun of the grouchy nigger, because the image has overturned the valorization. Paradoxically, in becoming aware of the reference, that is, of the fact that language exiles him, speaks in his place, the "I" also discovers that this same language forces him to make a choice he did not know existed. The women with whom he had exchanged a great complicitous smile are no longer a group whose privileges it is flattering to share; they are transformed into contemptible and hateful "members of the crew."

Conversely, the Antillean context enriches the reading of Baudelaire's poem with new historical references that give a more tragic meaning to the presence of the sailors. In proposing to the reader the association between the albatross and the nigger "finished off by poverty," the text invites a comparison between the generic ship and the slave ships that haunt Césaire's poetry: "le navire lustral [qui s'avance] impavide sur les eaux écroulées" [the lustral ship [advancing] fearlessly on the crumbling water] (*Collected Poetry*, 81) is also the reminder of the first voyage, the first exile, the first wrenching away: "le négrier craque de toute part . . . Son ventre se convulse et résonne . . . L'affreux ténia de sa cargaison ronge les boyaux fétides de l'étrange nourisson des mers!" [the slave ship cracks everywhere . . . its belly convulses and resounds. . . . The ghastly tapeworm of its cargo gnaws the fetid guts of the strange suckling of the sea!] (*Collected Poetry*, 79). Thus for a second time the poet crosses the sea, and the "pastime" of the crew members, like the "sneering" of the women and the poet, appear to be criminal violence. The hidden story of the first exile returns to haunt the text. The awareness of the reference thus has the consequence of forcing the narrator to accept that his identification with the women makes him guilty of an ignoble violence towards this "winged traveller" who, like him, has crossed the sea. The textual putting into relation forces him to recognize his own situation as an exile and the seriousness of the choice he makes in placing himself among the laughers.

All the more so since his laugh is marked by an enormous irony, an irony that the third repetition of "COMICAL AND UGLY" brings sharply into evidence: the third stage of textual "mise en relation" is no longer simply a more or less invisible reminiscence (an unconscious exile) or an oppressive reference (an unhappy exile), but the discovery of new alliances, of new relations of force, of new readings. In taking up for the third time the expression "comical and ugly," the text completely isolates it from the rest of the poem: "COMICAL AND UGLY for sure." Placed in apposition, without a noun, without a verb, the two adjectives seem apprehended by a narrative moment whose lucidity becomes superiority. The "for sure" can be read as an ironic illumination, the moment when the poet abruptly discovers another meaning in the parallel between the Albatross and the grouchy nigger.

Because not only does the image of the Albatross oppressed by the members of the crew underscore the alienation of the narrator who thought he would easily be able to side with the sailors, but also Baudelaire's poem enables us to push the parallel even further; the link between this wretched Black and the "I" becomes abruptly clearer, more complex, if we understand that the "grouchy nigger albatross" is also the symbol of the Poet. This "winged traveller" "tied to the deck" is not simply the exile who has lost his native land—he is also the narrator himself, insofar as he calls himself a poet. Therefore, it is not only because he makes himself the accomplice of the colonizers that the narrator may regret his laugh, but also because without knowing it, he has been making fun of himself. It is an image of himself that the narrator-Poet suppresses, without knowing that he has made himself both henchman and victim, again the Baudelairian "héauton-timoroumenos." He was "sneering" at himself. All his superiority caves in here, all alliances between "the assimilated," between "intellectuals," are ferociously denounced as illusory. In refusing to face his "désolidarisation," the poet is reduced to oppressing himself, not as a poor and ignorant man, not even as a Black, but as a Poet. The textual dialogue thus forces him to recognize that when he seeks to withdraw from class and racial solidarity (there is nothing in common between a "cultivated French student" and a "nigger finished off by poverty"), he repudiates in fact the Poet, "this monarch of the clouds." The textual putting into Relation reveals to him the extent of what Glissant calls "derision." The Antillean poet is "Exilé ou malade. Malade de cette absence dont le signe est si intarissable à établir: un palmarès de la dérision." [Exiled or sick. Sick because of this absence whose sign is so inexhaustible to establish: a prize list of derision] (Glissant, 119.)

The "I" who just discovered that he himself was guilty of oppressing the Other by the intermediary of a reference, was in fact falling into a paradoxical trap; ironically, the Baudelairian adjectives he used to poke fun at the "comical and ugly nigger" are in fact taken from a poem that, at the outset, pleaded in favor of the damned Poet, misunderstood by the crowd.

The reference to the poem by Baudelaire is therefore not necessarily a reactionary gesture forcing the poet to side with the colonizer. Certainly there is danger in speaking the language of the other, in assimilating it without questioning the quality of the relation uniting the "I" with the groups that form around him when he speaks French. Language may become the place of voluntary or unconscious exile, the place from which the poet renounces his own because he has transformed the world into violent binaries where only the oppressed, "winged travellers," and the oppressors, "members of the crew," any longer exist. But this passage illustrates the moment at which thought understands that there is a future far from this duality that resembles, to the point that it is difficult to tell them apart, the colonial situation as described by Fanon: a manicheanism without hope. The narrator need not choose between two equally detestable alternatives, cowardice or poverty, and will thus never be reduced to producing this parody of literature against which the journal *Tropiques* had declared war early in the century: "Littérature de hamac, littérature de sucre et de vanille. Tourisme littéraire. Guide bleu et CGT. Poésie, non pas" [Hammock literature, literature of sugar and vanilla. Tourist literature. Blue Guide and CGT. Poetry, not at all.][21]

The danger here would be what Glissant calls "mimetic annihilation" (Glissant, 64), which would be the pure and simple disappearance of a "homeland" other than Occidental culture and values. To the contrary, the inevitable intertextuality becomes textual "Entrée en Relation" (Glissant, 64), and the dialogue established little by little between the discourse of the "I" and the discourse of others becomes in itself a land that here makes the Poet a perpetual exile, but an exile conscious of his condition, capable of solidarity towards those whom he resembles. Of course this abstract "homeland" does not at all solve the problems confronting Antillean poets, nor does it prevent the poet from feeling exiled from his people of prosaic sailors or his position from making him suspect (rightly or wrongly) of an unbearable elitism.

---

21. Suzanne Césaire, "Misères d'une poésie: John-Antoine Nau" in *Tropiques* 1, 4.4 (January 1942), 50.

But at least this work of textual putting into relation offers proof that the poet can, in spite of the danger of assimilation, speak his own language, his own French. Sartre, describing the black/white hierarchy that forces the black poet to condemn himself, writes in "Black Orpheus":

> Dès qu'il ouvre la bouche, il s'accuse, à moins qu'il ne s'acharne à renverser la hiérachie. Et s'il la renverse en français, il poétise déjà: imagine-t-on l'étrange saveur qu'auraient pour nous des locutions comme "la noirceur de l'innocence" ou "les ténèbres de la vertu"?

> Let him open his mouth and he condemns himself, except insomuch as he sets himself to destroy the hierarchy. And if he destroys it in French, he poetizes already; let one imagine the strange savor which terms such as "the blackness of innocence" or the "shadows of virtue" would have for us. [Sartre, 27]

By putting his poetic word and language into Relation, Césaire goes even further than what Sartre proposed: he is not happy simply to invert the valorized metaphors separating whites and blacks, he calls into question the systems of inclusion and exclusion that make of some either exiles or full citizens. The narrator of the *Notebook* discovers the power of alternating between his language and that of the other. This contact obviously necessitates a perpetual wandering, but also provides the means of becoming aware of exile and of perceiving its tragedy. To claim the homeland of the "members of the crew" is quickly an untenable situation, and would also be an inhuman price to pay for the end of exile (and the scene reminds us that no one is immune from these moments of "cowardice"). This passage from the *Notebook* may thus be read as an allegory of the difficult process of recognizing the Negritude that presides over the creation of the text in its entirety; it is at once a warning against the deceitful "cowardice" constantly lying in wait for the narrator but also the discovery of the possibility of choice, of what Ronnie Scharfman calls his "engagement."[22] Textual relationality can be a strategy at the service of the "grouchy nigger" and grant him the power that language would like to

---

22. See Ronnie Scharfman's *"Engagement" and the Language of the Subject in the Poetry of Aimé Césaire* (Gainesville: University of Florida Press, 1987). The conclusion of this study stresses the multiplicity of positions that what the author calls "the subject" can occupy in Césaire's works: "poet, victim, slave, universe, spokesman, nigger, island. The other can be language, oppressor, master, lover, people, poem, country" (12).

take away from him. Despite the dangers of seeing oneself transformed into a passive vehicle of official ideology, "Un homme qui possède le langage possède par contrecoup le monde exprimé et impliqué par ce langage. On voit où nous voulons en venir: il y a dans la possession du langage une extraordinaire puissance" [A man who possesses language possesses as an indirect consequence the world expressed and implied by this language. My point may already be seen: there is extraordinary power in the possession of language] (Fanon, 14). In ascertaining the role that Baudelaire's language plays in his own poem, the narrator of the *Notebook* ran the risk of discovering that he has perhaps no other homeland than Relation, that is, an exile, that he remains a "winged traveller" incapable of walking. Certainly, the "return" to the "native land" is an indispensable step that redeems the temptation of "sneering." The "j'ai longtemps erré et je reviens vers la hideur désertée de vos plaies" [I have wandered for a long time and am returning towards the deserted hideousness of your wounds] (*Collected Poetry*, 44), keeps alive the hope that solidarity towards the grouchy nigger is possible in the name of a homeland of suffering and oppression. But the moments of textual putting into relation remind the poet that his words express above all this multiple I to which the French language had denied him access. In an interview with Jacqueline Leiner, Césaire tries to define his work as a poet:

> mon effort a été *d'infléchir* le français, de le transformer pour exprimer disons: "ce moi, ce moi-nègre, ce moi-créole, ce moi martiniquais, ce moi-antillais". C'est pour cela que je me suis plus intéressé à la poésie qu'à la prose et ce *dans la mesure ou c'est le poète qui fait son language.*

> My effort has been to *bend* French, to transform it so that we can say: "this I, this Black I, this Creole I, this Martinican I, this Antillean I." That is why I was more interested in poetry than in prose, *to the extent that the poet creates his own language.* [Leiner, XIV]

The poet finds a homeland only in the acceptance of his own exile. He is Black, Creole, Martinican, Antillean, he is elsewhere, forever.

Partir
Comme il y a des hommes-hyènes et des hommes-panthères, je serais
un homme-juif,
un homme-cafre
un homme-hindou-de-Calcutta
un-homme-de-Harlem-qui-ne-vote-pas

To go away.
As there are hyena-men, and panther-men,
I would be a jew-man
a Kaffir-man
a Hindu-man-from-Calcutta
a Harlem-man-who-doesn't-vote

[*Collected Poetry*, 43]

"Il y a encore une mer à traverser / oh encore une mer à traverser" [There still remains one sea to cross / oh still one sea to cross] (*Collected Poetry*, 81), he writes at the end of the *Notebook*. And his complaint seems to have rendered possible (and just as problematic) the conclusion of Maryse Condé, who at the end of her "Notes on a Return to the Native Land" asked a question without answer:

> Etre Antillais, finalement, je ne sais toujours pas très bien ce que cela veut dire! Est-ce qu'un écrivain doit avoir un pays natal? Est-ce qu'un écrivain doit avoir une identité définie? Est-ce qu'un écrivain ne pourrait pas être constamment errant, constamment à la recherche d'autres hommes? Est-ce que ce qui appartient à l'écrivain, ce n'est pas seulement la littérature, c'est-à-dire quelque chose qui n'a pas de frontières?

> To be Antillean, finally, I still don't quite know what that means! Does a writer have to have a native land? Does a writer have to have a defined identity? Couldn't a writer constantly be wandering, constantly searching for other men? Is that which belongs to a writer not something more than literature, that is, something without boundaries?

[Condé, 23]

—Translated by Robert Postawsko

ELISABETH MUDIMBE-BOYI

The Poetics of Exile and Errancy in *Le Baobab fou* by Ken Bugul and *Ti Jean L'Horizon* by Simone Schwarz-Bart[1]

> First the slave trade: being snatched away from our original matrix. The journey that has fixed in us the unceasing tug of Africa against which we must paradoxically struggle today in order to take root in our rightful land. The motherland is also for us the inaccessible land.
> —Edouard Glissant, *Caribbean Discourse*

> It may be that we shall be captured at the end of our itinerary, vanquished by our adventure itself. It suddenly occurs to us that, all along our road, we have not ceased to metamorphose ourselves, and we see ourselves as other than we were.
> —Hamidou Kane, *Ambiguous Adventure*

I

Journey and displacement are common motifs in the Francophone novel of Africa and the French Caribbean, and sum up the life experience of many a character. Journey embodies the quest of colonial and postcolonial subjects caught in epistemological ruptures and entangled in multicultural contexts. Whether alienated from their indigenous cultures or exiled from the hegemonic other's territory, they are in search of roots and ground, of new cultural and ethnic spaces in which to construct new identities for themselves. Their experience of exile may be geographical, psychological, cultural, or racial.

1. I would like to thank Robin Smith for her editorial assistance in transforming my Frenchlike style into a more readable English. Thank you also to the editors of the volume for their comments and suggestions.

Ken Bugul, *Le Baobab fou* (Dakar: Nouvelles Editions africaines, 1982). The English translation came out after this article was already completed. Trans. Marjolyn de Jaeger, *The Abandoned Baobab* (New York: Lawrence Hill Books, 1991). In reference to Schwarz-Bart's work, in the text I use the original French title: *Ti Jean L'Horizon* (Paris: Seuil, 1979). However, I will always refer to the English translation by Barbara Bray, *Between Two Worlds* (New York: Harper and Row, 1981). In references to other works, I refer to English translations where available; otherwise I offer my own translation.

YFS 83, *Post/Colonial Conditions*, ed. Lionnet & Scharfman, © 1993 by Yale University.

Ken Bugul is from Senegal and *Le Baobab fou* is her first and only published work. The book is about her geographical displacement, coupled with an intellectual and psychological journey from her native village to the urban environment in order to attend the Western school; from Africa to Europe in order to complete her higher education; a journey that finally culminates in the return to her native village. Simone Schwarz-Bart, without being the heroine of her book *Ti Jean L'Horizon*, has also lived a life of travel and displacements that brought her from her native Guadeloupe to Europe, from Europe to Africa and back to the homeland of Guadeloupe where she is living today. Both Bugul and Schwarz-Bart have been, since their childhood, at the confluence of different cultures, immersed in a context of multiculturalism and multilinguism. Their works are thus nurtured by their own experience and that of their society.

From a literary viewpoint, a similar thematic enables us to bring together the two writers. They both center their narratives on journey, exile, and errancy; memory, past and present. Finally, their two characters, Ken Bugul and Ti Jean L'Horizon, hold in common a virtual separation from their parents at an early age. Ti Jean was born and lived with his mother among the people of "Down Below," while his father had stayed "Up Above." In Ken Bugul's case, her mother left her after divorcing her father.

Similar formal structures also shape both *Le Baobab fou* and Schwarz-Bart's other novel, *Pluie et Vent sur Télumée Miracle*. In the first part of *Le Baobab*, "Préhistoire de Ken", the first-person narrator presents the history of her family at the time of their emigration from the North and their settlement at the place where the baobab tree will grow and she will be born. The second part, "Histoire de ma vie", is Ken's life story from childhood to her adolescent years. *Pluie et Vent* starts with "Présentation des miens" in which the narrating "I," Télumée, introduces the genealogy of her ancestry, all the way back to her great-grandmother, the founding mother on Caribbean soil of the family of the Lougandor women. Then follows "Histoire de ma vie", an account of the narrator's life from childhood to old age.[2] *Ti Jean*, al-

---

2. For a detailed discussion, see Elisabeth Mudimbe-Boyi, "Ken Bugul ou à la recherche de la mère perdue" paper presented at the African Literature Association's annual conference, Dakar, March 1988: to be published in English in Anne Adams, ed., *Fifty African and Caribbean Women Writers* (Westport, Conn.: Greenwood Press, forthcoming) and *"Pluie et Vent sur Télumée Miracle* de Simone Schwarz-Bart: mémoire du temps et prise de parole" in Ginette Adamson and Eunice Myers, ed., *Continental, Latin American, and Francophone Women Writers*, Vol 2. (University Press of America, 1990) 155–64.

though based on a different structure, presents a similar project since Ti Jean will embark on a journey to Africa in search of the birthplace of his father, the maroon Wandemba, and of his ancestor Obe, also a maroon. He too, like Schwarz-Bart and Bugul, is looking for a genealogy.

In *Lettres parisiennes*, the Franco-Algerian[3] writer Leïla Sebbar, talking about her relationship to writing, states forcefully:

> Et puis, pour moi la fiction c'est la suture qui masque la blessure, l'écart entre les deux rives. Je suis là, à la croisée, enfin sereine, à ma place, en somme, puisque je suis une croisée qui cherche une filiation et qui écrit dans une lignée, toujours la même, reliée à l'Histoire, à la mémoire, à l'identité, à la tradition et à la transmission, je veux dire à la recherche d'une ascendance et d'une descendance, d'une place dans l'histoire d'une communauté, d'un peuple, du regard de l'Histoire et de l'univers. C'est dans la fiction que je me sens sujet libre (de père, de mère, de clan, de dogmes . . .) et forte de la charge de l'exil. [138]

> And then, for me fiction is the stitch that covers the wound, the gulf between two shores. Here I am, at the crossroads, finally serene, at the proper place in fact since I am a mixed-race person seeking a filiation, and writing within a lineage, always the same one, connected to History, to memory, to identity, to tradition and its transmission. I mean, I am in search of an ascendance and a descendance, of a position in the history of a family, a community, a people, in relation to History and the universe. It is within fiction that I feel like a free subject (free of father, mother, clan, dogmas . . .), strengthened by the burden brought by exile.[4]

In this passage, Sebbar summarizes the problematics of identity in regard to journey and exile, and raises the question of historical continuity and discontinuity, the dialectical relationship between collective history and individual history. The collective history is embodied in binaries such as lineage and tradition, family and community, whereas individual memory, identity, and positionality connect the writer with a collective history and insert him/her into a historical continuity. If indeed Sebbar has found her place of anchorage through

3. I deliberately chose this identity in order to emphasize Sebbar's plural identity. Sebbar is Franco-Algerian, but not Beur, although she writes about the Beurs. See Michel Laronde, "La Mouvance beure," *The French Review*, 61:5 (April 1988): 689. See also Alec Hargreaves, *Voices from the North African Community in France: Immigration and Identity in French Beur Fiction* (Oxford: Berg Publishers, 1991).

4. Leïla Sebbar and Nancy Huston, *Lettres parisiennes: autopsie de l'exil* (Paris: Bernard Barrault, 1986). My translation.

writing fiction, her characters are engaged in a search for place: such is
the case with Shérazade in *Shérazade, brune, frisée, les yeux verts, Les
Carnets de Shérazade,* and *Le Fou de Shérazade* as well as with Dalila
in *Fatima ou les Algériennes au Square.*[5] Similar characters, such as
Ken and Ti Jean L'Horizon, are numerous in the Francophone novels
from Africa and the Caribbean. Their journey and their quest translate
what Edouard Glissant in *Caribbean Discourse* calls a "longing for
history" (79, 83).[6]

Sebbar's statement also brings about the examination of journey or
errancy, exile and identity in relation to culture and society, time and
space. In deconstructing Sebbar's quotation, one finds encoded the four
functions assigned to language by Henri Gobard, and which Gilles
Deleuze and Félix Guattari use in their *Kafka*[7] to analyze the linguistic
situation of Jews in Prague in Kafka's work: the vernacular, the vehicular, the referential, and the mythic. This typology is applicable here to
the language (*langage*) of the narrative rather than to language (*langue*)
itself. It is of interest to the examination of the poetics of exile and
errancy in so far as the categories of time and space are concerned in
relation to geography (exile, errancy), history, and memory. In effect,
the vernacular function refers to an *"ici"* [here], the vehicular to *"par-
tout"* [everywhere], the referential to a *"là-bas"* [over there], and the
mythic to an *"au-delà"* [beyond] (23). Each function is linked to a
sphere of life, respectively the maternal, the urban, the worldly or the
public, and the spiritual or the religious (23). In his glossary of contemporary criticism, Marc Angenot[8] presents the four functions and their
categories more clearly with a diagram (33) reproduced below (diagram 1).[9]

5. Leïla Sebbar, *Shérazade, brune, frisée, les yeux verts* (Paris: Stock, 1982); *Les
Carnets de Shérazade* (Paris: Stock, 1985); *Le Fou de Shérazade* (Paris: Stock, 1991);
and *Fatima ou les Algériennes au Square* (Paris: Stock, 1981).

6. Edouard Glissant, *Le Discours antillais* (Paris: Seuil, 1981). English translation
by Michael Dash, *Caribbean Discourse,* (Charlottesville: University of Virginia Press,
Caraf Books, 1989).

7. Gilles Deleuze and Félix Guattari, *Kafka: Pour une littérature mineure* (Paris: Les
Editions de Minuit, 1975). Translated into English by Dana Polan, *Kafka: Toward a
Minor Literature* (Minneapolis: University of Minnesota Press, 1986. Theory and Histo-
ry of Literature, Vol. 30).

8. Marc Angenot, *Glossaire pratique de la critique contemporaine* (Québec: Hur-
tebise HMH, 1979).

9. I focus on the vernacular, the referential, and the mythical. For the linguistic
relationship between the vernacular and the vehicular, see the works of Créolistes or
Créolophones such as Jean Bernabé (for example, his *Fondal Natal. Grammaire*

Diagram 1: ANGENOT

function	space	time	language (langue)
vernacular	*ici* [here]	*maintenant* [now]	maternal
vehicular	*partout* [everywhere]	*plus tard* [later]	urban
referential	*là-bas* [over there]	*jadis* [long ago]	national
mythical	*au-delà* [beyond]	*toujours* [always]	sacred

Based on Angenot's diagram, we can construct other diagrams that represent and compare Bugul's and Ti Jean's itineraries and experiences of exile and errancy (diagrams 2, 3, and 4): from "here" to "over there"; from "over there" to "here." In Angenot's diagram, the vernacular represents for the characters what Glissant calls *"pays réel"* [*real land*] and the referential "over there," the *"pays rêvé"* [dreamland],[10] as shown in diagram 2:

Diagram 2: EXILE

function	space			time	language
vernacular	here: real land	Ti Jean: Guadeloupe	Bugul: Africa	now	maternal
vehicular	everywhere	↓	↓	later	urban
referential	over there: dreamland	Africa	the Gauls	long ago	national
mythical	beyond: the Ancestors	↓ Africans	↓ the Gauls	always	sacred

While for Ti Jean, born in the new land into which his African father was transplanted, African space represents the referential and the

---

basilectale approchée des créoles guadeloupéens et martiniquais, 3 vols. [Paris: L'Harmattan, 1983]) and his research group the GEREC; Maximilien Laroche, *Littérature haïtienne. Identité, langue, réalité* (Ottawa: Editions Leméac, 1981) 57–122. For Africa, see Collectif, *Les Relations entre les langues négro-africaines et la langue française* (Paris: CILF-AUPELF, 1977); Raymond Relouzat, *Le Référent ethnoculturel dans le conte créole* (Paris: L'Harmattan/Presses Universitaires Créoles, 1989).

10. Edouard Glissant, *Pays rêvé, pays réel* (Paris: Seuil, 1985): title of a collection of poems in which the poet evokes Africa, the land of origins or the "land of before" (*pays d'avant*) as the "dreamland" (*pays rêvé*), and the Caribbean country as the "real land" (*pays réel*).

mythical, for Bugul, culturally alienated and assimilated through colonization, the country of the Gauls, her so-called ancestors, is the object of her aspiration and longing.

II

> Me too. The routine "our ancestors the Gauls" was pulled on me. But I was born in Algeria, and my ancestors lived in Spain, Morocco, Austria, Hungary, Czechoslovakia, Germany; my brothers by birth are Arab. So where are we in history? (...) What is my name? I want to change life. Who is this "I"? Where is my place? (...) Which language is mine? French? German? Arabic?[11]
>
> —Hélène Cixous, La Jeune née

The referential and the mythical functions allegorize the quest for the origins and for an ascendance, and thus establish a poetics of exile and errancy. The characters' psychological, intellectual, and geographical journeys, their oscillation between the Imaginary and the Symbolic[12] translate a desire for "inspiring influences,"[13] and a desire to inscribe themselves in a historical filiation in the hope of putting an end to their cultural nomadism and exile. Their journeys are thus a search for genealogy, history, and territorialization.

Both Ken and Ti Jean are wandering heroes: Ken moves from the village to the city, from Africa to the West, and Ti Jean departs his native Guadeloupe for Africa. If indeed expatriation constitutes a

11. Hélène Cixous and Catherine Clément, La Jeune née (Paris: UGE, 1975). English translation by Betsy Wing, The Newly Born Woman (Minneapolis: University of Minnesota Press, 1986) [Theory and History of Literature, vol. 24], 71.

12. Imaginary and Symbolic refer here to Lacan's dual relationship: mother-child for the Imaginary (Africa, as the mother, is the symbolic object of desire) versus the Symbolic, or the cultural order of the father (the colonial order). See Jacques Lacan, Séminaire I: Les Ecrits techniques de Freud (Paris: Seuil, 1975); Séminaire 2: Le Moi dans la théorie de Freud et dans la technique de la psychanalyse (Paris: Seuil, 1975).

13. In Poetry and Repression (New Haven: Yale University Press, 1976), Harold Bloom's "anxiety of influence" translates a revolt, a desire to distance and emancipate oneself from one's literary fathers. In his discussion of Black women's writing, Michael Awkward substitutes for "anxiety of influence" the term "inspiring influences." These terms refer to the anxiety of Black women writers to establish a connection with the women writers who precede them. See Inspiring Influences: Tradition, Revision, and Afro-American Women's Novels (New York: Columbia University Press, 1989), 8. See also Mircea Eliade, La Nostalgie des origines (Paris: Gallimard, 1971).

source of anxiety and questioning, it appears that an internal exile, thus an exclusion, intensifies anxiety and loneliness. In going to the French school Bugul is severed from her mother, and henceforth exiled from the world of childhood. Her years of schooling disconnect her from the indigenous culture, and, on the other hand, from her kin: they do not understand her commitment to the new school and nobody is interested in her good grades (130). Solitude and books populated with images and representations of a foreign culture become her companions, her refuge, her locus of identification. During her years in Europe, Bugul also lives in exile from within, alienated from her African fellows and alien to the milieu in which she moves. She soon realizes that contrary to what she had been taught and had internalized, the Gauls were not her ancestors. As for Ti Jean, once he reaches Africa, the land of the Ancestors, he experiences a powerful rejection by those very people he thought he belonged to. Instead of being welcomed, he is called "foreigner"[14] and summoned only to be sent away:

"Who are you and what do you hope to find among us? . . . Go back to your own people."

"Am I not among my people?"

"Among your own people? No. For us you are like the animals one sees sometimes in the bush, for which there is no name. For us your language is like the night, for us your words are like the hooting of an owl in the night. Listen, young man . . . We wish not for your death but for your life, and that is why we say to you again: Go. Go back to your own people." [134–35]

The dialectic of rejection and belonging thus plays an important role in Bugul's and Ti Jean's exile and errancy. In their respective errancies, Bugul, who is compared to a "lost lamb," and Ti Jean, who is compared to someone "shipwrecked without a compass," will both undergo other journeys of discovery and self-discovery. Bugul's frenzied new life in the West is a brutal initiation into the underground world of LSD trips and hard drugs, alcohol and prostitution, which splits her personality in making her play the role of a sought-after black

14. Juletane, the West Indian woman protagonist-narrator of *Juletane*, undergoes a similar rejection when she goes to live in West Africa with her African husband. She is called "toubabesse," meaning "white woman." See Myriam Warner-Vieyra, *Juletane* (Paris: Présence Africaine, 1982), 79. In much the same way, Zeïda, a young woman born of Moroccan parents who are immigrants in Belgium, longs for "là-bas," for Morocco, her homeland. But once she gets there, she is also rejected, called a "touriste," a "petite fille d'Europe" and is advised to return to Europe. See Leïla Houari, *Zeïda de nulle part* (Paris: L'Harmattan, 1985), 75.

beauty while hiding profound distress, desperately seeking for "the bond." If Ti Jean's itinerary follows a rather linear path, Bugul's psychological chaos is inscribed in the progressive-regressive movement of the narrative. The wandering back and forth in time here translates a destabilization of time that goes hand in hand with a destabilization of the character's identity. Ti Jean, in his turn, enters the underground world in the Kingdom of the Shades and in the Kingdom of the Dead, searching for a road to bring him back to Guadeloupe. He too experiences a splitting of his personality and meets characters who seem to be double, for the women in his life are beyond reach: at times his wife, the African Onjali, seems to be his Guadeloupean wife Egea. Similarly, his lover in the Kingdom of the Dead constantly metamorphoses herself from an ugly, dirty, old woman into a young, very beautiful and passionate lover. Ti Jean himself fluctuates in an indeterminacy of identity, embedded in the uncertainty of his status: living or dead person, human or bird, African or Caribbean.

The two protagonists' underground journeys, in both the literal and metaphorical senses, represent a period of trials and disturbances. As in myths and tales, the underground journey signifies here a symbolic death[15] from which they will rise with a new awareness: Gauls were not Bugul's ancestors and Ti Jean did not belong to the Ba'Sonanqué's people. As a result, they will disconnect themselves from the "pays rêvé" and start looking at the "pays réel". Ti Jean's metamorphosis equals Bugul's progressive-regressive development. For both, the oscillatory movement of wandering to and fro, which constructs and deconstructs their identities, does reflect a wrestling for stabilization and territorialization. In this process of self-discovery, awareness generates a discourse of identity and constitutes itself as a revelation about the ancestors, the origins, the filiation.

A poetics of exile and errancy also emerges from the formal and textual structure of the narratives and their development. *Ti Jean L'Horizon*, like *Pluie et Vent*, is at once folktale, epic, myth, as well as fictional narrative. *Ti Jean* belongs to a cycle of tales popular in the Caribbean[16] and espouses the circular structure of many traditional

15. Bugul and Ti Jean are bildungsroman characters. Their spiritual and geographical itineraries espouse Mircea Eliade's initiation process through which the individual emerges born again. See *Rites and Symbols of Initiation. The Mysteries of Birth and Rebirth* (New York: Harper and Row, 1958), x, xii, 3.

16. See Bernadette Cailler, "*Ti Jean L'Horizon* de Simone Schwarz-Bart, ou la leçon du Royaume des Morts" *Stanford French Review* 6 (1982): 263–97.

initiation tales: separation and departure, journey and trials, return. Journey brings the hero across time and beyond space into an underground world. Like mythical heroes, Ti Jean's birth is extra-ordinary: he was born from an incestuous relationship between his mother Awa-Eloise and his father Wandemba, who himself fathered Ti Jean's mother.

The narrative is enfolded in the traditional genres of oral literature which thus constitutes the matrix of the written text. Moreover, the textual indeterminacy, and the destabilization of genres reproduce the character's indeterminacy and instability of identity. *Le Baobab fou*, although not drawn from the reservoir of oral literature as is the case for *Ti Jean L'Horizon*, nevertheless espouses the form and the resonance of a story being told. Bugul's text is at times very emotional, and free from abstractions or theorizations. As a speaking subject and master of her discourse, Bugul speaks in the language of everyday life. What might be considered stylistic weakness is precisely what renders the immediacy and the naturalness of the spoken and construes the narrator as a dialogic voice, in communication with an anonymous interlocutor: the blank page, or a sympathetic future reader.

III

> Thus said the Ancients years ago, before that batch of creatures who know "neither high nor low, center nor source": So they called us, the Younger generation. And they would add, half sad, half mocking, "But what you chase after, on this forsaken island, is but the shade of the clouds, while your own you consign to oblivion." But I do not say, no, I do not say they were right.
> —Simone Schwarz-Bart, *Between Two Worlds*

The mythical dimension in *Le Baobab fou* and *Ti Jean L'Horizon* calls for a discussion of the question of memory and remembrance and its results: the reconstitution of the past and the appropriation of History. For most displaced and uprooted communities there is an urgent need, "a longing for history," to quote Glissant, which emerges from the oblivion of a *"là-bas"* buried under the layer of a new memory and an Other's history: the official written one. The people of "Down Below," Wandemba reminds Ti Jean l'Horizon, have "a short memory." Talking in a proverbial manner, Wandemba asserts that "of all the birds in the world they are the only ones who have forgotten their nest" (52). They do not remember things that are not recorded in books, such as the story of Obe, the maroon ancestor.[17] When told about past events and heroes from before abolition, they could not hide their skepticism and they

> laughed, a strange shrill little laugh, and said that these things were never of such great importance—they couldn't be, for where were the books they were written down in? Some of the villagers even cast doubt on the truth of the stories. [8]

Thus, knowing what had happened before and what had existed before, becomes itself a necessity for Ti Jean l'Horizon: his journey to Africa, the land of the ancestor, is meant to be a quest for the origins and a reconstruction of past history in order to bridge the gap between past and present, and to overcome the historical discontinuity introduced by the Middle Passage. When he lands on the African shores, the first story *told* to l'Horizon is from Maiari, a story of the origins and the ancient times: "Once upon a time, in a far, far country long years away from here on foot, there was . . . " (124). In the same way in *Pluie et Vent*, Télumée's grandmother reenacts the past in also *telling* her an aetiological tale (77).

In the progressive-regressive development of her narrative, Bugul proceeds to uncover the layers of cultural amnesia that had led her to embrace a false ancestry, and she dis-covers Africa, which becomes her reference point. But Bugul's Africa is one reconstructed from her childhood memories, during her agonizing days of exile in the West. As for Ti Jean, the Africa he is looking for is the one framed and enshrined in his father's memory and transmitted as such to his son. For both Ti Jean (46, 116) and Bugul (165), Africa emerges as a fixed, immutable, and unchanged image, as represented in picture books, postcards, and publicity pamphlets. For Bugul, alone, depressed, and disillusioned with her integration into the West, Africa as an "over there" has taken on an idyllic quality: it is the land where "life is pure" (121), the land of "poetry and rites" (143), where "everyone is integrated, concerned, surrounded" (87). The people in this land, and the ancestors, are im-

---

17. See Edouard Glissant, *Mahagony* (Paris: Seuil, 1987). In this novel, Glissant revisits a question previously addressed in *Le Quatrième Siècle* (Paris: Seuil, 1964), the question of oral history and the relationship between the written and the oral.

bued with a mystical presence, and cast in the mythical, such as the immoral Ancestor father who led the clan from the North to the new place: he was five centuries old (21). In Bugul's new awareness, Africa has thus become a mythical and idealized place.

The referential function points to an "over there," and thus actualizes an appropriation not only of history but also of writing. For centuries the Western tradition has linked History with writing. Michel de Certeau reflects on the tradition very clearly represented in the reproduction on the frontispiece of the 1724 edition of Lafitau's book *Moeurs des sauvages américains comparés aux moeurs des premiers temps:*[18] "To write is to make History" (51). If this is indeed so, then the narratives of Bugul and Ti Jean subvert the order of succession of History and writing. Ti Jean's ancestral history has been *told* to him, and Bugul is *telling* her story through the dialogic voice of a first-person narrative. The medium of transmission is clearly an oral one. The stories told here exist before being written and constitute History. They reenact the past of Bugul's and Ti Jean's ancestors.[19] Translated into a written medium, the nonofficial, marginal, oral history becomes the center of the narrative, and thus subverts the official function of writing.

In actuality, Ti Jean l'Horizon's story, although constructed as a third-person narrative, is transformed into a first-person narrative: the story of l'Horizon we read is in fact his own story as he is *telling* it to Old Eusebius, and it constitutes the material for the making of the novel itself.

> After that the mesmerizer's eye suddenly lost its gleam and Ti Jean went on, unreeling his little story without haste, as he had done before to the girl with the duck's beak, and as she herself had done to begin with, detaching each word one by one like grapes until her bunch of woes was completely exhausted. Eusebius just nodded his head gravely as if he had known all this for a long time, and was hearing of a country where he had lived for many years. Neither the fall into Africa nor the meeting with the boy with rings in his hair made his eyes light up again, and Ti Jean felt like a schoolboy being examined by an elderly teacher

18. See Michel de Certeau, "Writing vs. Time: History and Anthropology in the Works of Lafitau," *Yale French Studies* 59: 37–64; also *L'Ecriture de l'Histoire* (Paris: Gallimard, 1978). Frederich Hegel, *Lectures on the Philosophy of World History* (London: Cambridge University Press, 1973).

19. Jan Vansina, *Oral Tradition as History* (Madison: University of Wisconsin Press, 1985).

who knew much more than he did himself. . . . He passed swiftly over what happened to Wandemba, and was preparing to gallop straight on, without any twirls or flourishes, when something mysterious brought his tongue to a halt. . . . [Old Eusebius] fell quite silent and distant, showing no reaction either to the spear thrust into Ti Jean's chest, or to his long stay in the King's village, or the final stoning. But when Ti Jean came to his arrival in the Kingdom of the Dead, and the ancestors' rejection of him, he thought he saw Eusebius' lower lip tremble slightly: the old man had now let go of the brim of his hat. But Eusebius didn't say a word, and Ti Jean went on. . . . Ti Jean kept talking, but like someone dancing in front of a blind man, and he relived alone the underground galleries, the river, the sea and all the rest. [230–32]

In encapsulating the oral within a written form and transmitting it, the writers of the "peuple sans écriture" achieve an appropriation of the written, a medium from elsewhere. As Glissant states in *Caribbean Discourse*, they transform unofficial history, "nonhistory," into History, and thereby restore the collective memory (61–62).

Bugul's and Ti Jean's cultural experience is inscribed in the encounter between Africa and the West, in the uprooting of African populations and their transplantation to the New World. In the heroes' circular itinerary and the structure of the narrative, Africa is invested with a different meaning for Bugul and for Ti Jean, a meaning shown by the place Africa holds in the previous diagrams and the diagrams below (diagrams 3 and 4). For Bugul, Africa will mean the end of exile, and the final return to the "real land." For Ti Jean, Africa, formerly a destination, reveals itself to be only a stopping place during exile and errancy. The two protagonists, in search of ancestors, initially look for an elsewhere, or as the authors of *Eloge de la Créolité* put it, for an "exteriority" (20) that inscribes the subject in a cultural and/or ethnic space outside his/her present time and present space, generating an uncomfortable discrepancy and noncoincidence with self, leading precisely to exile and errancy.

In *Eloge de la Créolité*, the authors intend to go beyond Negritude, which, despite the inspiration it gave to a generation of Caribbean intellectuals, nevertheless creates an "illusion" of an identity enshrined in a faraway space [*extériorité*]. Negritude does not take into account the "here" and "now" of the Caribbean people. From this perspective "*Créolité*" echoes the concept of "*Antillanité*" Glissant is calling for in *Caribbean Discourse*. Following in the footsteps of Glissant, *Eloge* is an invitation to the Caribbean people to come to terms

Diagram 3: AFTER REJECTION

function		*space*		*time*	*language*
vernacular	here: real land	Ti Jean: ↓ Guadeloupe = Intcriority	Bugul: ↓ **Africa** = Interiority	now	maternal
vehicular referential	everywhere overthere: dreamland	Ti Jean: ↓ = Gaudeloupe	Bugul: ↓ **Africa**	later long ago	urban national
mythical	beyond: the Ancestors	Ti Jean: ↓ **Africa** = Exteriority	Bugul: ↓ **Africa** = Interiority	always	sacred

Diagram 4: EXILE AND EXODUS

	from	Interiority into	exile from Exteriority _____ return to →	Interiority
	from	real land to	from Dreamland _____ return to →	real land
Ti Jean		Guadeloupe	exile Africa errancy + exodus + return → the Ancestors: I am an African? ↓ deterritorialization	Guadeloupe (re)territorialization I am a Guadeloupean
Bugul		**Africa**	exile West errancy + exodus + return → the Ancestors: I am a Gaul? ↓ deterritorialization	**Africa** reterritorialization I am an African

with "*extériorité*," and to return to "*intériorité*," that is, to look at the "real land." This return to interiority will mark the end of exile (diagram 4).

To use the categories formulated by Bernabé et al., in *Eloge de la créolité*, there is for Ti Jean "the exteriority of aspirations (to mother Africa, mythical Africa, impossible Africa)" (889) and also "the exteriority of self-assertion (we are Africans)" (889).[20] Similarly, in *Le Baobab fou* Bugul's aspiration to exteriority is reflected in her desire to

20. Jean Bernabé et al., *Eloge de la créolité* (Paris: Gallimard, Presses Universitaires Créoles, 1989). English translation by Mohamed Taleb Khyar, "In Praise of Creoleness," *Callaloo* 13:4, (Fall 1990): 886–909.

go to the West, "the promised land" (35), "the referential North" (33). For her too, the promised land and an affirmation of the Self in terms of the dreamland "I am a Gaul" is an impossible dream. The outcome of the characters' experience of exile and errancy, and the rejection they endure, bring to light the falseness of their connection with an "over there" located in an exteriority which does not provide them with a cultural or an ethnic territorialization nor bestow upon them the identity they thought was theirs: "*Africanité*" for Ti Jean, "*Gallicanité*" for Bugul. If indeed Bugul can later redirect her aspirations to an African referential "over there" (100, 105) and an African "long ago" (Ken's prehistory) linked to nationality, if the space of "here" and "over there" and "beyond" as well as the maternal and the national do coincide, there is however a discrepancy in time: the "now" of the vernacular (today's Africa) being different from the referential (Africa of long ago). The death of the baobab thus symbolizes the disappearance of that Africa of "long ago" and upon returning, Ken will pronounce with sadness the eulogy of the baobab, "witness and accomplice of the mother's departure" (182). As for Ti Jean, after his rejection, he will also change his referential point in situating his "over there" in Guadeloupe, which he acknowledges as the space "where he belonged" (185), his "home" (197), linked to the national and to the maternal: Guadeloupe instead of mother Africa henceforth inaccessible, but still the space of "beyond," of the Ancestors (diagram 3).

In the coincidence between their present time and their present space, that is, their interiority, Bugul and Ti Jean settle finally in their proper place, which, as Michel de Certeau characterizes it in *The Practice of Everyday Life*,[21] is that locus which in a configuration of positions presents unity, completeness, and stability (117); in other words, a site of territorialization. Ti Jean's journey of initiation had started with the apparition of the Beast which engulfed him in its belly and immersed Fond Zombi, Ti Jean's village, in permanent darkness.[22] When Ti Jean returns to Guadeloupe, his final destination, he is restored to integrity in recovering his human age and his living human status. At the same time, with the killing of the Beast the universe of Fond Zombi is restored to its harmony, generating a new equilibrium

21. Michel de Certeau, *The Practice of Everyday Life* (Los Angeles: University of California Press, 1984).

22. For separation from the mother, being swallowed by a monster and symbolic return to the womb as stages of an initiation process, see Mircea Eliade, *Rites and Symbols*.

between Ti Jean and his world. The Beast's belly is described as watery and smooth, a clearly womblike locus. The killing of the Beast represents a symbolic killing of the mother, and thus constitutes an emancipatory gesture on Ti Jean's part. Once definitely severed from the mother (Africa), Ti Jean is able to settle into his present time and space: Fond Zombi. As for Bugul, upon her return home to her native village in Africa, she is applauded by the chief Baobab: although dead, it rises and joins the other baobabs in welcoming her back to the place she was born, which is her rightful place, where she had to live autonomously, henceforth severed from her mother who had left it.

The romantic desire for a return to an Africa of the origins, the longing for Africa as motherland, has shaped the Caribbean imaginary and its writing. As *"le pays d'avant"* [the country of before], Africa takes on a particular resonance for the Caribbean people, in the context of a double exile: exile from the original space and from the original culture. Novels such as Maryse Condé's *Hérémakhonon* and *Une Saison à Rihata*, as well as Myriam Warner-Vieyra's *Juletane*, Paule Marshall's *Praise Song for a Widow*, and Simone Schwarz-Bart's *Ti Jean L'Horizon* embody the Caribbean character's quest to render the intangible dreamworld physically real. In *Caribbean Discourse*, Glissant acknowledges the temptation of the *"retour"* [reversion] as "the first impulse of a transplanted population" (16). Since return is impossible, the transplanted subject has recourse to a *"détour"* [diversion] in the idealization of the "elsewhere." But, Glissant warns,

> Diversion is not a useful ploy unless it is nourished by reversion: not a return to the longing for origins, to some immutable state of Being, but a return to the point of entanglement, from which we were forcefully turned away, that is where we must ultimately put to work the forces of creolization[23] or perish. [26]

Ti Jean and Bugul, through their exile and errancy, acquire this new sense of what the return is: from exteriority to inferiority, to their "point of entanglement." Such a project is embodied in Aimé Césaire's *Cahier d'un retour au pays natal*. For Bugul, Ti Jean and the poet narrator of the *Cahier*, exile is transformed into exodus. As Daniel Chauvin rightly states it,

23. Glissant's original French reads: " . . . c'est là qu'il faut à la fin mettre en oeuvre les composantes de la *relation* ou périr." Dash renders *relation* as *creolization*. I prefer instead Françoise Lionnet's unofficial translation of *relation* in this context as *"contact."* See her *Autobiographical Voices: Race, Gender, Self-Portraiture* (Ithaca: Cornell University Press, 1989), 169.

Contrairement à l'exilé qui regarde en arrière et privilégie le passé, la terre d'origine, l'homme de l'Exode jette son regard en avant, vers l'avenir, vers l'issue de sa marche. L'Exode est donc entrée plus que sortie, installation plus que départ, fondation plus que dispersion. [21]

Unlike the exile who looks back and privileges the past, the land of origin, the man of the Exodus looks ahead, toward the outcome of his march. Exodus is thus an entering more than an exit, settlement more than departure, foundation more than dispersal.[24]

In other words, exodus itself already inaugurates a new beginning, present in the last chapter of *Ti Jean L'Horizon*, significantly entitled "the End and the Beginning." Exodus inaugurates also a new history which reconnects the time before the Middle Passage and colonization with the time of a "here" and a "now." To return to Sebbar's formulation, exodus covers "the gulf between two shores." Traces of this new history are sown all along the narrative of Ti Jean: first when his mother, Awa by her African name, becomes Ma Eloise and leaves the place of Up Above to go and settle in the place of Down Below, as did the Beluse family, contrary to the Longoué family, in Glissant's *Le Quatrième siècle*. This history starts with Ti Jean when his father Wandemba refuses to give him an African name. Those traces are also present in other Caribbean narratives, for example, in the matrimonial union of Minerve and Xango (Télumée's great-grandparents in *Pluie et Vent*), which is like the union of a Greek goddess with an African deity that founds a new dynasty of women, the Lougandor. Similarly, the marriage between Baindingue the African and the Bretonne Creole Anne de Lery in *Le Flamboyant à fleurs bleues* by Jean Louis Baghio'o[25] symbolizes the merging of two different cultural traditions. The forceful statement opening *Eloge de la Créolité* bears witness to that new history and proclaims a new identity, beyond *Négritude* and *Antillanité*, integrating the past and the present: "*Ni Européens, ni Africains, ni Asiatiques, nous nous proclamons Créoles*" (13) [Neither Europeans, nor Africans, nor Asians, we proclaim ourselves Creoles (886)]. For Ken Bugul in *Le Baobab fou*, if the old baobab of her childhood still has its branches, it is nevertheless dead, and this death inaugurates "the first morning of a sunrise without sundown" (182), a new era.

24. Daniel Chauvin, "Jérémie, Ezechiël, Isaïe: l'Exil et la Parole," in Jacques Mounier, ed., *Exil et littérature* (Grenoble: ELLUG, 1986) 17–30. My translation.
25. Jean Louis Baghio'o, *Le Flamboyant à fleurs bleues* (Paris: Editions Caribbéennes, 1981).

While the official history of colonized and transplanted people, the one recorded in textbooks, emphasizes discontinuity in erasing or obliterating precolonial and preslavery history and culture, the new history integrates both discontinuity and continuity represented by the journey into the past (Ti Jean's to Africa and Ken's prehistory), even a mythical past, thus reconnecting the characters with their ancestry and restoring for them a filiation broken by the irruption of colonization and slavery. If "when you kill the Ancestors you kill yourself" as Toni Morrison states,[26] the search for ancestors becomes a legitimate quest and strategy for survival. Far from being a paralyzing force, this search operates rather as a dynamic power in bringing awareness of one's "point of entanglement," that is one's present and interiority, and in leading to an exodus, that is, one's descendance and future.

Ti Jean L'Horizon and *Le Baobab fou,* in involving their characters in exile and errancy, allow them to confront themselves and engage them in a process of initiation and self-discovery. Moreover, the two narratives unfold a subtext which questions exteriority as well as cultural mimicry. They are an invitation to reject, or at least to relativize, the homogenizing discourse of an immutable and eternal African past. The exile and errancy of Bugul and Ti Jean in relation to their quest for identity underline the complexity of identity in a multicultural context and the necessity for a reconciliation with one's interiority. This in turn raises the following question: is it possible to construct for oneself an identity apart from memory, history, and geography? But this, of course is only a rhetorical question when considered in the context of Ti Jean's and Ken Bugul's journeys.

---

26. Toni Morrison, "Rootedness: The Ancestor as Foundation," in Mari Evans, ed., *Black Women Writers 1950–1980* (New York: Doubleday, 1984), 341.

BELLA BRODZKI

Nomadism and the Textualization of Memory in André Schwarz-Bart's *La Mulâtresse Solitude**

> Passive: the un-story, that which escapes quotation and which
> memory does not recall—forgetfulness as thought. That which, in
> other words, cannot be forgotten because it has always already fallen
> outside memory.
> —Maurice Blanchot, *The Writing of the Disaster*

The relationship between the Holocaust and André Schwarz-Bart's *La Mulâtresse Solitude*[1]—a novel about exile, slavery, and revolt in the Antilles at the end of the eighteenth century—may appear to be at the least gratuitous, at the most oblique. What are the moral and political implications of even positing such a relationship, as the author himself has done? What is the nature of this connection and how is it constructed, beyond the level of thematization? What kinds of reciprocal metaphorical exchanges are made possible by this figurative act? Which interpretive constraints are operative or set into motion by invoking the Holocaust as a figure or symbol of absolute horror in the context of imaging another people's catastrophe, especially one that preceded it historically? Is the Holocaust a privileged term—rhetorically as well as otherwise incomparable—not applicable or transferable?[2] To pursue this line of inquiry to any extent is to engage in some of

---

*I am grateful to Ronnie Scharfman and Françoise Lionnet for their very supportive and perceptive commentary throughout the preparation of this essay.

1. Although the English translation of the title *La Mulâtresse Solitude* retains her proper name, unfortunately it reduces the historical Solitude to an abstract and arbitrary, indefinitely modified, female subject. By contrast, the French original insists upon Solitude's identity being crucially inscribed in a racial category. Thus, I will retain use of the French title, although all citations will be taken from *A Woman Named Solitude*, trans. Ralph Manheim (San Francisco: Donald Ellis, 1985). For an incisive critique of the connotations of racial categories and terminologies, and an argument for the use of "métissage" as an aesthetic concept and analytic tool, see the introduction to Françoise Lionnet's *Autobiographical Voices: Race, Gender, Self-Portraiture* (Ithaca: Cornell University Press, 1989), especially 3–18.

2. For a superbly intelligent and sensitive analysis of the metaphorical character of the Holocaust, both its literalizing abuses by Nazi ideology and Jewish uses of meta-

YFS 83, *Post/Colonial Conditions*, ed. Lionnet & Scharfman, © 1993 by Yale University.

the most impassioned debates in contemporary theory surrounding the issues of particularism vs. universalism and essentialism vs. positionality.[3] In exemplary fashion, *La Mulâtresse Solitude* presents what is at stake in these debates: that which at every moment exceeds the theoretical, yet goes to the heart of the symbolic. My three-part essay begins by considering the kinds of responses and reactions Schwarz-Bart's project has generated; it then moves on to examine the role of memory and resistance in Guadeloupean and Holocaust history and literature, and closes with a discussion of the novel proper.

As evidenced by the minimal critical attention *La Mulâtresse Solitude* has received since 1972 when it first appeared, finding a place for this estranged, nomadic text—not quite a Holocaust novel, not quite a Caribbean slave narrative—has been remarkably difficult. Clearly, these are not disputes over generic classification. They point to deeper, thornier notions of racial identity and identification: whose history is it, anyway? Indeed. For the problem of identity/identification carries with it the interrelated problems of representation and appropriation, sexual as well as racial. Is this book an example of French colonialism and black slavery, cultural and sexual appropriation, as well as a book *about* it? How to read a modern, European white male's efforts to render into prose the disordered consciousness, the abject victimization of a deeply distressed black woman slave who lived in the Caribbean two hundred years ago? If compelling historical, ideological, and literary critical constraints made it previously impossible to receive this text in more enabling terms, perhaps now is the time to reexamine the issues it raises, enacts, not by the superimposition of one set of referents *over* another, but by the positioning of one set *alongside* another. By suggesting that a revisionary reading of *La Mulâtresse Solitude* is in order, my aim here is not to attempt to "resolve" or even defuse the problematic configurations presented in and by the text. Rather, it is to trace some recuperative and exclusionary, disfigurative and transfigurative discursive effects, in the context of shifting perspectives on subjectivity, identity, and experience offered by multicultural feminist studies, Holocaust studies, and postcolonial Caribbean discourse.

---

phor in Holocaust history and literature, see James E. Young, *Writing and Rewriting the Holocaust: Narrative and the Consequences of Interpretation* (Bloomington: Indiana University Press 1988), especially chapters five and six, 83–116.

    3. For an enlightening exposition of the problem of essentialism from the perspective of feminist poststructuralism, see Diana Fuss, *Essentially Speaking* (New York & London: Routledge 1989).

La Mulâtresse Solitude is not the first venture in which Schwarz-Bart, the French-born son of a Yiddish-speaking Polish family extermi-nated at Auschwitz, has textually or historically linked the victims of the Holocaust and those of the Atlantic slave trade. *Un Plat de porc aux bananes vertes* (1967), the dually inscribed, fictionalized life his-tory of a half-blind Martinican servant in a Parisian home for the aged, was coauthored with his Guadeloupean wife Simone Schwarz-Bart and dedicated to Aimé Césaire and Elie Wiesel. The novel was conceived as the first in a cycle about the blacks of Martinique and Guadeloupe from 1760 to the present, of which Solitude was to be the central figure. When *La Mulâtresse Solitude* appeared in print, it was designated the inaugural volume, while *Un Plat de porc aux bananes vertes*, the story of a woman who might have been one of Solitude's descendants, was identified retrospectively as its prelude. Although the collaborative project as a whole has since been abandoned, Simone Schwarz-Bart published *Pluie et vent sur Télumée Miracle* in 1972, the same year as *La Mulâtresse Solitude* appeared. It is perhaps because of all this cross-fertilizing that a sense of authorial indeterminacy hovers over the latter text, at least in the minds of certain bibliographers and critics. However, the means by which scholars have arrived at their different "resolutions" of the "problem" appear to be symptomatic of some-thing larger.

While the original Seuil edition names André only as author of *La Mulâtresse Solitude,* as does the English translation by Atheneum, Donald Herdeck's *Caribbean Writers: A Bio-Bibliographic Critical Encyclopedia* lists *La Mulâtresse Solitude* under Simone Schwarz-Bart, "with André Schwarz-Bart." The *Callaloo* Bibliography of *Fran-cophone Women Writers from Sub-Saharan Africa and its Diaspora* also lists *La Mulâtresse Solitude* under Simone Schwarz-Bart "and André Schwarz-Bart."[4] According to Charlotte Bruner, in an essay which compares the figure of Antoinette in Jean Rhys's *Wide Sargasso Sea* with Solitude (one of the very few critical studies of this text in English or French), Simone is the author "in collaboration with her husband."[5] After a nod to André as the Goncourt Prize-winning author of a "fictionalized history of a Jewish family from the year 1000" (239),

4. Donald Herdeck, *Caribbean Writers: A Bio-Bibliographic Critical En-cyclopedia* (Washington: 1979); *Callaloo* Bibliography of *Francophone Women Writers from Sub-Saharan Africa and its Diaspora* (1985).

5. Charlotte Bruner, "A Caribbean Madness: Half Slave and Half Free." *Canadian Review of Comparative Literature/Revue Canadienne de Littérature Comparée,* June (1984): 236–48.

Bruner refers thereafter to Simone only, possibly finding the notion of such a joint enterprise too difficult to negotiate. But not only does she progressively and effectively erase André from any association with the Caribbean project in her evolving discussion, she even removes *Le Dernier des Justes* from its own historical context by eliding the fatal specificity and closure signified in the title and fulfilled in the narrative—the Holocaust as crucial referent. (One can only deduce from this that she simply has not read the novel.) Whatever the particular reasons for such manoeuvering, the rhetorical effects are unmistakable. Ultimately, the comparative/feminist orientation of Bruner's textual analysis, which involves a pairing of the *authors* of these "West Indian novels" as well, depends on the notion that Rhys and Schwarz-Bart be "two contemporary Caribbean women . . . coming from similar islands but from different worlds . . . ," and that they "emphasize some common reactions to the rejection, oppression, and exploitation of women" (236, 248).

On the other side of the divide, Sidra DeKoven Ezrahi's study of the Holocaust in literature, while making reference to *La Mulâtresse Solitude* as performing the same kind of "reconciliatory" gesture as *Le Dernier des Justes*, describes the former as "the story of the massacre of the slaves of West Africa."[6] As in the case above, this "imprecision" suggests a lack of familiarity with the text's content. As evidence of how identical facile reductionism of authorial identity to thematic content can serve different ideological interests, the Centre de documentation juive contemporaine in Paris considers André to have authored only *Le Dernier des Justes*. As far as its bibliographers are concerned, Simone is the single author of *La Mulâtresse Solitude*, as well as of the other "Caribbean" texts with which her name is associated. One begins to wonder if the set of readers of "Holocaust" novels and the set of readers of "Caribbean" novels are self-defined in mutually exclusive terms, and if the problem posed by *La Mulâtresse Solitude* is that its modes of identification are not reducible to either/or binary terms.

Yet it would be tempting to attribute this "confusion" over joint or single authorship to André Schwarz-Bart's article in *Le Figaro Littéraire* (1967) entitled "Pourquoi j'ai écrit *La Mulâtresse Solitude*," in which he retraces the path from *Le Dernier des Justes* to *Un plat de*

6. Sidra DeKoren Ezrahi, *By Words Alone: The Holocaust in Literature* (Chicago: University of Chicago Press 1980), 136.

porc aux bananes vertes (whose over-arching title is *La Mulâtresse
Solitude*).[7] The referential ambiguity stems not only from the novels'
overlapping titles, but also from the impression given by the use of the
past tense that *La Mulâtresse Solitude* was a completed action; revealed instead in this rich autobiographical meditation is the unfold-
ing of a process of coming-to-writing-again, the emergence of a work in
progress which will become five years later the novel *La Mulâtresse
Solitude*. It is not merely on the level of an expressed poetics of intentionality that this essay touches and fascinates the reader of *La
Mulâtresse Solitude*, but as an example of the move towards "diversity" that Edouard Glissant calls "the human spirit's striving for a
cross-cultural relationship, without universal transcendence."[8] What
is especially striking in Schwarz-Bart's assertion of a principle of inter-
connectedness between two histories of exile, oppression, and resistance is that it actively seeks a way out of the totalizing and esen-
tialist approach to Jewish identity that Holocaust survivors and their
texts characteristically, and understandably, embrace.

The *Figaro* article begins in 1955 with Schwarz-Bart's reflection on
the nature of his affinity with the emigré Caribbean community in
Paris, an affinity that originates in a sense of existential identification
with a displaced population whose history is haunted by slavery, and
whose daily lives are plagued by racism and the marginalizing, debilitating effects of colonialism. (Since Martinique's and Guadeloupe's
"accession" to departmental status in 1946, massive migration to the
Metropole has produced a phenomenon Glissant calls "genocide by
substitution.") It closes with a celebration of collaborative work and
the signalling of Aimé Césaire's final approval of *Un Plat de porc aux
bananes vertes*. Thus, *how* rather than *why* Schwarz-Bart's identification with the African diaspora was translated into a literary production—within the context of his intimate relationship with a Guadeloupean woman—comprises the real narrative here.

Supremely conscientious and fearful of violating the integrity of
the other, of appropriating difference for one's own ends, but fully
committed to "the possibilities inherent in all communication",
Schwarz-Bart wrestles with the rhetoric of traditional humanism and
is reassured when his undertaking is sanctioned by Alioune Diop,
Jacques Rabemananjara, and ultimately Aimé Césaire. His own life

7. André Schwarz-Bart, *Le Figaro Littéraire* (26 January 1967).
8. Edouard Glissant, *Caribbean Discourse: Selected Essays*, trans. Michael Dash
(Charlottesville: University of Virginia Press, 1989), 98.

and writing steeped in the Jewish tradition of responses to catastrophe, he recounts the immense technical challenge of now combining "vérité historique" and "vérité romanesque," using wholly different coordinates. From both oral and recorded histories of Guadeloupe, notably those of Oruno Lara and Henri Bangou, he found in the mythical-historical "mulâtresse Solitude" a figure capable of carrying the symbolic weight of a narrative devoted to the reconstitution of African-Caribbean collective memory.

Schwarz-Bart's commemorative project is by necessity and design a form of counterdiscourse. Propelled by the desire to challenge the received or interpretive model—in this case, official French history, of which Caribbean history is merely a reflection or refraction—it takes as its point of departure the notion that writing is an invocation, and that its task is to recover and reclaim that which has been lost, taken away by force, or has yet to be inscribed. In Glissant's account, metaphorically reminiscent of Foucault's archaeologies, the primal psycho-historical trauma that continues to plague the Antillean imagination is emblematic of an entire cultural condition:

> The French Caribbean is the site of a history characterized by ruptures and that began with a brutal dislocation, the slave trade. Our historical consciousnes could not be deposited gradually and continuously like sediment, as it were, as happened with those peoples who have frequently produced a totalitarian philosophy of history., for instance European peoples, but came together in the context of shock, contradiction, painful negation, and explosive forces. This dislocation of the continuum, and the inability of the collective consciousness to absorb it all, characterize what I call a nonhistory. The negative effect of this nonhistory is therefore the erasing of the collective memory. [61, 62]

The "ruptures" referred to here are not the result of the experience of slavery as such, but the "brutal dislocation" that was the *slave trade*, begun by the Portuguese in the fifteenth century and lasting until the middle of the nineteenth when it was finally abolished in Brazil and the United States. (The actual practice of slavery in "the New World" continued, however, for another twenty or so years.) The prime mover of colonialism, the international slave trade was "one of the most significant population displacements in the history of humanity, the deportation of somewhere between twelve and fifteen million men and women," of which a million and a half died in transport.[9] In the collec-

---

9. Jean Meyer, *Esclaves et Négriers* (Paris: Gallimard, 1986) 21, my translation.

tive Caribbean imagination, this original commercial triangle—Europe-Africa-America—functions as a symbolic, if not actual web of interrelations, signifying multiple origins and affinities based on a shared, discontinuous, tragic past.

Glissant's charge against a "totalitarian philosophy of history" implicitly opposes, on the metanarrative level, concomitant assumptions about the writing and reading of history as neutral, objective, comprehensive, and exempt from the conditions that govern other kinds of narrativizing. Of course, whether such histories are seen as "universalist" or "particularist" is a matter of one's position. As marginalized and oppressed groups increasingly view History as the ground on which competing versions of history are fought and relativized, the power that accrues to certain complicit interpretations and investments in those interpretations is contested correlatively. And as C. L. R. James has demonstrated in *The Black Jacobins*, such rewriting can become the script for social change.[10] To press the case further, it may even be a requisite for cultural survival. Perhaps cultural identity or its extinction ultimately depends on understanding history and memory not as static repositories of archival content or unmediated experience, but rather as complex, often conflictual, symbolic, interactional processes.

In the spirit of Nietzsche, who grasped so well the idea that competing interpretations can be put to a variety of ideological uses, we note the "life-providing, life-preserving, and perhaps even species-cultivating"[11] potential of current metahistorical narratives that have moved away from equating oppression with passive victimization. Africanist and feminist historians, respectively, have increasingly stressed the role and symbol of resistance in slave culture, thus challenging racial and sexual stereotypes and emphasizing the notion that subjugated groups exercise subjective agency and resourceful survival strategies even in the most repressive and dehumanizing of systems.[12] In her

10. C. L. R. James's account of the Haitian Revolution (1791–1803), "the only successful slave revolt in history," had a dramatic effect on Third World liberation movements. See *The Black Jacobins: Toussaint L'Ouverture and the San Domingo Revolution* (New York: Vintage, 1963), preface to the first edition.

11. Friedrich Nietzsche, *Beyond Good and Evil* (New York: Random House, 1966), 4.

12. See Selwyn R. Cudjoe, *Resistance and Caribbean Literature* (Athens, Ohio: Ohio University Press, 1980), especially Part I, which provides a brief history of resistance in the Caribbean. For recent gender-inflected studies of Africans enslaved in the Western Hemisphere, see Jacqueline Jones, *Labor of Love, Labor of Sorrow: Black*

introduction to a volume of *Nouvelles Questions Féministes* devoted
to the condition of women in the Antilles, Arlette Gautier reaffirms
this point in fine: "Did women consent to the horror of slavery or
colonial oppression? Although most historians or novelists silently
overlook examples of female resistance, others invoke legendary figures such as the famous *mulâtresse Solitude,* Guadeloupean rebel
against the reestablishment of slavery in 1804."[13] Figured anywhere on
a continuum between imaginative intervention and overt revolt, resistance signifies—in its elaboration of appropriative and subversive
emancipatory strategies—changing configurations in identity politics.

II

> I call disaster that which does not have the ultimate for a limit: it
> bears the ultimate away in the disaster.
> —Maurice Blanchot, *The Writing of the Disaster*

In all its variety, literature in the late twentieth century reflects an
almost global obsession with the transmission, preservation, repression, and potential effacement of memory as an instrument of historical consciousness. Contemporary theorists and philosophers of history analyze the "reflexive turning of history upon itself" in a "historical
age that calls out for memory because it has abandoned it,"[14] recog-

---

Women, Work and Family from Slavery to the Present (New York: Basic Books, 1985);
Rosalyn Terborg-Penn's "Black Women in Resistance: A Cross-Cultural Perspective" in
Gary Okihiro, ed., *In Resistance: Studies in African, Caribbean, and Afro-Caribbean
History* (Amherst: University of Massachusetts Press, 1966), 188–209; Marietta Mor-
issey, *Slave Women in the New World: Gender Stratification in the Caribbean;* Barbara
Bush, *Slave Women in Caribbean Society, 1650–1838* (Bloomington: Indiana University
Press, 1990); and especially relevant to the present essay, Arlette Gautier, *Les Soeurs de
Solitude: histoire des esclaves femmes aux Antilles françaises, 1635–1848* (Paris, 1985).

13. *Nouvelles Questions Feministes* 9–10 (1985): 5–8. My translation.

14. Pierre Nora, "Between Memory and History: *Les Lieux de Mémoire,*" *Representations* 26 (Spring 1989): 7–25. In this special issue on Memory and Counter-Memo-
ry, the editors Nathalie Zemon Davis and Randolph Starn stress the seemingly opposed
collective tendencies of amnesia and obsession, the conflictual but productive "interdependence of memory and history" (1–6). Three compelling projects which testify
further to the recent preoccupation with memory and representation are Lawrence
Langer's *Holocaust Testimonies: The Ruins of Memory* (New Haven: Yale University
Press, 1991); Shoshana Felman and Dori Laub's *Testimony: Crises of Witnessing in
Literature, Psychoanalysis, and History* (New York & London: Routledge, 1992); and
Saul Friedlander's edited collection, *Probing the Limits of Representation: Nazism and
the 'Final Solution',* (Cambridge & London: Harvard University Press, 1992).

nizing the marked response of those who have experienced, personally and collectively, the worst horrors of our age and who dread history's tendency to consign to oblivion that which "escapes quotation."

If all writing is a form of memorializing, and contemporary writing especially so, none may be as determined (in every sense of the word) as that which remembers the Holocaust. Beginning with Lamentations, which mourned the Destruction of the First Temple in 586 B.C., "the writing of the disaster" has functioned as a collective performative utterance within the Jewish textual tradition, predicated on a fear of remaining unwritten or written out of history, human or divine, and perceived as an act of social survival. However, when exile—understood theologically to be the transcendent category and historically to be the normative condition of Jewish experience—became genocide in the Final Solution, paradigmatic or archetypal representations were challenged radically. Among Jewish theologians and philosophers debates rage: is the Holocaust an apocalyptic event, without analogy or precedent in history, a unique catastrophe in nature and degree wholly unlike any other? Or is it another episode to be absorbed in a long cyclical history relentlessly punctuated by suffering, and necessarily subject to the same critical models of remythification and ritualization?[15]

This problem, posed in a variety of ways, constitutes one of the principal themes in Holocaust writing. Schwarz-Bart's *Le Dernier des Justes*, which won the Prix Goncourt in 1959 and attracted a wide audience, uses a Medieval paradigm to wrestle with the fact that Jews were singled out by racial criteria for extermination by the Nazis.[16] His semifictional chronicle of the Levy family of Just Men traces a genealogy based on self-sacrifice and suffering, one which originates with the suicide of Yom Tov Levy in York in 1185 and ends with the martyrdom of Ernie Levy in the gas chambers at Auschwitz. Sidra DeKoven ex-

15. For a rich introduction to the intertextual commentary on this central problem in Jewish interpretation, see David G. Roskies, *Against the Apocalypse: Responses to Catastrophe in Modern Jewish Culture* (Cambridge, & London: Harvard University Press, 1984); Alan Mintz, *Hurban: Responses to Catastrophe in Hebrew Literature* (New York: 1984); Yosef Hayim Yerushalmi, *Zakhor: Jewish History and Jewish Memory* (Seattle & London: University of Washington Press, 1982); and James E. Young, op cit.

16. Although homosexuals and other social and political "deviants" and "undesirables" were deported, interned, worked to death, and killed, only Gypsies and Jews were destined for genocide because of their race, that is, considered unfit for human existence.

plains that "[i]n its focus on persecution as the organizing principle of communal memory, *The Last of the Just* is a fictional derivative of the medieval lamentation literature," but that it goes beyond that interpretive tradition by seeking redemption or consolation in human compassion. For Lawrence Langer, the text's desperate effort to situate the crematoria within a universal design of signification is best understood in Ernie Levy's "last instinctive gesture" inside the gas chamber itself, as he attempts "to vindicate the terror of the present by somehow uniting it with the past." However, parallels and precedents are lacking here; the text signals "the end . . . of a redemptive tradition of suffering," and "the meaning of [Ernie's] death, and that of six million others, is transferred to the imagination of the survivors. . . . [T]he only living memorial to Ernie Levy is *The Last of the Just* itself."[17] Thus, the text's challenge to a tradition steeped in martyrology resides precisely in its ambivalence; both faith and futility underwrite a prayer for the dead that mourns, blasphemes, and praises divine will all at once. For even as the litany of names of concentration camps recited by the narrator, a "friend" of Ernie's, constitutes a defamation of God's creation and a deformation of his discourse, it is nonetheless a reclamation:

> And praised. Auschwitz. So be it. Maidanek. The Eternal. Treblinka.
> And praised. Buchenwald. So be it. Mauthausen. The Eternal. Belzec.
> And praised. Sobibor. So be it . . . [18]

In an extraordinary final gesture that crosses historical, spatial, and racial boundaries, Schwarz-Bart's *La Mulâtresse Solitude* enjoins the tragic destinies of Caribbean blacks and European Jews by linking two heroic events in the French Revolution and the Holocaust: first, a suicidal black slave insurrection against Republican and Bonapartist efforts to reinstate slavery after the legislators of the Revolution had proclaimed "les droits de l'homme et du citoyen" in 1789 and decreed the abolition of slavery in 1794, and second, the suicidal Jewish resistance to the Nazis in the Warsaw Ghetto in 1943. Recounted in the

17. Sidra DeKoven Ezrahi, op cit., 132; Lawrence Langer, *The Holocaust and the Literary Imagination* (New Haven: Yale University Press, 1975), 263. For an excellent study devoted entirely to *The Last of the Just*, see Francine Kaufmann, *Pour relire "Le Dernier des Justes"* (Paris: Meridien Klincksieck, 1987).

18. André Schwarz-Bart, *The Last of the Just*, trans. Stephen Becker (New York: Atheneum, 1960), 408.

penultimate and final chapters is the celebrated last stand at Fort Matouba, Guadeloupe, of Colonel Louis Delgrès, the leader of the insurrection, his three hundred rebels, and the countless women and children who preferred death to surrender to the six thousand French soldiers surrounding them. Recounted also is the butchery that followed this doomed revolt.

The recuperation of this significant event by official French historians and its erasure in the Caribbean collective memory are dramatically illustrated in Schwarz-Bart's reconstructed life story of one of the survivors of the resistance, the legendary slave heroine Solitude. Her ultimate fate is already inscribed in the novel's epigraph, a one-sentence entry in Oruno Lara's *Histoire de la Guadeloupe,* the first national history written by a Guadeloupean: "The mulatto woman Solitude was with child at the time of her arrest; she was executed on 29 November 1802, immediately after the delivery of her child."[19] Solitude's legacy is both singular and emblematic: although she herself did not survive slavery or resistance, her child was "spared" death so as to be preserved for life as a slave.

Solitude's public execution closes Schwarz-Bart's narrative proper which, reinforced by the logic of analogy and continuity, is sublated in the explicit leap that constitutes the novel's epilogue: here the Matouba slave revolt and the Warsaw Ghetto Uprising converge symbolically in the imagination of a certain predisposed contemporary "traveler." Visiting the "remains of the old Danglemont plantation," the site of the battle on the heights of Matouba at the edge of the Soufrière volcano, he comes upon a "remnant of a knee-high wall and a mound of earth intermingled with bone splinters." Because of the teleological terms in which the narrative has been cast, "traveler" here seems oddly casual and deliberately understated, evoking rather the archetypal image of the Jewish wanderer, the figure of the nomad who, having no place, finds himself momentarily in this one. But it calls up as well the image of the pilgrim who has come to this site in search of something particular, although everything points to a collective memory "concealed" and "dispersed," at best randomly buried and dug up again by "the innocent hoes of the field

---

19. See Oruno Lara, *Histoire de la Guadeloupe* (Paris: L'Harmattan, 1921). For other novelistic versions of this tragically eclipsed episode in Guadeloupean history, see Michèle Lacrosil, *Demain Jab-Herma* (Paris: Gallimard, 1967) and Daniel Maximin *L'Isolé soleil* (Paris: Seuil, 1981).

workers." Against this leveling, his mediation attempts a purposeful, meaningful restoration.

> If he is in the mood to salute a memory, his imagination will people the environing space, and human figures will rise up around him, just as the phantoms that wander about the humiliated ruins of the Warsaw ghetto are said to rise up before the eyes of other travelers. [178, 179]

In this landscape of martyrdom and extinction, Schwarz-Bart's vision is a testimony to the sheer will to remember, or the inability to forget, what has happened there. Through a kind of "commemorative vigilance," his transfiguration of the monumental ruins of wall, bone, and ashes makes possible—indeed, creates—what Pierre Nora has called *les lieux de mémoire*. Nora's elaboration of the difference between memory and history relies on the notion that "there are *lieux de mémoire*, sites of memory, because there are no longer *milieux de mémoire*, real environments of memory" (7).

If, as Clarisse Zimra has noted, "in the Caribbean, topography is destiny,"[20] and the volcano is a dominant Caribbean metaphor for both the "explosive" and the "blanked past" of African-Caribbean collective experience, then perhaps the Matouba landscape is a text resistant to certain kinds of interpretation. The presence of ashes helps psychically to link two highly dissimilar landscapes (without eliding the distinction between volcanic ashes and those produced by bodies burnt in crematoria), because what truly links them is a likeness of effect. "The traveler" invokes that place definitively named by David Rousset in one of the first Holocaust narratives to emerge following the war, a universe in which total, self-contained horror and merciless human devastation has occurred, all the while coextensive with the familiar, quotidian one: "*L'Univers concentrationnaire* shrivels away within itself. It still lives on in the world like a dead planet laden with corpses."[21] But in uniting the image of the phantoms that haunt the site of the Matouba slave revolt with the image of the spirits that move about the "humiliated ruins" of the Warsaw Ghetto, Schwarz-Bart is memorializing not only persecution, terror, and suffering, as he did in *Le Dernier des Justes*.

---

20. See the illuminating introduction by Zimra in the translation of Daniel Maximin's novel *Lone Sun* (Charlottesville: University of Virginia Press, 1989), xxxviii.
21. David Rousset, *The Other Kingdom*, trans. Ramon Guthrie (New York: Reynal & Hitchcock, 1947).

The symbolic significance of the Warsaw Uprising insists upon a double legacy: of destruction certainly, but more importantly, of heroic resistance against the final round-up and liquidation of Warsaw Jewry. Lasting over six weeks, and involving more than 50,000 Ghetto Jews, only a handful of whom survived, the Warsaw Ghetto Uprising was, "outside of Yugoslavia's national uprising . . . the largest and longest armed resistance in Nazi-occupied Europe during World War II."[22] Unlike the Matouba slave revolt, which has never been memoralized, a monument marks both the place and the event of the Uprising. The site, now completely urbanized, has changed drastically over the years, as recounted by James Young:

> Dynamited, torched, and then bulldozed by the Germans, the Warsaw Ghetto had been demolished one block at a time. In 1948 all that remained was a moonscape of rubble, piled sixteen feet high, covering hundreds of acres. Anchored in this landscape of debris, the granite blocks in the monument appeared on its unveiling to rise out of the broken stones, emerging from them almost as congealed fragments of the destruction itself. As a singular tombstone rooted in this great burial mound, it seemed initially to draw its strength, massiveness, and authority from its relatively solitary placement amid the very destruction it commemorated. Location would reinforce here the sense of this memorial's link to events as a metonymical fragment of the event it commemorates, not just its displacement. Today the monument still stands alone in a large, well-kept square, but it is now surrounded by block-style apartment buildings, which diminish its earlier monolithic impact. Instead of seeming to pull order together out of the mounds of rubble around it, even being vivified by these ruins, from a distance it is now one rectangular block among many others. The trees, green lawns, and sun bathers during the summer combine to domesticate this memorial a little . . . [87–88]

By so strongly identifying with the events and symbolism of the Matouba slave revolt as a *lieu de mémoire,* Schwarz-Bart is not drawing merely upon a private associative memorial network. As Sander Gilman has pointed out in his study of "culturally determined patterns of Otherness," Jews and blacks are often seen as analogues of each other. Incorporated into the modern rhetoric of race, the "blackness of

---

22. James E. Young, "The Biography of a Memorial Icon: Nathan Rapoport's Warsaw Ghetto Monument," in *Representations* 26 (Spring 1989): 79. For a fascinating account of the complex political history (past and current) of the monument to the Uprising, see the article in its entirety, 69–106.

the Jew" can be understood as "the synthesis of two projections of Otherness within the same code." The black and the Jew were associated, argues Gilman, "not merely because both were outsiders but because qualities ascribed to one became the means of defining the difference of the other."[23] Such an analysis helps advance the present inquiry because it focuses not only on the nature and construction of stereotypes by privileged groups, but also on the ways in which the qualities projected are internalized by those so objectified.

III

> Off the coast of Senegal, Gorée, the island before the open sea, the first step toward madness.
> —Edouard Glissant, *Caribbean Discourse*

Schwarz-Bart's indictment of colonialism and slavery is a decidedly genealogical project, in which the history of Guadeloupe is mapped onto the reconstructed life story of Solitude; significantly, however, the text seeks to restore collective memory by beginning not with "the one-way passage of the deportation of Africans to the Americas,"[24] but with the portrayal of life in precolonial West Africa. Thus, the first of the novel's two sections is entitled "Bayangumay" and is devoted to the childhood and youth of Solitude's mother, Bayangumay; the second, entitled "Solitude," continues in Guadeloupe and treats the two stages of Solitude's life, slavery and *marronnage*. The African point of the triangle figures here, as it does in many French Caribbean texts, as the lost mother from whom Bayangumay will be brutally separated, while for her *métisse* daughter Solitude, conceived in violence and confusion, symbol herself of absolute estrangement in the New World,

---

23. Sander Gilman, *Difference and Pathology: Stereotypes of Sexuality, Race, and Madness* (Ithaca: Cornell University Press, 1985), 35. The qualities most strongly associated with both groups have been violent change and sexual excess; the images have, at points in history, been interrelated and even interchangeable. See the introduction on stereotyping, 15–35; and for a discussion of the convergence of images of Otherness and its relationship to language as a sign of difference, see his *Jewish Self-Hatred: Anti-Semitism and the Hidden Language of the Jews* (Baltimore: The Johns Hopkins University Press, 1986), especially 5–16.

24. "Pourquoi j'ai écrit *La Mulâtresse Solitude*" (my translation).

mother/Africa remains an abstract object of desire, the unknown continent.

Solitude's own child, fathered by the Mozambican "wandering soul" Maimouni, symbolizes the tragic irony of her sweet but ill-fated momentary reunion with Africa. For once again, generativity is cursed: not only is Solitude condemned to death and her execution delayed until she can deliver her child into slavery, but the imprint of exile already marks her unborn offspring. In Maimouni's prescient realization, *dépaysement* is encoded morphologically:

> But he was never able to say what sort of heart he wanted for the child. He could not wish it an African heart, which would be useless in a foreign country, and still less could he resign himself to a white, black, or mulatto heart beating to the obscure rhythm of Guadeloupe. [152–53]

Read allegorically, the violation of Bayangumay's body and psyche, her *refoulement* and renunciation of the product of her pain, and Solitude's anomalous beauty and madness—that is, the deformation of the maternal legacy—recount the narrative of colonial penetration of Africa, the deportation and enslavement of its people in the West Indies, and the overall *dépaysement* of subsequent generations of Antilleans, who continue to struggle to constitute a nonderivative, nonmimetic cultural identity.[25]

Despite the polymorphism and polyvalence that are woven into the very texture of this quintessentially nomadic narrative, *La Mulâtresse Solitude's* precise blending of discursive elements and practices of myth, folktale, proverb, documentary, and psychological realism, and its restrained, distanced classical style and deeply ironic tone produce an effect quite dissimilar from "un style antillais." Put another way, what is absent in its mode of expressivity is both the tension between

25. Glissant's analysis of "dispossession" of identity utilizes two models of exile. The first response, based on an obsession with return to a single origin, he calls "reversion"; the second, which involves "try[ing] to exorcise the impossibility of return," he calls "diversion" (16–26). He points to a significant "difference between the transplanting (by exile or dispersion) of a people who continue to survive elsewhere and the transfer (by the slave trade) of a population to another place where they change into something different, into a new set of possibilities. . . . [T]his difference between a people that *maintains its original nature* and a population that is transformed elsewhere *into another people* . . . is what distinguishes, besides the persecution of one and the enslavement of the other, the Jewish Diaspora from the African slave trade" (15).

and fusion of the written and the oral, French and Creole. Most often,
Creole words or phrases are presented parenthetically or are translated,
as if to stress the problem of cultural transmission, itself a problematic
in the text. Whether by design or not, the narrative relies most heavily
on formal description and allusion rather than linguistic interpella-
tion: the reader must infer that which Maryse Condé has identified as
"the civilization of the bossale," the oral heritage of slaves in the
Caribbean.[26] This is evident in Schwarz-Bart's reconstruction of Diola
culture in the mideighteenth century, opening—in the valley of the
Casamance River in Senegal, southwest of the Gambia River in Gambia—with a fairy-tale description of cyclical rhythms, oral traditions,
and island beauty:

> Once upon a time, on a strange planet, there was a little black girl by the
> name of Bayangumay. She had made her appearance on earth about
> 1755 in a calm and intricate estuary landscape, where the clear water of
> a river, the green water of an ocean, and the black water of a channel
> mingled—and where, so it is said, the soul was still immortal. [3]

Already suggested here is a gently insistent rhetoric of myth, in which
the tragically ironic perspectives of the fabulist and historian are pur-
posefully interfused. A pervasively lyrical tone, dependence on condensation of image, and frequent ellipses impress upon the reader a
sense of elemental harmony, a density of congruence, spiritual calm,
immanence. This impression is only heightened by the intrusion of
Bayangumay's approximate date of birth in the second line, which jars
stylistically and functions more as sign than mere "information": the
reference to the Western time line suggests the imminent, cataclysmic
incursion of History. Alerted, the reader learns that in this actual and
symbolic geography where water is generative source, the natural setting for rice-growing, shell-fishing, "shade and quiet luxury," water is
also the gateway through which, unbeknownst to the spirited young
woman coming of age in this chapter, this world is being infiltrated by
"the sellers of men" (32), ultimately to be consumed by "the evil that
had been instilled in its blood" (31).

---

26. Condé classifies the *bossale, créole,* and *marron* in the following way: "the
bossale is not simply the slave newly debarked from Africa, but s/he who develops in a
slave universe. The *créole,* the black from the postslavery colonial period. According to
the same logic, the *marron* is s/he who refuses the rules of colonial society as her/
his ancestors had refused slavery" (my translation). *La Civilisation du Bossale* (Paris:
1978), 7.

What stuns the reader of this text is its peculiar blend of aesthet-icism and atrocity, an identifiable characteristic of certain kinds of Holocaust writing. Gorée, situated in the bay of Dakar, was the center of the French slave trade in this region. Schwarz-Bart, invoking Lamen-tations, recounts the transformation of the name of "the big city on the river" Sigi, meaning "Sit down," into Sigi-Thyor, meaning "Sit down and weep." As the slave hunters extend their network and penetrate deeper and deeper into the interior, "the Elders likened the new body of Africa to an impaled octopus losing its substance drop by drop while its tentacles squeeze and rend each other without mercy, as though to punish each other for the stake that traverses them all" (31). For Schwarz-Bart, it is imperative that this experience of absolute *déchire-ment* be conveyed from its first ravages of consciousness to final dis-olution. Thus he does not gloss over the raid of Bayangumay's village, the fires, the round-up, the massacres, the march ("shackled and col-lared") to the coast, or the captivity on Gorée, but attempts painstak-ingly to render the horror and utter incomprehension of these events as they would be perceived by the young woman. What begins as Bay-angumay's dream of death ends with her desperate effort to convince herself that she is human; the narrator's depiction of the grotesque and agonizing experience of transport renders the sense of psychic and physical dislocation, the terror of loss, of sensibility and of identity, of bodily control, shame, and pain. Her rape during the collective bestial ritual of the "Pariade" when the female prisoners, newly washed in seawater but still chained, were given over to the drunken crew, is depicted as a series of disconnected sensations and animist images, for she is haunted by spirits she cannot understand. What she does under-stand, however, in this horrific Babel of languages that was Middle Passage, is the process of dehumanization upon which the system of slavery depends. The unexpected acuity of her response is rendered in this simultaneous attempt at self-redemption and suicide:

> trembling as though with fever, she awoke to her miseries—hunger, thirst, vermin, the lack of air, the smell of others, and the smell of her own feces that had escaped during the night. Yes, she was wholly human and alive again. Inspired by this marvelous thought, she tried to swallow her tongue. [45]

If Bayangumay signifies the intentionality, self-possession, and em-powerment that draws from her identity as a Dialo, the *métisse* daughter born to her on the du Parc plantation signifies total divestment, both of tribal identity and subjectivity. As the product of that infelicitous union of the races, Rosalie (whose name, through the mere act of substitution, is taken from the "Permanent Register") has two differently colored eyes: "one dark, and one light-green, as though belonging to two different persons" (50). Indeed, the irreparable split between body and consciousness, history and identity that is reflected in Rosalie's eyes is inscribed in the slaves' own classification system of "saltwater" blacks and "freshwater" blacks. For Bayangumay, renamed "Man Bobette" by her white owners, and the other "saltwater" African-born slaves, the loss of the African homeland is absolute; for the "freshwater" slaves like Rosalie, who are born in captivity, the sense of loss is somehow more destructive because impossible to localize. Thus in this context, to be *métisse* is to be doubly cursed; scorned by the pure blacks and rejected by her mother for whom the child embodies the whites' appropriation of her shame, Rosalie is a more highly valued commodity and thus susceptible to greater exploitation by her masters. The other slaves have another name for her, "Two-Souls," in reference to her differently colored eyes, mulatto body, and disintegrated psyche. Eventually, after a succession of degenerative metamorphoses, the *mulâtresse*, object of derision and desire, renames herself "Solitude." Ultimately, she triumphs over abjection by linking her destiny with others, through an act of solidarity with the rebels of Matouba.

The history of Guadeloupe's collective trauma is represented in the harrowing if heroic story of "la *mulâtresse* Solitude." Hovering between schizophrenia and catatonia in an unrelentingly bleak universe, Solitude's range of possibilities is severely limited. Thus, although there is something fundamentally awful about Schwarz-Bart portraying her "activism" as the expression of an almost vacated subjectivity, rather than of agency, to dwell on the implications of such symbolism is to forget that there are many different kinds of revolt. Solitude is the daughter of a woman who, in response to having survived unspeakable horror, "tried to swallow her tongue." As a testimony to the struggle for historical memory, this text so obsessed with dispossession is also its own commentary on the disfigurative and mutative effects of exile and cultural nomadism.

Contributors

Hédi Abdel-Jaouad teaches French at Skidmore College. He is a regular contributor to CELFAN Review. He is currently working on a book tentatively entitled, *L'Afrique des psychologues*.

Tahar Ben Jelloun, the Moroccan novelist, essayist, and journalist, is the author of many works of fiction, including *Harrouda, L'Enfant de sable, La Prière de l'absent*, and *La Nuit sacrée* (Prix Goncourt, 1987).

Réda Bensmaïa teaches French, film theory, and Francophone literature at Brown University. He has published widely on contemporary French philosophy—Deleuze, Roland Barthes (*Barthes à l'essai*), and on Maghrebian literature.

Bella Brodzki is a member of the Senior Literature Faculty at Sarah Lawrence College, where she teaches courses in modern fiction and autobiography, literary theory, and feminist studies. Coeditor, with Celeste Schenck, of *Life/Lines: Theorizing Women's Autobiography*, she has published articles on Borges, contemporary criticism, and autobiography. Among her current projects is a study of the politics of subjectivity in Francophone African and Carribean women's writing.

Maryse Condé is a Guadaloupean novelist and critic; among her many novels and essays are *Hérémakhonon, Segou, Parole des femmes, Moi, Tituba, Sorcière de Salem*, and *Traversée de la Mangrove*.

Catherine Dana is a Ph.D. candidate in the Department of French at Yale University. She is working on memory in the nineteenth and twentieth centuries.

YFS 83, *Post/Colonial Conditions*, ed. Lionnet & Scharfman, © 1993 by Yale University.

JOAN DAYAN teaches at the University of Arizona. She is author of *Fables of Mind: An Inquiry into Poe's Fiction* and is completing a book called *Haiti, History, and the Gods.*

RENÉ DEPESTRE, Haitian poet, essayist, and novelist, has lived in France for many years. His works include *Un Arc-en-ciel pour l'occident chrétien, Minerai noir, Bonjour et adieu à la négritude,* and *Hadriana dans tous mes rêves* (Prix Renaudot, 1988).

JENNIFER CURTISS GAGE was awarded the American Literary Translator Association's Gregory Rabassa Prize for her translation of Dominique Rolin's novel *The Deathday Cake.* Her other translations from the French include Jean-Joseph Goux's *Symbolic Economies,* André Weil's *Apprenticeship of a Mathematician,* as well as creative and critical works by other authors.

ABDELKEBIR KHATIBI is a Moroccan novelist, poet, essayist, critic, and sociologist. He teaches at the Collège de Philosophie, in Paris. His works include *La Mémoire tatouée, Amour Bilingue, Maghreb pluriel, Un Eté à Stockholm.*

FRANÇOISE LIONNET teaches French and comparative literature at Northwestern University. During 1991–92, she was a Senior Rockefeller Fellow at the Center for Advanced Feminist Studies at the University of Minnesota, and she also participated in The University of California Humanities Research Institute project on "Minority Discourse." She is the author of *Autobiographical Voices: Race, Gender, Self-Portraiture* (Cornell, 1989), and is completing work on *Spiralling Tensions,* a book-length study on women writers and universalisms.

CAREN LITHERLAND is a Ph.D. candidate in the Department of French at Yale University.

LUCY STONE MCNEECE received her doctorate from Harvard University. She teaches twentieth-century French and Francophone Literature at the University of Connecticut at Storrs, where she is a member of the Executive Board of African Studies.

ELISABETH MUDIMBE-BOYI is associate professor of French at Duke University. She is the author of a book on the Haitian writer Jacques-Stephen Alexis in a second edition: *Jacques Stephen Alexis: Une Ecriture poétique, un engagement politique* (Montreal, 1992). She is currently working on a book dealing with cultural encounters.

H. ADLAI MURDOCH is assistant professor of French and Francophone literature at Wellesley College. He holds degrees from the University of the West Indies, Howard University, and Cornell University, where he completed his Ph.D. in the Department of Romance Studies. His particular areas of scholarly interest are the nineteenth-century French novel and the field of postcolonial discourse, especially as it is represented in the twentieth-century French Caribbean novel. His articles have appeared in *Callaloo* and in *entralogos.*

ROBERT POSTAWSKO is assistant professor of French at the University of Tulsa. He works on eighteenth-century travel literature.

MIREILLE ROSELLO teaches French at the University of Michigan. She is the author of *L'Humour noir selon André Breton* (Corti, 1987), *L'Indifférence chez Michel Tournier* (Corti, 1990), and the forthcoming *Tactique et Opposition dans la littérature.*

RONNIE SCHARFMAN is associate professor of French language and culture at SUNY Purchase. She is the author of the award-winning *Engagement and the Language of the Subject in the Poetry of Aimé Césaire,* (University of Florida) as well as numerous articles on Francophone Literature.

THOMAS SPEAR teaches French and Francophone literature at Lehman College. He has just translated Leslie Kaplan's *Brooklyn Bridge,* forthcoming at Station Hill in 1992. He is working on an anthology with Rosemary Scullion, *Céline and the Politics of Difference,* and a book on French autofiction.

Why stand still...

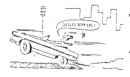

When you can take *ACTION!*

French in Action

Mireille, Robert, Professor Pierre Capretz, and a colorful cast of *personnages* are ready to lead you and your class through this unique approach to the instruction of French language and culture.

For the past five years, **French in Action**, *the* complete multi-media course, has effectively combined **video**, **audio**, and **text** to help students learn *real, unsimplified* French in the dynamic context of actual *communication*.

The **French in Action** program includes:

- 52 Half-hour Video Programs
- Textbook
- Workbooks
- Study Guides
- Instructor's Guide
- 52 Audiocassette Programs

Contact Yale University Press for full information on the **French in Action** system and to request examination copies. Be sure to ask about Teacher Support Workshops!

Yale University Press
92A Yale Station, New Haven, CT 06520   (203) 432-0912

The following issues are available through **Yale University Press**, Customer Service Department, 92A Yale Station, New Haven, CT 06520.

63 The Pedagogical Imperative: Teaching as a Literary Genre (1982) $17.00

64 Montaigne: Essays in Reading (1983) $17.00

65 The Language of Difference: Writing in QUEBEC(ois) (1983) $17.00

66 The Anxiety of Anticipation (1984) $17.00

67 Concepts of Closure (1984) $17.00

68 Sartre after Sartre (1985) $17.00

69 The Lesson of Paul de Man (1985) $17.00

70 Images of Power: Medieval History/Discourse/ Literature (1986) $17.00

71 Men/Women of Letters: Correspondence (1986) $17.00

72 Simone de Beauvoir: Witness to a Century (1987) $17.00

73 Everyday Life (1987) $17.00

74 Phantom Proxies (1988) $17.00

75 The Politics of Tradition: Placing Women in French Literature (1988) $17.00

Special Issue: After the Age of Suspicion: The French Novel Today (1989) $17.00

76 Autour de Racine: Studies in Intertextuality (1989) $17.00

77 Reading the Archive: On Texts and Institutions (1990) $17.00

78 On Bataille (1990) $17.00

79 Literature and the Ethical Question (1991) $17.00

Special Issue: Contexts: Style and Value in Medieval Art and Literature (1991) $17.00

80 Baroque Topographies: Literature/History/ Philosophy $17.00

81 On Leiris (1992) $17.00

Special subscription rates are available on a calendar year basis (2 issues per year):
Individual subscriptions $24.00   Institutional subscriptions $28.00

ORDER FORM   **Yale University Press,** 92A Yale Station, New Haven, CT 06520

I would like to purchase the following individual issues:

_____

_____

For individual issue, please add postage and handling:
Single issue, United States $2.75   Each additional issue $.50
Connecticut residents please add sales tax of 6%
Single issue, foreign countries $5.00   Each additional issue $1.00

Payment of $_____ is enclosed (including sales tax if applicable).

Mastercard no. _____

4-digit bank no._____Expiration date_____

VISA no._____Expiration date _____

Signature _____

SHIP TO _____ _____

_____

_____

See the next page for ordering issues 1-59 and 61-62. Yale French Studies is also available through Xerox University Microfilms 300 North Zeeb Road, Ann Arbor, MI 48106.

The following issues are still available through the **Yale French Studies Office,** 2504A Yale Station, New Haven, CT 06520.

19/20 Contemporary Art $3.50

23 Humor $3.50

33 Shakespeare $3.50

35 Sade $3.50

38 The Classical Line $3.50

39 Literature and Revolution $3.50

41 Game, Play, Literature $5.00

42 Zola $5.00

43 The Child's Part $5.00

44 Paul Valéry $5.00

45 Language as Action $5.00

46 From Stage to Street $3.50

47 Image & Symbol in the Renaissance $3.50

49 Science, Language, & the Perspective Mind $3.50

50 Intoxication and Literature $3.50

52 Graphesis $3.50

53 African Literature $3.50

54 Mallarmé $5.00

57 Locus: Space, Landscape, Decor $6.00

58 In Memory of Jacques Ehrmann $6.00

59 Rethinking History $6.00

61 Toward a Theory of Description $6.00

62 Feminist Readings: French Texts/American Contexts $6.00

Add for postage & handling

Single issue, United States $1.75

Single issue, foreign countries $2.50

Each additional issue $.50

Each additional issue $1.50

YALE FRENCH STUDIES, 2504A Yale Station, New Haven, Connecticut 06520

A check made payable to YFS is enclosed. Please send me the following issue(s):

Issue no.   Title   Price

_____

_____

                                             Postage & handling   _____

                                                          Total   _____

Name_____

Number/Street _____

City_____State _____Zip_____

The following issues are now available through Kraus Reprint Company, Route 100, Millwood, N. Y. 10546.

1 Critical Bibliography of Existentialism

2 Modern Poets

3 Criticism & Creation

4 Literature & Ideas

5 The Modern Theatre

6 France and World Literature

7 André Gide

8 What's Novel in the Novel

9 Symbolism

10 French-American Literature Relationships

11 Eros, Variations...

12 God & the Writer

13 Romanticism Revisited

14 Motley: Today's French Theater

15 Social & Political France

16 Foray through Existentialism

17 The Art of the Cinema

18 Passion & the Intellect, or Malraux

21 Poetry Since the Liberation

22 French Education

24 Midnight Novelists

25 Albert Camus

26 The Myth of Napoleon

27 Women Writers

28 Rousseau

29 The New Dramatists

30 Sartre

31 Surrealism

32 Paris in Literature

34 Proust

48 French Freud

51 Approaches to Medieval Romance

36/37 Structuralism has been reprinted by Doubleday as an Anchor Book.

55/56 Literature and Psychoanalysis has been reprinted by Johns Hopkins University Press, and can be ordered through Customer Service, Johns Hopkins University Press, Baltimore, MD 21218.

Imagining Paris

Exile, Writing, and American Identity

J. Gerald Kennedy

This book explores how living in Paris shaped the careers and literary works of five expatriate Americans: Gertrude Stein, Ernest Hemingway, Henry Miller, F. Scott Fitzgerald, and Djuna Barnes. Kennedy shows that the writings of each author reveal their various struggles to accommodate themselves to a complex, foreign scene, to construct an expatriate self, or to understand the contradictions of American identity. He treats these figures and their narratives as instances of the profound effect of place on writing and on the formation of the self.

"The story of these five representative Americans is told by Kennedy so clearly that it seems obvious, as truth always does when it is said right."
—Michael Reynolds   Illus. $30.00

Atget's Seven Albums

Molly Nesbit

This stunning book—the first complete reproduction of Eugène Atget's seven photographic albums of Paris at the height of its belle époque—is at once a new kind of history of photography, and a social history of art and of Paris in the early twentieth century.

"This brilliantly researched and argued book will shed a great deal of light on the history of photography."—Rosalind Krauss
158 b/w illus. + 420 duotones $55.00
Yale Publications in the History of Art

Watteau's Painted Conversations

Art, Literature, and Talk in Seventeenth- and Eighteenth-Century France

Mary Vidal

This innovative study shows that images of sociability and conversation were central to Watteau's paintings and that his focus on conversation was related to developments such as the redefinition of the nobility, the flourishing of women's salons in Paris, and the development of the literary genre of the written conversation.
133 b/w + 47 color illus. $50.00

Yale University Press

92A Yale Station, New Haven, CT 06520